John Brown

The Pilgrim Fathers of New England and their Puritan Successors

John Brown

The Pilgrim Fathers of New England and their Puritan Successors

ISBN/EAN: 9783742809988

Manufactured in Europe, USA, Canada, Australia, Japa

Cover: Foto ©ninafisch / pixelio.de

Manufactured and distributed by brebook publishing software (www.brebook.com)

John Brown

The Pilgrim Fathers of New England and their Puritan Successors

THE
PILGRIM FATHERS
OF NEW ENGLAND
AND THEIR
PURITAN SUCCESSORS

BY
JOHN BROWN, B.A., D.D.
AUTHOR OF "JOHN BUNYAN, HIS LIFE, TIMES AND WORK"

WITH INTRODUCTION BY
REV. A. E. DUNNING, D.D.
EDITOR OF *The Congregationalist*

WITH ILLUSTRATIONS FROM ORIGINAL SKETCHES
BY CHARLES WHYMPER

FLEMING H. REVELL COMPANY
NEW YORK   CHICAGO   TORONTO
Publishers of Evangelical Literature

COPYRIGHT, 1895
BY
FLEMING H. REVELL COMPANY

INTRODUCTION TO THE AMERICAN EDITION.

EVERY loyal American ought to know the principles and motives which led to the founding of this Republic. These cannot be understood without an acquaintance with the men and women who first came to New England. Their work was greater than beginning a nation. Dr. John Fiske says: "Among the most significant events which prophesied the final triumph of the English over the Roman idea, perhaps the most significant—the one which marks most incisively the new era—was the migration of English Puritans across the Atlantic Ocean."

But the character of these pioneers of New England was largely formed in old England and in Holland; and it can best be interpreted by a sympathetic student of their history who has lived long among the scenes of their earlier years. For this task no one living is better fitted than Dr. John Brown, of Bedford, Eng. For more than thirty years he has been the beloved minister of the church at Bunyan meeting, in that ancient town. The first edition of his elaborate biography of John Bunyan, published about ten years ago, was exhausted in a few weeks, and successive editions since that time have not only greatly increased the interest in the life and works of the immortal dreamer, but have spread the fame of his biographer on both sides of the Atlantic.

Dr. John Brown is one of the best known and most honored of English Nonconformist ministers, and one of the most trusted authorities on the important historical topics he has treated. His broad sympathies with all honest men of every denominational name have made his judgment impartial, while his popular literary style and his enthusiasm as a student of history have clothed with life the facts he has discovered in many dry and dusty MSS. He is skillful in unraveling facts and fiction long woven together by custom, in showing how both have taken hold of present life, and in giving due weight to fact while he puts fiction aside. His address on the Historic Episcopate, which he delivered in London in 1891, as president of the Congregational Union of England and Wales, is one of the most incisive and convincing utterances yet made on that topic, and is still extensively quoted. He gave the first address at the reception of the International Congregational Council in London in the same year, and was one of the most prominent Englishmen in the deliberations of that body. His repeated visits to the United States have made him widely known and loved in this country. In October, 1892, he represented the Congregational Union of England and Wales at the National Council of Congregational Churches in Minneapolis.

During all his mature life Dr. Brown has been interested in the Pilgrims and Puritans who first settled New England. He has inherited and manifested their spirit, though with none of the intolerance which sometimes qualified the Puritans. Living within easy reach of the homes of the Pilgrims, he has familiarized himself with every nook and corner in which their conventicles used to be held. His access to both public and private libraries of England and Holland, and his extensive acquaintance with historians and antiquarians, have given him rare opportunities to learn the details of the lives of those once obscure men whose unselfish loyalty to great principles of religion and liberty were destined to make them famous to coming generations: and he has availed himself of these opportunities to make the Pilgrims of the sixteenth and seventeenth centuries live anew, and to introduce them so fittingly to their descendants as to give fresh interest to their principles and new strength to the virtues they have bequeathed to us.

Dr. Brown has followed the Pilgrims eagerly to their earliest homes in America, and has studied their footprints and memorials along the shores of New England. He was an intimate friend and correspondent of Dr. Henry M. Dexter, the foremost authority in this country on Pilgrim history and life; and he is hardly less familiar with the literature on this subject in our libraries than with that on the other side of the ocean.

The story of the Pilgrims has all the elements of a fascinating romance. When it is read in the light of what they have produced and in the spirit of sympathy which appreciates and enjoys the religious and civil liberty we inherit, it is fitted beyond most uninspired records, to kindle exalted ideas of citizenship and to stimulate young and old to self-denying service of our country and of mankind. The years of perplexity and persecution in England during which honest yeomen and their families met in secret and worshiped God and entered into covenant to live worthy of him; the escape to Holland and the experiences which there shaped their purpose to begin a new life in a new world; the struggles with stormy seas, with the wilderness and winter cold; the encounters with Indians; the sturdy manhood which courted loneliness and defied starvation and death, esteeming loyalty to God and to conscience above all other ambitions; the wonderful providences which changed defeat into victory, which turned the wilderness into a garden, and made the humble Plymouth Colony the beginning of a great nation standing proudly in the forefront of Christian civilization—all these are materials which give to the beginnings of the youngest of the nations an interest unsurpassed by the ruins of the oldest.

The characteristics of New England life and the impress it has given to the whole country cannot be rightly appreciated without a knowledge of the first settlers and the sources whence they drew the inspiration to turn from the civilization of Europe and to make for themselves a higher civilization in a new land. The genius of American self-government was born in the minds of the Pilgrims, began to be realized in Plymouth Colony, and joined itself to men of like spirit and love of liberty controlled by law, as they faced the difficulties of organizing a new nation and overcame its foes; till they became fitted for the great struggle by which they separated themselves from their mother country and established themselves a people free and independent. It is a most welcome evidence of the strong ties that bind England and America together that an Englishman has here chronicled the noblest chapter in our early history, with so genuine an insight into its character and dignity that in both nations it will be read with equal interest. The Pilgrim spirit has reproduced itself in mountain and valley and on the prairie all the way from Massachusetts Bay to the Golden Gate. It has helped to unite in high aims people of widely different histories and languages, as they have together laid foundations in new lands for this rapidly growing Republic. This same spirit is ever bringing nearer the two peoples which once were one, which drew apart for a time, but which can never forget that they have the same ancestry, the same language and literature, the same inherent love of liberty, the same purpose to serve mankind, and that the hand of divine Providence is directing them to the same ways of fulfilling that purpose. May this book help to cement more closely these ties of kindred and service between two great nations which rejoice in the same inheritance.

A. E. DUNNING.

Boston, October, 1895.

DE MINIMIS MAXIMA.

Great things from small, for God works ever so,
That so behind all causes he may stand
Revealed omnipotent.
J. H. B. MASTERMAN.

Well worthy to be magnified are they
Who, with sad hearts, of friends and country took
A last farewell, their loved abodes forsook,
And hallowed ground in which their Fathers lay;
Then to the new-found World explored their way,
That so a Church, unforced, uncalled to brook
Ritual restraints, within some sheltering nook
Her Lord might worship and His Word obey
In Freedom.
WORDSWORTH.—Ecclesiastical Sonnets.

PREFACE.

PLACING in the forefront of this work, what an Elizabethan writer called 'a brief ingresse to the Christian reader,' it may be well to state that it is now more than forty years since the latest previous history of the Pilgrim Fathers, printed on this side of the Atlantic, was given to the public. Therefore, as might be expected, since the appearance of Mr. Bartlett's book in 1853, important contributions have been made to the literature of the subject, which have had the effect of placing it in clearer light and giving it fuller meaning. Notably the discovery in 1855 of the original manuscript of Governor Bradford's *History of Plymouth Plantation* may be regarded as a matter of prime importance.

It was known that such a history had been written, although never published, for it was freely used by Nathaniel Morton in his *New England's Memorial*, published in 1669; Thomas Prince, in the preface to the first volume of his *Annals*, printed in 1736, had cited it as one of his manuscript authorities; and Governor Hutchinson had also used it in the preparation of the second volume of his *History of Massachusetts* in 1767, he being the last man who, till the present century, was known to have seen it. While in the possession of Prince, who died in 1758, the manuscript was deposited in the New England Library in the tower of the Old South Church in Boston, from which, after the siege of the city, it mysteriously disappeared, and as time went on, was given up as hopelessly lost.

The next step in the history brings us to the year 1845, when Samuel Wilberforce, afterwards Bishop of Oxford, published a *History of the Protestant Episcopal Church in America*. In the preparation of this work he made researches for original documents in the library of the Bishop of London's palace at Fulham, from one of which he made several extracts, the references for which were given in the footnotes. The book became fairly well known, and passed through other editions, but no one seems to have taken special note of it for about ten years after its first publication. At length, in the month of February, 1855, the Rev. John S. Barry happened to consult it when engaged upon the first volume of his *History of Massachusetts*, when he was struck again and again by reading in the extracts from the Fulham MS. passages he remembered to have seen cited as from Bradford's *History* by Morton and Prince. He at once took the volume to his friend, Charles Deane, Esq., of the Massachusetts Historical Society, to whom he communicated his suspicion that Wilberforce's extracts were taken from the manuscript which had been so long missing, and which, after all, might possibly still be found in the Bishop of London's library. This turned out to be the case. Here at last was the *History of Plymouth Plantation*, written by William Bradford, one of the Pilgrim Fathers, and afterwards largely used by Morton and Prince. How it came to be transferred from the library in the tower of the Old South Church to that in the episcopal palace at Fulham can only be matter of conjecture, but the probability is that it was brought over by the English soldiers when the Revolutionary War was ended.

This invaluable and interesting record being thus, happily, once more brought to light, I have made use of it in all those portions of the history for which it is the sole authority, supplementing it by such State Papers, Domestic and Colonial, as throw light on the subject, and also by such other MSS. as have in recent years become available for historical purposes.

I have been greatly helped also by many of the numerous works issued in recent years both in this country and in America on the history of New England. To the more important of these I have acknowledged my obligations in the references given; but where one has been making notes extending over a lengthened period it is not always easy to remember the source from which many points of detail were taken. If, therefore, I have not always made due acknowledgment, I can only crave lenient indulgence beforehand.

In the hope that the re-telling of an old story, under the new lights of a later time, may not be without interest, instruction, and stimulus for ourselves, I leave these pages to the kindly judgment of such readers as love to linger over the record of brave deeds wrought by brave men in bygone days.

JOHN BROWN.

THE MANSE, BEDFORD,
July 25, 1895.

BOSTON.
(*From a sketch by* CHARLES WHYMPER.)

CONTENTS.

	PAGE
I. PRECURSORS OF THE PILGRIM FATHERS	15
II. SCROOBY AND AUSTERFIELD	40
III. BEGINNINGS OF CHURCH LIFE	73

CONTENTS.

	PAGE
IV. THE EXILES IN HOLLAND	110
V. THE WRITINGS OF JOHN ROBINSON	136
VI. WHERE LIES THE LAND?	158
VII. THE SAILING OF THE MAYFLOWER	184
VIII. PLYMOUTH PLANTATION	209
IX. AT THE END OF SEVEN YEARS	238
X. ARRIVAL OF NEW NEIGHBOURS.	265
XI. MASSACHUSETTS BAY AND CONNECTICUT VALLEY	295
XII. THE UNITED COLONIES	327

OLD KITCHEN, GUILDHALL, BOSTON.
(*From a sketch by* CHARLES WHYMPER.)

LIST OF ILLUSTRATIONS.

	PAGE
THE OLD MANOR HOUSE, SCROOBY. *From a sketch by Charles Whymper*	*Frontispiece*
BOSTON. *From a sketch by Charles Whymper*	9
OLD KITCHEN, GUILDHALL, BOSTON. *From a sketch by Charles Whymper*	11
SCROOBY—VIEW FROM THE RIVER. *From a sketch by Charles Whymper*	14
GOVERNOR BRADFORD'S COTTAGE AT AUSTERFIELD. 1. Cottage. 2. Steps to cellar. 3. Cellar. *From sketches by Charles Whymper*	41
ANCIENT PEWS IN SCROOBY CHURCH	47
SITE OF THE OLD STOCKS, SCROOBY CHURCHYARD. *From a sketch by Charles Whymper*	49
SOUTH DOORWAY, AUSTERFIELD CHURCH	67

LIST OF ILLUSTRATIONS.

	PAGE
SCROOBY MANOR HOUSE. *From a sketch by Charles Whymper*	72
THE BRIDGE, GAINSBOROUGH „ „ „	73
RICHARD BERNARD. *From an old print*	79
THE OLD HALL, GAINSBOROUGH. *From sketches by Charles Whymper*	89
THE GUILDHALL, BOSTON. 1. Cells in which the Pilgrims were confined. 2. Passage and stairs leading to cells. 3. Guildhall, front view	101
THE STABLE OF SCROOBY MANOR HOUSE. (Probable place of meeting in 1607.) *From sketches by Charles Whymper* .	111
BOSTON STUMP AND MARKET-PLACE. *From a sketch by Charles Whymper* . . .	136

SCROOBY—VIEW FROM THE RIVER.
(*From a sketch by* CHARLES WHYMPER.)

THE PILGRIM FATHERS.

I.

PRECURSORS OF THE PILGRIM FATHERS.

THE sailing of the Mayflower from Plymouth to New England, in 1620, was one of those epoch-making events in history which are at once the fruit of the past and the seed of the future. The hundred exiles who in simple heroic fashion crossed the Atlantic in their little barque of a hundred and eighty tons, while merely aiming at freedom of worship for themselves and their children, were really bringing to new and pregnant issue the long and resolute struggle of centuries. We can see now that they were almost unconsciously pointing the way to a broader, freer life for the English-speaking people on both sides of the sea. For the time in which they lived was, in a special sense, a time of transition. In the Tudor days, only recently ended, England had been under the personal government of monarchs who, though not uninfluenced by the opinion of their people, were yet practically absolute and irresponsible. Other forces, however, were now coming into play, and the nation was to make its way to a fuller life as a community of free self-governing men. This transition from mediæval to modern life was brought about by the combined action of religious enthusiasm with the spirit of personal independence.

The modern movement of government by the people began, not, as is sometimes supposed, with the eighteenth century but with the sixteenth, and was religious in its origin. It was, indeed, the child of the Reformation. For the two principles by which the power of Rome was assailed were, free inquiry as opposed to the absolute authority of the Church, and the universal priesthood of all believing men as opposed to that of a clerical caste of priests. When these two principles came to be applied, they proved to be farther-reaching than even their own advocates realised at first. The principle of free inquiry turned out to mean more than the mere right of the laity to read the Bible for themselves, it meant the right of free and independent search in every department of human thought and life; and the universal priesthood of believers carrying with it, as it did, the power of the people in the government of the Church, carried with it also the principle of the sovereignty of the people in the government of the State.

On the Continent, democracy, as springing out of the Reformation, was arrested by the power of the princes, and delayed for centuries; in England also it came into conflict with the aristocratic forces of the time, and was defeated for long in its struggle against ancient laws and institutions; but carried across the Atlantic by the Pilgrim Fathers, it there found a virgin soil in which it spread its roots freely, and grew vigorously. American self-government was not the sudden birth of the Declaration of Independence. For a century and a half the idea and political habits from which its strength was drawn had been gradually developed. It really sprang from the organisation which the Pilgrim Fathers gave to the first colony, an organisation which determined the shape and character of the State constitutions which followed.[1]

[1] *Rise of Modern Democracy.* By Charles Borgeaud, LL.D. 1894.

The modern movement in the direction of freedom and the sovereignty of the people being, as we have said, religious in its origin, can best be understood in connection with the struggle for faith and freedom made from earliest times. Steady and stifling as had been the pressure of the priestly system of Rome, it never quite succeeded in crushing out all aspirations after liberty or all strenuous endeavour after a purer faith. Again and again there were those who, weary of superstition and unreality, freed themselves from ecclesiastical bondage, and set forth in search of the true fountains of life. It is as a continuation of this honoured succession that the Pilgrim Fathers of New England take their rightful place. It may be well, therefore, to set their story in its true light at the outset by tracing the roots and beginnings of their movement in the generations which went before them.

There may have been others, but looking back through the dim mists of time, the earliest pioneers of independent thought we come upon on English soil are thirty weavers in the diocese of Worcester, who were summoned before the council of Oxford as far back as A.D. 1165. William of Newburgh, in Yorkshire, in that chronicle of his which he wrote at the request of Ernald, the abbot of the neighbouring monastery of Rievaulx, tells us that when these people were under examination, they answered that they were Christians, and reverenced the teachings of the apostles. Inasmuch, however, as they made light of sacraments and priestly power, they were condemned, were scourged and branded as heretics, and then driven out of the city, to perish in the winter cold; and thus, says the chronicler, the pious firmness of this severity not only cleansed the realm of England from the pestilence which had now crept in, but also prevented it from creeping in again. But as at the Assize of Clarendon, held some time after, Henry II. forbade any one to receive *any of the sect* of the renegades who had been excommunicated at Oxford, it is not so clear that the realm was cleansed from this so-called pestilence. And as at the same time he also caused an oath to be taken of all sheriffs that they would see to the execution of these commands, and that 'all his officers, dapifers and barons, together with all knights and freeholders, should be sworn to the same effect,'[1] it would appear that the opinions of these people were not confined to the diocese of Worcester, but were widely sympathised with elsewhere through the kingdom. These outcasts who declared themselves to be believers in the Holy Trinity, in the canonical Scriptures, and also 'in the one true Church,' but who repudiated the catholic doctrine of sacraments and rejected the ecclesiastical ceremonies, seem to have been the first to greet the morn,

> Or rather, rose the day to antedate,
> By striking out a solitary spark,
> When all the land with midnight gloom was dark.[2]

How the seed grew secretly and the leaven worked silently during the next century and a half it may not be easy to show. But such secret, silent working there must have been. Our countryman, William of Occam, born about 1270, was excommunicated by the Pope in the early part of the fourteenth century, for asserting in dialogues and tractates the freedom of the law of Christ against the plenitude of papal power. He maintained the authority of Scripture as the supreme arbiter of all things in the Church, and sought after that which was eternal as opposed to that which is merely of human ordinance. In that same century, also, we have in the *Vision of Piers Plowman*, a prophet who, though no Lollard, made nought of pilgrimages, penances, and oblations, in comparison with holiness and charity, appealed to the plainest Scriptural

[1] Camden Society, *Assize of Clarendon.*
[2] Wordsworth's *Ecclesiastical Sonnets*, xiv.

truths, and installed reason and conscience as the guides of the self-directed soul. Even Chaucer's voice was a voice of freedom, and of more or less covert hostility to the priestly system of the Church.

But if to any one man more than another we may trace the origin of the Free Church influences most potent in our modern life, that one man was John Wickliff of Lutterworth. He not only gave to Hus his ruling ideas, and sowed the seeds of Reformation in Germany, but in his own land also did much to change the emphasis in religion from the ceremonial to the ethical and spiritual. He carried the appeal from the organised authority of the priesthood to the authority of the Church's Invisible Head. As a Reformer his inspiration came from returning to the primitive faith. For religious thought must ever return to the essential ideas which Jesus created, and every such return is the beginning of new life, and so the Founder of Christianity remains the most recreative force in the religion He founded.

While John Wickliff and his followers may not have been the first to assail priestly pretensions, they appear to have been the first to carry out a definitely-organised movement in the way of ecclesiastical reform. Wickliff contended that the official clergy alone are not the Church, for, said he, 'the temple of God is the congregation, living religiously, of just men for whom Jesus shed His blood.' He held to the free and immediate access of believers to the grace of God in Christ; in other words, to the general priesthood of believers. In accordance with these principles, secret assemblies were gathered of those who were of like mind in the faith of Christ; and preachers were sent forth, as in 1382 Archbishop Courtenay complained in the House of Lords, going through the realm from county to county, and from town to town, preaching from day to day, not only in churches and churchyards, but also in market-places and public thoroughfares. They contended with great emphasis that for the ministry of the Church the Divine call and commission are perfectly sufficient; that the true installation of the preacher is that by God Himself. It has been asserted that the Lollard movement was premature, and came to an untimely end. On the contrary, it may safely be maintained that the life then created never died out, and that without the Lollards of the fourteenth century the Reformation of the sixteenth would not have been possible. Wickliff died in 1384; but seventeen years later the preamble of the Act of 1401, for the burning of heretics, states that 'divers false and perverse people of a certain new sect . . . usurping the office of preaching, do perversely and maliciously, in divers places within the realm, preach and teach divers new doctrines and wicked erroneous opinions; and of such sect and wicked doctrines they make unlawful conventicles.' Even this Act, stern and terrible as it was—the first statute that consigned Englishmen to the flames for their opinions—was powerless to arrest the convictions of earnest men. From a list of authenticated trials for heresy, drawn up by Bishop, then Canon, Stubbs, at the request of the Royal Commission on Ecclesiastical Courts (1881-1883), it appears that, beginning with the trial of Wickliff, and ending with that of William Balowe, who was burned in 1466, more than a hundred and twenty persons were tried for heresy—even this list being far from complete.

Thirty years later we still find the movement at work. In the registers of the bishops of Lincoln and Salisbury is a series of confessions and abjurations extorted from various persons by fear of death. While mainly referring to pilgrimages, transubstantiation, and other Romish practices and doctrines, they indicate at the same time a more organised separatism in church life than is usually supposed to have existed before the Reformation. These extracts belong for the most part to the year 1499, but twenty years later, as we find from the register of the Bishop of London, Thomas Man was cited for 'teachings and practices contrary to the determination of the Holy Church.' From the report of this case it appears that the defendant had spread his teachings in East Anglia, and also in the western counties. As he went westward he found 'a great company' who had cast off the superstitions of the time, 'especially at Newbury, where was' (as he confessed) 'a glorious and sweet society of faithful favourers, who had continued the space of fifteen years together,' but who were at last betrayed by an informer, and some of them burnt. At Amersham, also, he came upon 'a godly and great company of "known men," or "just fast men," who had continued in that doctrine and teaching for twenty-three years,' this 'congregation of the faithful brethren' being duly organised under the care of four principal teachers. This was sixteen years before the Act of Supremacy of 1534, which severed the Church of England from the See of Rome, and therefore some time before the Reformation was an accomplished fact. Nor were these the only pre-Reformation witnesses to a purer faith and simpler polity, for, as Foxe goes on to tell us, 'there were secret multitudes who tasted and followed the sweetness of God's Holy Word, and whose fervent zeal may appear by their sitting up all night in reading and hearing.' He speaks, also, of their earnest seekings, their burning zeal, their watchings, their sweet assemblies, their love and concord, and their godly living.

Even after the Reformation had come in, being but a halting measure, it did not put an end to separate gatherings. In the Privy Council Register of Edward VI. it is recorded that one Upcharde of Bocking was examined touching a certain assembly of some sixty persons, who had met at his house on a recent Sunday at midday, in 1551. Sixteen of the sixty were apprehended, who, on 'being examined, confessed the cause of their assembly to be for talk of Scripture, not denying that they had refused communion (at the parish church) above two years upon very superstitious and erroneous purposes.' In the reactionary days of Queen Mary, which came in with 1553, the Separatists appear to have increased in numbers and influence. There were secret gatherings by night in Lancashire and in the adjacent county of York, and more numerous gatherings still in those eastern counties which furnished so large a contingent to the roll of the Marian martyrs. Through nearly the whole period of the persecution a congregation met in Colchester; and at Much Bentley, near to Colchester, there was a company of Christian men, who, as an informer tells us, 'assembled together upon the Sabbath day in the time of divine service, sometimes in one house and sometimes in another, and kept their privy conventicles and schools of heresy.' There was also a congregation at Stoke, in Suffolk, 'so numerous and held together in such mutual concord of godliness, that without much ado none well could be troubled.'

But there were two Separatist communities in London itself, one in Queen Mary's reign and the other in the time of Elizabeth, if indeed they were not the same church in continuity, which seem to form a link between the Protestant martyrs of Mary's time and the Pilgrim Fathers themselves. Governor Bradford in his *Dialogues* tells us that 'in the days of Queen Elizabeth there was a separated church whereof Mr. Fitz was pastor, and another before that in the time of Queen Mary, of which Mr. Rough was pastor or teacher, and Cuthbert Symson a deacon, who exercised among themselves, as other ordinances, so church censures, as excommunications, etc.' When Bradford, with the rest of the exiles from Scrooby, reached Amsterdam in 1608, there was in the church already established there one who had been connected with this London brotherhood. This interesting fact, forming a link between the Pilgrim Fathers and the brethren of the earlier generation, we gather from Henry Ainsworth's *Counterpoyson* (1608). He says that John Bolton was an elder of 'that separated church whereof Mr. Fitz was pastor in the beginning of Queen Elizabeth's reign. This is testified to me by one yet living among us who then was member of that church.'

For all that we know concerning the Marian church to which Governor Bradford refers, we are indebted to John Foxe's *Acts and Monuments*. From this we gather that the members at first were about forty, that they then rose to a hundred, and sometimes to two hundred. Roger Sergeant, an informer, who went to their meetings to betray them, tells us that they had reading and preaching, their minister, at the time he was there, being a Scotchman; 'they have also,' he says, 'two deacons that gather money, which is distributed to the prisoners, their brethren in the Marshalsea, the King's Bench, the Lollards' Tower, and in Newgate, and also to the poor that cometh to the assembly.' A second informer reports that Cuthbert Symson was the officer or deacon who made the collection when the reading was done, who was the paymaster of the prisoners, and was also the executor of such of the brethren as happened to die in gaol or at the stake. One Brooks, of Queenhithe, a salter and a rich man, who went not to the parish church, was also a collector and keeper of money for the prisoners. From the testimony of these informers we learn further that the meetings of the brotherhood were held in various places on both sides of the river and at varied times, to avoid detection. They addressed each other as 'brother,' read together, talked together, and elected their own officers. Towards the end of 1557, after many previous hairbreadth escapes, they were arrested in Islington when met 'for their godly and customable exercises of prayer and hearing the Word of God.' John Rough, the minister mentioned by Roger Sergeant, and Cuthbert Symson, the deacon, were among those arrested and sent to Newgate, and ten days later the former was burnt at Smithfield. Cuthbert Symson was not put to death till the following March, for it was known that he had in his possession the official list of the members of the church, and he was thrice put to the torture of the rack to compel him to give up the names of his brethren. When the Constable of the Tower and Sir Roger Cholmley demanded these names, Cuthbert Symson says, 'I answered I would declare nothing. Whereupon I was set in a rack of iron the space of three hours, as I judge.' Again and again they tried by force to subdue his fortitude, but tried in vain; so on March 28, 1558, this good deacon, standing in the succession and true to the spirit of Stephen, was sent by way of the Smithfield fires to the martyr's crown.

Eight months later Mary herself vanished from the scene, but on into the reign of Elizabeth this persecuted community continued still to hold its meetings. Thomas Lever, one of the Protestant exiles who had fled to Zurich, describes their fellowship as he found it on his return to England in 1559. Writing in August to his friend Bullinger, he says:—'There had been a congregation of faithful persons concealed in London during the time of Mary, among whom the Gospel was always preached, with the pure administration of the sacraments; but during the rigour of the persecution of that Queen they carefully concealed themselves, and on the cessation of it under Elizabeth they openly continued in the same congregation. . . . Large numbers flocked to them, not in churches, but in private houses. And when the Lord's Supper was administered among them no strangers were admitted except such as were kept free from popery, and even from the imputation of any evil conduct; or who, ingenuously acknowledging their backsliding and public offence, humbly sought pardon and reconciliation in the presence of the whole assembly. I have frequently been present on such occasions, and have seen many returning with tears, and many too, in like manner, with tears receiving such persons into communion, so that nothing could be more delightful.'[1]

Of the existence of the church under the pastorate of Richard Fitz we have intimations in Bradford and Ainsworth, as we have already seen; there are also references to it in a little anonymous volume printed in 1611; but in recent years three documents have been found together among the State papers which place its existence beyond all manner of doubt. The most important of these documents is a petition to the Queen for ecclesiastical reform. It bears no date, but a reference to the thirteenth year of Elizabeth's reign fixes it as belonging to the year 1571. It is described as from Whitechapel Street, and is signed by twenty-seven persons. After having pleaded for the removal of all superstitious and unscriptural practices in the Church, they described themselves as: 'We a poor congregation whom God hath separated from the Church of England and from the mingled and false worshipping therein,' and say that, 'as God giveth strength at this day we do serve the Lord every Sabbath day in houses, and on the fourth day come together weekly to use prayer and exercise discipline on them that do deserve it, by the strength and true warrant of the Lord God's word.' They state also, incidentally, that the maintainers of the Canon Law have 'by long imprisonment pined and

[1] *Zurich Letters.* Second Series, 1558–1602; pp. 29, 30. Parker Society.

killed the Lord's servants—as our minister Richard Fitz, Thomas Bowland, deacon, one Partryche and Gyles Fouler, and besides them a great multitude.' In addition to this written petition there is a small printed sheet in black letter, entitled *The trewe Markes of Christ's Church*, etc., and commencing thus: 'The order of the Privye Churche in London, which by the malice of Satan is falsely slandered and evil spoken of.' The true marks of Christ's Church are declared to be these three: (1) The glorious Word and Evangel are preached freely and purely; (2) The sacraments are administered according to the institution and good word of the Lord Jesus; and (3) Discipline is administered agreeably to the same heavenly and almighty word. The name 'Richard Fytz, Minister,' is appended. The remaining document, also in black letter, sets forth reasons for separation from the Anglican Church, and prays that 'God may give them strength still to strive in suffering under the cross, that the blessed Word of our God alone may rule and have the highest place.'[1]

The days in which these Elizabethan Separatists bore their testimony on behalf of Scripture truth and a more earnest spiritual life, were days when such testimony was sorely needed. In many parts of the country the Reformation was more a name than a reality. Most of the clergy who had celebrated mass in Mary's time continued to serve the parishes under Elizabeth. When the Oath of Supremacy was tendered after the accession of the latter, out of nine thousand four hundred clergy less than a hundred and eighty refused it altogether, and of these more than half were dignitaries. The majority of those who took the oath had probably done the same under Henry and Edward, as well as Mary, and quite as probably

---

[1] *State Papers, Domestic.* Elizabeth. Addenda. Vol. xx., No. 107, 1571?

remained the papists they had always been. Passing from the clergy to the laity, the effect of priestly influence and teaching for generations was but too plainly seen in the Romish ideas and practices prevailing. In the north especially, large districts had scarcely been even touched by the Reformation, and many of the great county families with their retainers still held tenaciously by the ancient forms of worship. Grindal tells us that when he first went down to his province as Archbishop of York, the Church he came to scarcely seemed to be the same with the one to which he had belonged as Bishop of London. The people among whom he now found himself in 1570 still observed the old Romish fasts and festivals; still, under the influence of the old ideas of purgatory, brought offerings of money and eggs at the burial of the dead; and still counted their beads as they went through their prayers. As archbishop he found it necessary to issue a commission to the four archdeacons of the diocese 'for the pulling down and demolishing those *sustentacula*, commonly called rood-lofts, placed at the door of the choir of every parish church, as footsteps and monuments of the old idolatry and superstition.' As his register shows,[1] he also had to issue injunctions against crossing, breathing over the sacramental bread and wine, the elevation of the elements for adoration, and against the use of oil, or chrism, tapers, spittle, and other popish ceremonies at baptism. Hand-bells were still rung at burials to drive away evil spirits; the people still observed 'months minds,' or monthly and yearly commemorations of the dead, when dirges were sung and prayers offered for the repose of their souls; pedlars continued to set forth their wares in church-porch and church-yard on Sundays as well as holidays; superstitious observances were still kept up in connection with the perambulation of the parish bounds

[1] Folio 155. Cited by Strype, *Life of Grindal*, p. 167.

in cross-week or gang-days; lords of misrule or summer lords and ladies, minstrels and morris dancers came at Christmas and May-day, or at rush-bearings into church as well as church-yard, playing unseemly parts with wanton gesture and ribald scoff; while at the Feast of the Purification or Candlemas-day, as many as two hundred candles were lighted in the church in honour of the Virgin, in addition to from ten to twenty torches.

The truth is that in many parishes there had been little, if any, religious teaching of Scriptural sort for generations. The President and Council of the North informed the Privy Council that in several of the churches there had literally never been a sermon for years; that many of the ministers were utterly unable to teach, and that the backwardness of the people in religion and their insurrection in the Northern Rising really rose rather from ignorance and lack of convenient instructing, than from stubbornness or wilful disobedience. To remedy this state of things, the preachers in the cathedral churches were ordered to divide themselves in the diocese where they dwelt, and travel from place to place preaching the Word of God to the people; letters also were despatched to all justices of the peace requiring them to receive these preachers, assist them and accompany them to the places where they were to preach, remain at their sermons and procure sufficient and orderly audience to their encouragement.[1]

During the reign of Edward VI., several of the nobility had come into possession of monastic lands on the understanding that they should continue the payment of life-pensions to the monks who were dispossessed. In order to rid themselves of this liability and get these men off their hands, they presented them to the livings they happened to have in their gift, and so men were thus

[1] *State Papers, Domestic.* Elizabeth. Vol. xiv., 32, November, 1568.

introduced to the sacred office who were ignorant and altogether unfit for the discharge of its duties. These monks thus suddenly called upon to fill positions to which they were not accustomed, did not preach simply because they could not. In this way it came about that in many parishes besides those in the northern province, there were churches where there had not been a sermon for years. It was a step in advance, therefore, when it was laid down by authority that a sermon must be preached once every quarter. To this some of the more godly in the nation replied with disappointment that four sermons in the year were as little likely to make perfect men in Christ Jesus, as four strokes of an axe were to fell a mighty oak, or as four showers an hour long were to moisten the hard dry earth and make it fruitful the whole year long.[1]

From a report of the diocese of Chichester made in 1569, it would appear that some parts even of the province of Canterbury were not much more enlightened than the province of York, as Grindal described it. From that report we find there were churches where there had not been a sermon once in seven years, or even once in twelve. Some churches had 'neither parson, vicar nor curate, but only a sory reder.' In the deanery of Midhurst there were beneficed men who preached in Queen Mary's days, but who did not and would not preach now in Elizabeth's time, and yet had kept their livings all the ten years since Mary died. When the preacher in the town of Battle spoke against popery, the people, it is said, 'will not abide, but get out of the church.' In some other parishes when the rood was taken away the parishioners retaliated by drawing a figure of the cross with chalk in its place; and when that in return was painted over, crosses were drawn upon the church walls, within and without, and also upon

---

[1] *The lamentable Complaint of the Commonaltie.* Parte of a Register, p. 216.

pulpit and communion-table; in other churches where the rood-lofts were taken down by authority, they were defiantly set up again.[1]

It was in days like these, when the land had scarcely emerged from beneath the power and superstitions of Rome, that the early Congregationalists raised their testimony on behalf of what they held to be a more scriptural faith and polity than prevailed in the National Church. For our purpose they may be most conveniently described as falling into three groups, these groups being determined by the localities in which they carried on their operations. Thus we have those in Eastern England, those in London, and finally those in the churches at Scrooby and Gainsborough, from which the Pilgrim Fathers took their rise.

The leader of the Congregationalists in East Anglia was Robert Browne, a man of ability and force of character, and, so far as social position was concerned, of aristocratic connections. By a strange irony of fate, he is by one side persistently described as the founder of Congregationalism, and as persistently repudiated by the other. From having advocated Congregational principles at one part of his career, and withdrawn from them at another, he has received scant justice from both sides. Ardent and impulsive, but too unstable to stand the stress of the storm which gathered round him year after year—he was, he says, in the course of his life in no fewer than thirty prisons, in some of which he could not see his hand at mid-day—he scarcely seems to have deserved all the hard things that have been said of him. No doubt he had more capacity for expounding the principles of Congregationalism than for working them out in actual life, but no one can dispassionately read the five books he published between 1582 and 1584, without feeling that at that time

[1] *State Papers, Domestic.* Elizabeth. Vol. lx., 71 : 1569.

at least he was an earnest-minded man, of strong and clear convictions in favour of popular government in the Church.

But, whatever may be his merits or demerits, he was certainly not the founder of Congregationalism in England. For, to say nothing of the community in Queen Mary's days, under the pastorate of John Rough, there is, as we have seen, indisputable evidence of the existence of a Congregational Church in London as early as 1571, which must have been in existence there for some years, for its pastor Richard Fitz had already died in prison, probably died there before Robert Browne had even entered Cambridge as an undergraduate, for he did not take his degree till 1572. There is strong probability indeed that it was from these very people that he first derived the principles of Congregationalism. For on leaving Cambridge he went to London, where he was engaged in teaching 'schollers for the space of three years,' as he tells us himself. It was during these same three years, he says, 'he wholly bent himself to search and find out the matters of the Church, as to how it was to be guided and ordered, and what abuses there were in the ecclesiastical government then used.'[1] It was also during this time of mental conflict we find him speaking on Sundays to scattered companies of Christian people who were accustomed to gather in the fields and gravel pits about Islington. It was here that the Separatists had gathered and continued to gather. Here John Rough and Cuthbert Symson were arrested; here on into Elizabeth's reign they continued to meet, and here in June 1592 fifty-six persons were arrested on Sunday, and sent to prison 'for hearing the Word of God truly taught, praying and praising God.' A petition presented to Parliament on their behalf says that 'they were taken in the very same place where the persecuted Church and martyrs were enforced to use like

[1] *True and Short Declaration.*

exercises in Queen Mary's days.'[1] Finding Robert Browne 'lecturing' to Sunday gatherings in the fields and gravel pits of Islington at a time when his mind was in a state of ferment on the subject of Church government, it is not difficult to see where and how he was first initiated into the principles of Congregationalism.

The plague drove him from London, and we find him again in Cambridge, where he continued to preach till inhibited by the bishop. Just then it came to his ears that some good people in Norfolk were 'verie forward' in the matter of religion, and he 'thought it his duetie to take his voiage to them.' While he was so resolving there came up from Norfolk, Robert Harrison, an old Cambridge acquaintance, who had been going through the same kind of mental conflict as Browne himself. After much intercourse and free talk on matters ecclesiastical they went to Norwich together, where they gathered a congregation of believers into church fellowship. They did not, however, confine their labours to Norwich, for in 1581 the bishop forwarded to Lord Burleigh articles of complaint against Browne, who was his kinsman, to the effect that he had been lately apprehended at Bury St. Edmunds on the charge of gathering people to hear him in private houses and conventicles to the number of a hundred at a time. It would appear that Harrison also was arrested at the same time as his friend, for he tells us in a *Little Treatise*, published by him in 1583, that he could have escaped in time, but that he did not think it lawful to withdraw into any other place for his own liberty's sake till he had borne open witness for the good cause. After their release they with their followers left England for Middelburg in Zealand, where they established a Congregational church, and from whence they sent over from time to time the

---

[1] Petition reprinted in *More Work for the Dean*. Thomas Wall. 1681.

books they published, and against which a proclamation was issued in 1583. It is conjectured that Harrison died about 1585, and the following year Robert Browne returned to England, where he again joined the Episcopal Church, in the communion of which he remained till his death.

In 1581, as we have seen, the Bishop of Norwich informed Lord Burleigh that Robert Browne had more than once taught 'strange and dangerous doctrine' at Bury St. Edmunds. He was not, however, the earliest exponent of Congregational principles in that ancient East Anglian town. For at the very time he was gathering people into conventicles there, John Copping was a prisoner in the old gaol in the market-place, where he had already lain for five years for his advocacy of these principles; and two years later this man and his friend Elias Thacker were to die on the scaffold for their fidelity to them. It seemed fitting, perhaps, that here in the town where for generations the great Abbey of St. Edmunds had been the centre of all life and influence, where ecclesiastical authority had been supreme and paramount, that the first martyrs for Free Church principles should lay down their lives for their testimony.

In the old time Bury was one of the most powerful strongholds of the ancient faith. The royal abbey was the burial-place and shrine of King Edmund; its conventual bell was the largest in England, and its porphyry altar had privilege of mass when all the rest of the kingdom was under interdict. Its abbot had liberty of coinage, sat among the peers in Parliament, and had great officers under him: prior, sub-prior, sacrist, and the like, besides eighty monks, fifteen chaplains and one hundred and eleven attendants within the walls of the monastery. The great west gate now remaining was only one of three with their high walls and towers, while within the precincts were the palace, the monastery, the chapter house, a hundred feet long, and besides the abbey church three other churches, one of which, St. Margaret's, is said by Leland to be equal if not superior in length and stateliness to old St. Peter's at Rome. But if the townspeople knew something of the splendours of ecclesiasticism they knew something of its superstitions and something of its oppressions and tyrannies too. Pilgrims came from far and near to see wonder-working relics: drops of the blood of the martyr Stephen; some of the coals on which St. Lawrence was broiled; skulls of ancient saints and martyrs; the boots of St. Thomas of Canterbury and the bones of St. Botolph, which, if carried in procession, would be sure to bring rain when rain was needed; there were wax candles too, which, if carried round the cornfields in seed-time, would work in such wondrous way that neither darnel nor noisome weed of other sort would grow that year to the discomfort of faithful husbandmen. But if priestly candles did ever save the labour of the toiler in the fields, that labour was rigorously exacted in other ways about which there could be no manner of doubt. Every serf within the jurisdiction was bound to plough a rood of the abbot's land, to reap his harvest field, to fold his sheep, and to help to bring the annual catch of eels to his table. Within the abbot's wide domain the land and water were his; the townspeople had to pay him for the pasture of their cattle on their own common; and if the fullers refused him the loan of their cloth, the use of the stream was refused and their looms were seized. So it came to pass that in the very town where the first Congregationalists were brought as martyrs to the scaffold, plain burgesses, centuries before, rose up and won in detail the liberties of Englishmen, even before the Great Charter claimed them for the realm at large. When the exactions of the abbot grew to be more than English folk could bear the very women turned out, distaff in hand, and put his officers to flight; and in later times surging masses of angry men, women and children poured in from all the villages round to wreck the abbey in their wrath, and break the yoke of the tyranny under which they had groaned too long.

The men of Bury in the sixteenth century were no more willing to submit to ecclesiastical domination than their ancestors in the centuries before. In 1581 an Act was passed inflicting a fine of twenty pounds a month upon those who refused to come to church; but when the commissary of the archdeacon proceeded to enforce the Act he was seriously molested. He complained that when he swore in six questmen to bring presentments against such as came not to church ever, some of the justices sent for him, 'called him Jack and Knave he knew not how often,' and threatened to send him to gaol. The bishop drew up twelve articles against the justices, which he laid before Lord Burleigh, charging them with favouring John Copping and one Tyler, who were in prison for spreading Robert Browne's books, and trying to get them liberated. He further complained that these justices were for nothing but Geneva psalms and sermons, in reply to which they said they could not but marvel at the bishop speaking thus, for the psalms were David's, and as for the sermons, his lordship knew the necessity there was for them. Eventually the bishop and other members of the Ecclesiastical Commission visited the town in person, and described the two Puritan ministers, Mr. Handscomb and Mr. Gayton, as 'the men that blew the coals whereof this fire was kindled.' Further, at the Assizes held June 1583, before the Lord Chief Justice, Sir Christopher Wray, Elias Thacker and John Copping were put upon their trial for dispersing the books written by Robert Browne and Robert Harrison, and being convicted were sentenced to death. That there might be no time for appeal, they were hanged at once, while the Assizes were still being held, Thacker one day, and Copping the next. They were both willing to acknowledge the civil authority of Her Majesty, but no further; and though Dr. Still, the chaplain, tried to convince them that the Queen was head of the Church as well as of the State, 'yet they were at that very time of their death immovably of the same mind.' Before their execution 'their books, as many of them as could be found, were burnt before them.' It is easier, however, to stretch men by the neck and burn their books than to suppress their opinions. In his official report the Lord Chief Justice had to tell the Lord Treasurer that there were still many remaining of Copping and Thacker's way of thinking, that, indeed, he had had to send one minister to prison for saying that if it had been known when Elias Thacker was to have suffered, there would have been five hundred good fellows more than there were at his execution.[1]

While Robert Browne's books were coming over from Middelburg by stealth, and men were being hanged for spreading them, there were great searchings of heart going on in a certain east country parsonage in the county of Norfolk. John Greenwood, on leaving Cambridge, where he had graduated in 1581, had been ordained by the bishop. He had been greatly influenced, however, by opinions of freer sort, which were ripe at the university in that seething time; he had also met with Robert Browne's *Treatise of Reformation without Tarrying for anie*, which came over the year after he had entered upon his living, and the more he thought upon these questions the less satisfied he became, and at length in 1585 he was deprived of his benefice by the bishop 'for the disliking he had to the Order of the Book of Common Prayer.' We next find him acting as chaplain to a Puritan nobleman, Lord Rich, at

[1] *Lansdowne MSS.*, xxxviii., 64.

Rochford Hall, in the county of Essex. The services he and Robert Wright carried on jointly in the great chamber of the hall proved so attractive that the people of the neighbourhood forsook those at the parish church to attend them. This brought down the displeasure of the bishop, and Greenwood had to flee, seeking refuge in what was even then the great wilderness of London life. Here he found companionship with those who composed the secret church in London, the successors of those who ever since the Reformation had striven for a simpler worship and a more scriptural faith. He joined their gatherings, until in the month of October 1587 he was arrested along with twenty others 'for being at private conventicles in Henry Martin's house in St. Andrew's, in Wardropp.'[1] After examination before the Bishop of London he was sent to the Clink prison, there to abide till further order was taken.

While John Greenwood lay in the Clink he received a visit from one whose name was to become memorable in Free Church history. This was Henry Barrowe, the son of a country squire at Shipdam, in Norfolk. He had been trained for the law, and during the years of his London life had lived in wild and wanton way, but passing a London church and hearing the preacher's voice, he turned in in freakish fashion and heard that which changed everything for him. Lord Bacon, who knew him, says that 'he made a leap from a vain and libertine youth' to a life of earnest purpose, 'the strangeness and suddenness of which alteration made him very much spoken of.' The change was as permanent as it was sudden, and introduced him to new companionships of godly sort. In this way he came to be associated with John Greenwood, and hearing of his friend's arrest he went down to the prison one Sunday

[1] *State Papers, Domestic.* Elizabeth. Vol. cciv., 10, 1587. Particulars of several Brownists.

morning to visit him. No sooner was he within the walls of the Clink than he himself was arrested by the gaoler and sent up the river the same afternoon to Lambeth Palace, where he was examined before the archbishop and other officials. Examined again and again from time to time, he was at length consigned to the Fleet prison, where he and his friend Greenwood shared the same chamber. Here the years passed slowly away, the two prisoners engaged in writing books for the assertion and vindication of their principles. In 1592 there was some relaxation after five years' imprisonment. Greenwood was released, but not for long. On December 5 that same year, he along with Francis Johnson was arrested while worshipping at the house of Edward Boyes on Ludgate Hill, and between one and two o'clock in the morning conveyed with bills and staves to prison once more.

The end was now not far off. On March 23, 1593, Barrowe and Greenwood were put upon their trial at the Old Bailey, and that night the Attorney-General reported to the Lord Keeper of the Great Seal, that the Court had proceeded against these men for devising seditious books, that they were attainted by verdict of judgment, and direction given for execution to-morrow, as in cases of like quality.[1] Next morning they were brought out of their dungeon, their irons struck off, and they bound to the cart, at which moment a reprieve arrived. Again, a week later, as Barrowe says, 'my brother Greenwood and I were very early and secretly conveyed to the place of execution,' that is, to Tyburn, 'where being tied by the necks to the tree, we were permitted to speak a few words.' These few words ended, they then joined in prayer for the Queen, the magistrates, and the people, and like their Master before them, for their enemies also. Their last words, as they supposed, were almost reached, when at the fateful moment

[1] *Harleian MSS.* 6848 ; 7, 9, 11, 14, 191.

a messenger with a reprieve from her majesty made his way through the crowd to the scaffold, and again their lives were spared. Cheers and rejoicing rose from the multitude, both all round the place of execution and all the way back, from ways, streets, and houses, as they returned to their prison chamber. The reprieve, however, was not for long. They had had 'two near and miraculous escapes'; twice had they gone through the bitterness of death, and twice been sent back to the hopes of life. But the end came at last. On April 6, 1593, stripped of their irons and bound to the cart once more, they went forth to Tyburn again, two aged widows with them bearing their winding sheets. This time there came no reprieve; from this journey there was no return. The conflict ended, as it has often ended, before and since:

Truth for ever on the scaffold, Wrong for ever on the throne,
Yet that scaffold sways the future, and behind the dim unknown
Standeth God within the shadow, keeping watch above His own.

II.

SCROOBY AND AUSTERFIELD.

HAVING briefly traced the course of the struggle for spiritual freedom on English soil to the end of the sixteenth century, we now turn to the church in the north Midland shire from which the Pilgrim Fathers sprang. We make our way therefore to the village of Scrooby, nestling amid quiet meadows and by the side of tranquil streams, where the three counties of Nottingham, York and Lincoln meet. After two centuries of oblivion this village sprang to fame as the birthplace of the Pilgrim Church. Half a century ago all that was known of the local beginnings of that church was gathered from some brief sentences of Governor Bradford, to the effect that those who formed this historic community 'were of several towns and villages, some in Nottinghamshire, some in Lincolnshire, and some in Yorkshire, where they bordered nearest together'; and next, that 'they ordinarily met at William Brewster's house on the Lord's day, which was a manor of the bishop's.' To find out where these conditions applied was an inviting problem to solve, and in 1842, during a visit to England, the Hon. James Savage submitted that problem for solution to the Rev. Joseph Hunter, the author of a history of South Yorkshire, of which district he was a native. Mr. Hunter was at that time Assistant Keeper of Her Majesty's Records, and therefore it was with special training and with special advantages that he addressed

GOVERNOR BRADFORD'S COTTAGE AT AUSTERFIELD.
1. Cottage. 2. Steps to cellar. 3. Cellar.
(*From sketches by* CHARLES WHYMPER.)

himself to the consideration of the question. After careful investigation he pointed out that the required conditions as to locality were met in the village of Scrooby, in the hundred of Basset-Lawe, in the county of Nottingham, that being the only place comprising an episcopal manor which was near the three counties mentioned by Bradford. Since the publication of his *Collections Concerning the Early History of the Founders of New Plymouth*, in 1849, the question as to locality may be considered as finally settled.

Scrooby, one of those places of far less importance now in railway times than in the old coaching days, is situated in Nottinghamshire, about a mile and a half south of Bawtry, a market-town within the Yorkshire border on the great north road from London to Berwick. The village has a railway station of its own, but the traveller from the south who would approach Scrooby aright should go on to Bawtry, and return by the high road lined with elm-trees, leading from Bawtry Hall to Scrooby Mill. This is both more picturesque and is the road along which William Bradford came from Austerfield to the gatherings of the brethren in William Brewster's house. Bawtry itself also has its memories of those olden times as well as Scrooby, on which it may be pleasant to linger as we saunter through. The same John de Builli who in the reign of Henry II. gave to the neighbouring convent of Blyth the chapel of Austerfield, in which William Bradford was baptised, gave to that convent the chapel of Bawtry too. At the southern extremity of the town also is the hospital of St. Mary Magdalen, founded in 1390 by Robert Morton of Bawtry, and endowed for a priest there to have residence, 'to keep hospitalitie for poore people, and to pray for the Founder's Soule and all Christian Soules.' By way of further acknowledgment 'a free rente of a pound of peper' was to be paid out of the hospital yearly to the Mortons, as descendants of the founder.[1] These Mortons continued long after the Reformation to be strenuous supporters of the ancient faith. In the days of William Brewster's boyhood he may have more than once seen along the road the hasty movements of the disguised priest, Nicholas Morton, as from time to time he passed between Rome and Bawtry, 'a notable busy factor for the Pope in England.' Strype tells us that 'his resort was to Bautrie, where he lived obscurely at that town of danger, half a mile from the highway and open along the north road to all parts of England and Scotland.[2] Soon after Elizabeth's coronation this man fled to Rome, but during the next thirty years he was often to and fro on secret errands, coming sometimes by way of Boston and sometimes by Grimsby, and remaining months at a time for purposes of intrigue. He was involved in that Catholic rising when, on November 14, 1569, the Earls of Northumberland and Westmoreland entered Durham in arms, passed into the cathedral, tore the Bible and Prayer-book to pieces, set up the old altar, and had the mass said once more at the altar of St. Cuthbert, after which they pushed on to Doncaster with an army which soon swelled to thousands of men. This same Nicholas Morton was also the man who, at the peril of his life, brought over in 1570 the papal bull by which Pius V. declared Queen Elizabeth a heretic, and as such cut off from the communion of the faithful, and her crown and kingdom forfeited; and as he and his nephew Robert Morton at Bawtry were only some fifteen or sixteen miles from Fotheringay Castle, where Mary Queen of Scots was prisoner, there they were often the medium of communication between her and her Catholic friends across the sea.

---

[1] *An Account of the Hospital of St. Mary Magdalen, near Scrooby.* MS. in the possession of Thomas Frewer, Esq. Hearne's Works. Vol. iv., 1810.

[2] *Annals*, 1575. Vol. II., pp. i., 577-579.

With these sixteenth-century memories in our minds we pass the elm-trees round Bawtry Hall, with their lively colony of rooks, and half a mile farther on we come to Gibbet Hill, with its gruesome associations of a dark and evil deed wrought at the old toll-gate more than a century ago. At this point we are in sight of Scrooby spire, and before crossing the bridge we had better leave the present high road, which is of modern date, and keep to the picturesque old road to the left, which goes past the clump of fir-trees and the slopes of red sandstone bright with golden furze, and so by the banks of Ryton stream as it goes its quiet way to the Idle and on to the Trent at Idle Stop. The old road comes out more and more distinctly as we go till it reaches the ford below the water-mill, and across this we pass into the centre of the village, as kings and nobles and long lines of meaner folk have passed before us, sometimes with the waters of the ford high up the wheels of the lumbering coach.

The village of Scrooby, situated 146 miles north of London, in the Bassetlawe division of Nottinghamshire, with its population of some two hundred souls, though small in extent, is of ancient fame. As far back as *Domesday Book* the manor belonged to the Archbishops of York, who had a palace here as well as at York, Bishopthorpe, Cawood, Southwell, Beverley, and elsewhere. It is not known when they first came here, but as early as 1178 John the Constable of Chester granted the town of Plumtree to Roger, Archbishop of York, and his successors for ever; and in 1537 Edward, a successor in the archbishopric, 'demised to Geoffrey Lee, Esquire, his brother, all that his great close, paled about, called Plumtree field, besides Scrooby Park with the lodge upon the same, together with all his warren and game of conies in the parishes of Scrooby and Harworth for forty-one years.'[1]

[1] Raine's *History and Antiquities of the Parish of Blyth.* 1860.

The parish church, which Leland described more than three centuries ago as 'not big but well builded,' is dedicated to St. Wilfrid, and is an embattled building in the Early English and Decorated styles, having a tower surmounted by four pinnacles and a lofty octagonal spire. It is somewhat one-sided in appearance, having an aisle on the south side, but none corresponding to it on the north. Two of the three bells in the tower go back farther than William Brewster's time, bearing date upon them 1411 and 1511; the third was not placed till 1647. The spire has been twice struck by lightning, once in 1817 and again in 1831; and the interior of the church was restored in 1862, about which time the old font disappeared, having found its way, it is said, to the American side of the Atlantic. Two massive benches, one on each side of the chancel, and having the backs and ends covered with carvings of the ancient Christian symbol, the grape vine, are remnants of the former majesty of the manor pew. The parish register, unfortunately, does not go back to the days of the Pilgrim Fathers; the oldest tombstone that is decipherable is that of Theophilus Torre, who died in 1620, and there is a monument to the memory of the daughter of Archbishop Sandys; but for the rest, when the churchyard was restored in recent years the gravestones were grouped together without respect to the bodies which lay beneath. Near the north-eastern gate are the old vicarage, the parish pound, and all that remains of the parish stocks. The quaint cottage known as the vicarage, built of small bricks, without a staircase except that furnished by an uplifted ladder, has for generations been the abode of the parish clerks, the vicar, having charge of three churches, residing in the neighbouring parish of Sutton-cum-Lound.

The primary interest, however, which now draws pilgrims to Scrooby, is neither the village nor the village church, so much as what remains of the old manor house and the

ANCIENT PEWS IN SCROOBY CHURCH.

field where still lie buried the foundations of the ancient palace. The latter building probably began to fall into decay about the time the little community of Christian men came to worship at William Brewster's house. Thoroton, writing of Scrooby in 1677, says :—' Here *within memory* stood a very fair palace, a far greater house of receit and a better seat for provision than Southwell, and had attending to it the North Soke, consisting of very many towns thereabouts ; it hath a fair park belonging to

SITE OF THE OLD STOCKS, SCROOBY CHURCHYARD.
(*From a sketch by* CHARLES WHYMPER.)

it. Archbishop Sandes caused it to be demised to his son Sir Samuel Sandes, since which the house hath been demolished almost to the ground.' The building whose decay and downfall were thus chronicled by the Nottinghamshire historian was one of the palaces held by the Archbishops of York in the days when they moved from one part of their diocese to another, administering various civil as well as ecclesiastical functions, dispensing hospitality and taking with them a numerous and splendid retinue.

It was of great antiquity. The letter by which Archbishop Gray granted to the brethren of the Hospital of St. John, Nottingham, the power to elect their own warders, was thus endorsed: 'Given at Scrooby by the hands of Master Simon of Evesham, the fourth of December, in the seventeenth year [of our pontificate.' December 11, 1232.][1] Being also near to one of the post stations on the great north road, it was not infrequently a hospice for distinguished travellers on their way south or north. It is recorded that Margaret, Queen of Scotland, daughter of King Henry VII., slept here on the 12th of June, 1603, on her way to Scotland.

For the space of several weeks also, towards the close of his strangely chequered career, Cardinal Wolsey made the old manor house his abiding-place, planting the mulberry-tree in the garden which till recent days was associated with his name. More a statesman than an ecclesiastic, he has been described as 'probably the greatest political genius whom England has ever produced; for at a great crisis of European history he impressed England with a sense of her own importance, and secured for her a leading position in European affairs.'[2] Though raised to the Archbishopric of York in 1514, it was not till 1530 that Wolsey visited the province over which he had been placed. When the royal favour was gone and his fortunes were broken, with a desolate heart, at the beginning of Passion week, he set out on his journey to York. After spending some time at his other manor house at Southwell, towards the end of the summer he removed from Southwell to Scrooby, where 'he continued until after Michaelmas, ministering many good deeds of charity.' In his retinue at this very time was an ecclesiastic who was to gain a notoriety of his own in later days. Bonner, afterwards

---

[1] Archbishop Gray's *Register*. Ed. Raines, p. 35.
[2] *Twelve English Statesmen*: Cardinal Wolsey, p. 2.

Bishop of London in Mary's reign, dates a letter to Thomas Cromwell 'at Scrooby with my Lord's grace,' in 1530.[1]

In this quiet interval at Scrooby, before the end came, Wolsey seems to have turned to simpler and more guileless pursuits than those so long congenial to him, of baffling kings and statesmen in the political game. One writing in 1536, says of him: 'Who was less beloved in the north than my lord cardinal before he was amongst them? Who better beloved after he had been there a while? He gave bishops a right good example how they might win men's hearts. There were few holy days but he would ride five or six miles from his house, now to this parish church, now to that, and there cause one or other of his doctors to make a sermon unto the people. He sat among them, and said mass before all the parish; he saw why churches were made, and began to restore them to their right and proper use. He brought his dinner with him, and bade divers of the parish to it, when he enquired whether there were any debate or grudge between any of them, and if there were he would, after dinner, send for the parties to the church and make them all one.' All this would be pleasant to read, were it not for the fact that behind all these pastoral simplicities there was a weary aching heart. For it was during these same Scrooby days Wolsey learnt that all his most cherished plans had come to nothing; that the king had dissolved his college at Ipswich, seizing all its lands and possessions; and that at Oxford the name of Christ Church had obliterated that of Cardinal College. 'I am put away from my sleep and meat,' he wrote, 'for such advertisements as I have had of the dissolution of my colleges.'

After three months spent at Scrooby, towards the end of September, the fallen minister set out for York, and two

---

[1] Ellis's *Original Letters*, III., vol. ii., p. 178.

months later he had taken that longer journey from which there is no return. As the end drew near he sent a message to the king, requesting 'His grace in God's name that he have a vigilant eye to depress this new pernicious sect of Lutherans, that it do not increase within his dominions through his negligence.' As if either king or cardinal could keep back the oncoming tide! Little did Wolsey dream that from that same manor house at Scrooby he had so lately left there would, in process of time, go forth a little band of earnest men who would carry across to the new world beyond the Atlantic the principles of freedom and self-government born of that very Reformation he was trying to crush with his dying hand. He could not foresee this, nor could he anticipate that even when, eleven years later—in 1541—the king himself slept a night at Scrooby on his way to the north the mighty change would have come, and that 'this new pernicious sect of the Lutherans' would be supreme in the State. Yet so it was. In that brief space the king had become a Lutheran himself, the Act of Supremacy had become law the monasteries were dissolved, the nation had passed over to the Protestant faith, and England was severed from the See of Rome.

We happen to be able to reproduce to our own mind's eye the palace, its appearance and equipment, as it was seen at the time. Leland, the antiquary, was there the same year as the king. Speaking of the year 1541, he says:—'In the meane townlet of Scrooby I marked two things—the parish church, not big but very well builded; the second was a great manor place, standing within a moat, and longing to the Archbishop of York; builded in two courts, whereof the first is very ample and all builded of timber, saving the front of the house that is of brick, to the which *ascenditur per gradus lapideos.* The inner court building, as far as I marked, was of timber building, and was not in compass past the fourth part of the outer court.'[1] So much for the exterior. The interior arrangement and equipment we gather from an official source. After their visitation of the province of York, Doctors Richard Layton and Thomas Legh presented their report to Cromwell. Describing the 'implements remayning at Scrooby,' they state that in the Hall there were three screens, six tables, nine forms, one cupboard, etc.; 'in the Chapell oone alter Tymber, oone lectionary and superalles, a payer of Organes, a Clock without plometts and ropes.' They tell us also what was in the 'dynyng chambre,' which was 'ceiled and dressed with waynscot,' what was in the 'winpholler's chambre and the four oodre chambres above and beneath,' and so on through all the thirty-nine chambers and apartments, even to 'the court between the galerie and the kitchen,' and including all the furniture, even to 'the olde tymbre of a shed over the well.' William Warener, the receiver, valued the rents of the archbishop's lordship of Scrooby at £167 11s. 4¾d., in purchasing value a far greater sum, of course, in those days than in these.[2]

After the Reformation and the visitation of the religious houses consequent thereon, the place seems to have lost something of its ancient stateliness, and to have entered upon its period of decline. In 1557 Archbishop Heath granted a lease of 'all his manor house or chief manor place of Scrooby with the park and lands' for twenty-one years at about £21 per annum, to James Bryne, the steward of his household. In 1575 Archbishop Grindal again leased the said manor for the same length of time and at the same rent to William Marshall of Much Hadham, co. Hertford, an arrangement which, however, seems to

---

[1] *Itinerary*, I. 36.
[2] *Letters and Papers* of the Reign of Henry VIII.: 27 Henry VIII., January 12, 153⅚.

have fallen through; for the following year, Archbishop Sandys, then recently elevated to the see of York, leased the same manor to his son, Sir Samuel Sandys, of the Middle Temple, at a yearly rent of £65 6s. 8d. By this time the Brewsters, with whom this narrative will be intimately concerned, appeared upon the scene; for in the month of January, 1575-6, Archbishop Sandys appointed William Brewster—the father of the Elder Brewster of later days—his receiver of Scrooby and all its liberties in Nottinghamshire, and also bailiff of the manor house, to hold both offices for life. The family were there even earlier still, for on the 'administration of the estate of William Brewster of Scrooby' being granted to William Brewster his son, in 1590, it is noted that the widow Prudence held the office of Post when he died, and that the father of the deceased man had held it before him. The connexion of the family with the office was therefore of long standing. In 1545, on the death of Sir Brian Tuke, who had been Master of the Postes, a letter was sent from the Privy Council to Mr. Mason, his successor, 'for the contynuance of Adam Gascoyne in the office of the Postship of Scrobye,' and a warrant to him the following year, 'that he shuld paye to Adam Gascoynes his dailye wages of iiijs. from the last of his payes.'[1]

As William Brewster's grandfather had probably succeeded Gascoyne, and been in turn succeeded by his own son, we may take it for granted that the future leader of the Pilgrim Fathers first saw the light in the old manor house which was the residence of the 'Post' for the time being. As he deposed at Leyden, June 25, 1609, that he was then forty-two years of age, he was born somewhere in 1566-7. After spending his early life at Scrooby and receiving education at some neighbouring school, William Brewster, as Bradford tells us, 'spent some small time

[1] *Privy Council Register*, 1545, p. 267; 1546, p. 363.

at Cambridge,' where he matriculated at Peterhouse, the oldest of the college foundations, December 3, 1580.[1] As he was at this date only about fourteen years of age, college could have been little more than a grammar school, and he appears not to have remained there long enough to take his degree. The next point in his history of which we have definite knowledge is that he was in the service of William Davison, Her Majesty's representative in the Netherlands when the cautionary towns of Brill and Flushing were delivered up to England in 1585. According to Bradford's narrative: 'After being first seasoned with the seeds of grace and virtue he went to the court, and served that religious and godly gentleman, William Davison, divers years when he was Secretary of State.'

The connexion between these two men thus referred to is interesting, as being one of the master facts of Brewster's life. The acquaintance probably first sprang up as Davison passed through Scrooby on his way to and from Scotland on business of State. We know that he was along the great North Road at the beginning of 1583 on a diplomatic mission to Scotland, together with Robert Bowes, for there is a letter of his to Lord Burghley, dated January 3, 1582-3, in which he describes how he met M. de la Mothe Fénélon, the French envoy, on the road, and discussed Catholicism with him. The object of the envoy was to arrange with James VI. an alliance with France, while Davison's object was to checkmate him. At that very time William Brewster would be at home from Cambridge, and as Davison would certainly have to change horses at the manor house at Scrooby—may possibly have had to stay the night there—it is probable the acquaintance then sprang up between them which led to Brewster entering

---

[1] Mr. Franklin B. Dexter, of Yale University, found the record of this fact in the general Matriculation lists preserved in the Registry at the Pitt Press.

Davison's service. This was an important step in the young man's life, bringing him into contact with some of the leading men of the time. In August 1585 he accompanied Davison to the Netherlands, where he went to negotiate an alliance with the States-General, and when on their return Davison became assistant to Walsingham, the Queen's Secretary of State, from the autumn of 1586 till the following February, Brewster was with him in the court at Richmond, where, as his correspondence shows, Davison was in daily attendance upon the queen.

As an official of the State, Davison was greatly esteemed and trusted, doing his work veraciously and resolutely. It was seldom that his advice to his own country on matters pertaining to the Netherlands did not prove to be the wisest that could be offered; and, on the other hand, Prince Maurice said of him that he was one of the best and most certain friends that the House of Nassau possessed in England. He was not only a capable and honest statesman, he was also a godly man, the esteemed elder of a Puritan church. In days when the bishops were pressing the Puritans with increased severity, many of them fled to Antwerp, which has been described as at that time the Pella of the Puritan refugees; and a church was formed in that city by the English and Scottish Merchant Adventurers. The church records of this community are still in existence, and it is from these we learn that Davison sustained an official relation to the church. Under date May 21, 1579, there is an entry to the effect 'that upon Mr. Davison's occasion to depart for England' it became necessary for the church to choose some additional elders. The records also mention that 'divers children borne to Mr. William Davison, Ambassador of Queen Elizabeth in Antwerp, and christened in the English church there, were afterwards naturalised in England.'[1]

[1] Additional MSS., 6394, pp. 113, 142.

On the 21st of the following January the grant was made to him of the office of the Clerk of the King's Bench and Keeper of the Records in the Treasury House at Westminster.[1] Davison's connexion with the Christian men who had gone to the Low Countries, partly for purpose of commerce and partly also for larger range of religious freedom, while it throws light on his character, throws light also indirectly on that of William Brewster in these early years. For their personal relations seem to have been not merely intimate, but even affectionate. Bradford tells us that the elder man found the younger 'so discreet and faithful as he trusted him above all that were about him, and only employed him in all matters of greatest trust and secrecy. He esteemed him rather as a son than a servant, and for his wisdom and godliness (in private) he would converse with him more like a friend and familiar than a master. He attended his master when he was sent in ambassage by the queen into the Low Countries (1585) in the Earl of Leicester's time, as for other weighty affairs of State, so to receive possession of the cautionary towns; and in token and sign thereof the keys of Flushing being delivered to him in Her Majesty's name, he kept them some time, and committed them to this his servant, who kept them under his pillow on which he slept the first night. And at his return the States honoured him with a gold chain, and his master committed it to him, and commanded him to wear it when they arrived in England, as they rode through the country till they came to the court.'[2]

Distinction so flattering coming thus early seemed to have in it the promise of a brilliant political future. Certainly it then seemed far from probable that the young man thus basking in the world's sunshine would

[1] *State Papers, Domestic.* Elizabeth. Addenda, 1566–1579.
[2] *History of Plymouth Plantation*, pp. 409, 410. Boston. 1856.

yet choose and that for a long lifetime 'to suffer affliction with the people of God.' Yet so it was. He who shapes our lives for us had other thoughts for William Brewster than that he should spend his days in royal courts, where, as Sir Walter Raleigh, one of his contemporaries, says: 'Strain'd sardonic smiles are glosing still; where mirth's but mummery, and sorrows only real be.' The change in his career came in manner most unexpected. Within two years of that triumphal return from the Netherlands Secretary Davison's fortunes came down with a crash, bringing with them the brilliant prospects of his younger friend. It seems strange to connect events apparently so wide apart, yet it is almost certain that but for the execution of Mary, Queen of Scots, there would have been no Pilgrim Church at Scrooby or at Leyden, no voyage of the Mayflower, and no Elder Brewster in Plymouth Church, with all his far-reaching influence in American life. The way the death of the Scottish queen came to affect the whole course of Puritan history may be briefly explained. Elizabeth had resolved upon the death of Mary, but hesitated long before taking the final step. For months a warrant for the execution had been drawn up, waiting for that signature which the queen's ministers urged her again and again to give. At length, when the Scotch and French ambassadors were gone, and with them the last excuse for delay, she did sign it in the presence of Davison, who had lately become co-secretary with Walsingham, and having signed it directed him to have it sealed. It is clear now that she meant the execution to take place, but meant at the same time to throw the responsibility on someone else. Davison says that she 'forbade him to trouble her any further, or let her hear any more thereof till it was done, seeing that for her part she had now performed all that either in law or reason could be required of her.' But signing the death warrant, as both of them knew, was not enough; there must also be formal delivery of it to some person, with direction to carry it out. This the queen contrived to evade, and when, on February 9, 1587, news of the execution arrived, and she found it convenient to throw the responsibility of the deed upon her subordinates, she stormed at Davison for exceeding her instructions, and made him the scapegoat of the transaction. Tried before a special commission on the charge of divulging State secrets, he was fined ten thousand marks, deprived of his secretaryship, and sent as prisoner to the Tower.

With this fall of Davison came, as we have said, the fall of his friend and favourite, William Brewster, so far at least as his position at court was concerned. Bradford tells us that 'afterwards he went and lived in the country, in good esteem amongst his friends and the gentlemen of those parts, especially the godly and religious.' In other words, he went back to Scrooby, towards the end of 1587, at a time when, as it turned out, his services began to be greatly needed at home. His father had for several years held the responsible position of 'Post' on the great North Road at Scrooby, but now his health was failing, and he was unequal to the discharge of its duties, indeed, within a year and a half, in the summer of 1590, he was taken away by death. During these later months, the younger Brewster came back opportunely to fill his father's place. So completely did he do this, that his name appears to have been enrolled on the official list of Posts, and for a year and a half he received the emoluments. Nothing seemed more natural, therefore, than that he should receive the appointment when the position became formally vacant by the death of his father. In this, at first, he was disappointed. That same summer, in the month of June, Sir John Stanhope was made Postmaster-General, and he appointed one Samuel Bevercotes, a lawyer of Gray's Inn, to the vacant position. He had two reasons for preferring this man to William Brewster; first, he was his kinsman, and next, Brewster had not shown him that deference he expected—'All this while, and to this hour,' says he, 'I never heard one word from young Brewster, he neither came to me, being in town, nor sent to me being absent, but as though I were to be overruled by others made his way according to his liking. I know my interest such as whether he had the place or no I can displace him, and thynk him worthily displaced for his contempt of me in not sekyng me at all.' This was in answer to an earnest letter from ex-secretary Davison, strongly urging the prior claim of his friend William Brewster. Sir John Stanhope's letter is among the State Papers. It is dated Oatlands, August 22 [1590], and on the back are notes in William Davison's handwriting, showing 'Why young Brewster ought to bee appointed.' He says that he 'was possessed of the place longe before his father's death, as may appeare by the enrolment of his name on the rolls among the other Postes; by receipt of the fee for a year and a half; by the testimony of Mr. Mills, who was privie to the grant, and did both register his name and pay him the wages; and his exercise of the place for above a year and a halfe, which may be testified by the Postes his next neighbours. Neither is there any just cause to except against him, either in respect of his honestie, sufficiency for the service, discharge thereof hitherto, or other wayes whatever.'

Other reasons also are noted at the back of this letter why Brewster should not be displaced, such as: 'the charge he hath been at provision this hard year for the service; the loss he would sustain, or rather, utter undoing by being suddenly dispossessed, and the harmes of the example' to Her Majesty's Service.[1] It may be safely assumed that these strong reasons written by Davison at the back of

---

[1] *State Papers, Domestic.* Elizabeth. Vol. ccxxxiii., 48. 22 August [1590]. Sir John Stanhope to Sec. Davison.

Sir John's letter, were rough notes afterwards expanded into a reply sent to the Postmaster-General; for Bevercotes' appointment seems shortly after to have been cancelled, and William Brewster made Post of Scrooby. Indeed, Sir John had prepared the way in his own letter for a retreat, possibly from some misgiving as to the equity of his procedure: 'If I find cause, and may, without disgracing my cousin [*i.e.* Bevercotes] and touch to myself, I will revoke my grant, if you shall not rest satisfied that he have any other that shall fall void with the first. You shall hear and see ere long what I will do to satisfy you.' The outcome of it all was that Davison's chivalrous devotion to his friend, devotion as honourable to one side as to the other, carried the day against the nepotism of the Postmaster-General, and for the next eighteen years of his life William Brewster filled the office at Scrooby his father and grandfather had filled before him.

As everything relating to one so eminent among the Pilgrim Fathers of America as William Brewster came to be is of interest to us now, it may be worth while to look at the nature of his occupation as Post of Scrooby, from the time when he was a young man of twenty-three, till he reached the age of forty. Until the reign of Henry VIII., or perhaps even earlier, there was no regular system of posts in England, and for long after that the only four that were established were for the exclusive use of the sovereign. In 1572, Thomas Randolph, the immediate predecessor of Sir John Stanhope as Master of the Post to Queen Elizabeth, rendered an account of the charges to which he had been put in the execution of his trust during the preceding five years. In this account, no single post is mentioned without connecting it in some way closely with the person of the sovereign. It was 'a post daily serving Her Majesty,' 'a post for Her Majesty's Service and affairs,' 'a post during the time of Her Majesty's progress,' or 'a post for the conveyance of Her Majesty's letters and those of Her Council.' These posts were always spoken of as journeys of the court, thus: 1. 'The Courte to Barwick,' that is, the post to Scotland; 2. 'The Courte to Beaumaris,' that is, the post to Ireland; 3. 'The Courte to Dover,' that is, the post to the Continent; and 4. 'The Courte to Plymouth,' that is, the post to the Royal Dockyard. But the conveyance of the sovereign's letters was not the only purpose these posts were originally designed to serve. Another purpose of an important kind was that there should be stationed in constant readiness, and at given distances along these four main roads of the kingdom, a relay of horses, by which persons travelling on the affairs of the State might pass from place to place. So that it was rather as a means of travelling than as a means of correspondence that the post came to be used by others not employed on affairs of the State.[1] Indeed, the increasing number of such persons making use of the posts for this purpose became an embarrassment to the public service. In the Privy Council Register, under date Feb. 12, 1566-7, there is the following entry:—

'The Lords this day considering how much trouble daily groweth unto the realm abrode by continual granting from their lordships of letters for post-horses to diverse noblemen and gentlemen being not sent for any case of the Queen's Majesty's Service, but travelling in their own private business, have thought good to order that from henceforth no warrant or passport be signed for any posthorses, except the same be for the Queen's Majesty's Service.'

The earliest instructions we have for the regulation of the post were issued about the time the elder Brewster

[1] *History of the Post Office down to* 1836: by Herbert Joyce, C.B., of the Post Office. 1893.

officiated at Scrooby. Every 'Post' was to keep and have constantly ready two horses at least, with suitable 'furniture'; he was also to have at least two bags of leather well lined with baize or cotton, and a horn for the driver to blow 'as oft as he meets company,' or four times in every mile. After receiving the packet entrusted to him, the driver was to start within fifteen minutes, and to run in the summer at the rate of seven miles an hour, and in winter five. The address of the packet of State letters and the day and hour at which it was received were to be carefully entered in a book to be kept for the purpose.[1] The pace prescribed for travelling was not always kept even in summer, for in 1589, when the younger Brewster was acting for his sick father, there was a charge of negligence as to the transmission of a despatch sent from Berwick to London by Sir Henry Wodrington on the 25th of August. It appears from the Articles of Charge that the one hundred and fifty-five miles between Berwick and Newark took eighty-three hours to travel, so that the pace was less than two miles an hour. The despatch in question left Doncaster 'at ij in the morninge and reached to the post of Scrobie,' that is, came into young William Brewster's hands, 'the same day at iiij in the morning. Soe in riding vij miles ij houres,'[2] which came nearer to the regulation pace.[3]

[1] Joyce's *History of the Post Office.*
[2] *State Papers, Domestic.* Elizabeth. Addenda, Vol. xxxi., 40, 1589.
[3] This was not the first time that complaint had to be made concerning the dilatoriness of the Northern Post, as the following extract from the Privy Council Register shows : ' 29 August, 1558. A lettre to Sir John Mason signifying unto him the usual slackness of the Postes layed northwarde in the conveyance of letters hither, and the opening of them by the way, and therefore requiring of him to give orders forthwith for their reformation on that behalf, or else the Queen's Majesty must be enforced to discharge them every one, and to seek some new means to be served from time to time with a through Poste.'

The office of 'Post' on the four great roads was one of more importance and responsibility than that of a country postmaster of our time. As we have seen, the position at Scrooby was sought for by Samuel Bevercotes, who is described as a lawyer of Gray's Inn. In Brewster's days also, Rowland Whyte, who was a correspondent of many of the nobility of the time, was the 'Post of the Court.' Nicholas Heyford, and after him Ralph Aslaby, was post at Doncaster, and Heyford and Aslaby were both names of respectable families in the south part of the West Riding of Yorkshire, corresponding in social position, as we may suppose, with the Brewsters.[1] The emoluments of the office were from £275 to £325 a year in present value. From Sir John Stanhope's account, declared before Lord Burghley, the Lord High Treasurer, and Sir John Fortescue, Chancellor of the Exchequer, March 31, 1597, for the three preceding years, we find that from April 1594, to April 1597, 'William Brewster, Post of Scrooby, for his ordinary wages, serving Her Majesty all the time aforesaid, at 20*d.* per diem, £91 6*s.* 8*d.*' From the 1st of July, 1603, Brewster's wages were advanced from 20*d.* to 2*s.* a day,[2] as is shown by the following entry: 'William Brewster, Post of Scrooby, for his wages as well, at 20*d.* per diem for 640 days, begun the 1st of July, 1603, and ended the last of March, 1605, £102.' The latest account in which Brewster's name occurs brings us to the very time when, as we shall see hereafter, the members of the church at Scrooby had to flee from persecution to Holland. This entry is interesting, therefore, as telling us precisely when

[1] Hunter's *Collection*, p. 70.
[2] It has been seen that Adam Gascoyne was to have four shillings a day in 1546 till further order taken. The varying scale of payment may be explained by the following extract from the Privy Council Register: 'At St. James. 19 Oct. 1557. It was the day agreed by the Boarde that the Postes serving northerwarde shal have from the xvth of this present moneth, *during the warres* xxd. a pece by the daie for theire better reliefe and enterteignement.'

William Brewster went into exile, and who his successor was at Scrooby. 'William Brewster, Post of Scrooby, for his wages at 2s. per diem for 183 days, begun the 1st of April, 1607, and ended the last of September, 1607, £18 6s.; and then Francis Hall succeeding him at 2s. per diem for 548 days begun the 1st of October, 1607, and ended the last of March, 1609, £73 2s.'[1] This at a time when a skilled workman's wages were fixed at eightpence a day[2] would amount to from £275 to £325 a year. There would seem also to have been additional income accruing from other sources besides State payment. In 1605, Sir Timothy Hutton, the son of the Archbishop of York, journeying to and from London, paid to the 'post' at Scrooby, who must have been William Brewster, for a conveyance and guide to Tuxford, ten shillings, and for a candle, supper, and breakfast, seven shillings and tenpence, so that he slept under Brewster's roof. On his return he paid to the post at Scrooby eight shillings for conveying him to Doncaster, and two shillings for burnt sack, bread, beer, and sugar to wine, and threepence to the ostler.[3] Thus the postmaster, while enlarging his income as hotel-keeper at the old manor house, was again brought into frequent contact with some of the most distinguished persons both of Church and State, who as they travelled the great North Road came to abide under his roof.

Before proceeding to speak of the fortunes of the Pilgrim Church at Scrooby, there is one other man, the life-long friend and biographer of William Brewster, scarcely second in interest to Brewster himself, to whom we may turn for a moment or two. This was William Bradford, afterwards Governor Bradford of Plymouth Colony, and the historian of Plymouth Plantation. He was born at Austerfield—in Domesday it is called *Oustre-*

---

[1] Quoted in Hunter's *Collections*, pp. 66–68.
[2] *Hatfield MSS.*, iv., 455.
[3] *Surtees' Society Publications.* Vol. xvii., pp. 197–204.

feld, whether from the Scandinavian word *oster*, for east, or whether because the Roman Ostorius was here defeated by the Romans, it may not be easy to say. This is an ancient village about three miles from Scrooby on the Yorkshire side, consisting of a few houses inhabited by a population of about three hundred and fifty persons, chiefly engaged in agricultural pursuits. There is still a Roman camp near the village, and there was a chapel here even before 1229 which belonged to the canons of Blyth, to whom it was given by John de Buslis. Probably the present quaint old church of the place, dedicated to St. Helen, is substantially the same as that erected by De Buslis. It is a stone edifice partly Norman in style, consisting of a chancel and nave under a single roof, having a porch on the south side, and surmounting the western gable a bell-cote similar to that of the beautiful church at Wycliffe, containing two small bells. The chancel arch is Norman, and the south doorway of the same period has two nook shafts with cushioned caps, supporting an arch enriched with zigzag and beak-headed moulding, in the tympanum being a rude figure of a dragon with other ornaments. The interior was re-pewed in an excruciating manner about sixty years ago, but the outside remains probably much as it was when on March 19, 1589 (N.S. 1590), William Bradford was brought to be baptised by Henry Fletcher, who in his own neat, clear hand entered the record in the old register, which goes back to 1559.

Bradford, born in the same year that Brewster was appointed Post at Scrooby, was thus his junior by some three-and-twenty years, and was only a youth of about seventeen when he began to consort with the brethren meeting in Scrooby Manor House. The house in which he is reputed to have been born is still shown by the side of the road as we make our way to the church. His father seems to have been a yeoman of fairly good position; but he died when William was little more than a year old,

SOUTH DOORWAY, AUSTERFIELD CHURCH.

leaving him, as Cotton Mather tells us, a comfortable inheritance. The fatherless child thus left was committed to the care of his grandfather, who also died some five years later, after which the boy was brought up by his uncles William, Thomas, and Robert Bradford, or Bradfurth, 'who devoted him, like his ancestors, unto the affairs of husbandry.' Some idea of the social position of the Bradfords may be gathered from the fact that William's maternal grandfather, John Hanson, shared with old William Bradford the honour of being the only subsidymen at Austerfield; and also from the will of his uncle, 'Robert Bradfurth, of Austerfield, yeoman.' In this the testator, who was of the yeoman class—the class in the reign of Elizabeth next to the acknowledged gentry, using coat-armour of right—sets out with declarations of his Christian faith in more energetic terms than usual, and then leaves bequests to Austerfield Chapel, and to Thomas Silvester, clerk. He leaves to one of his servants, Grace Wade, the free use of a dwelling-house, and to others small legacies; to his son Robert he gives his best iron-bound wain, the cupboard in the 'house'—the apartment corresponding to the modern parlour—and one long form, with his best yoke of oxen, also the 'counter wherein the evidences are.' He leaves him also the piece of armour known as the corslet, with all the furniture thereto belonging. While he divides the residue of his property equally among all his four children, he directs that his son Robert shall have the reversion of two leases; the one of all the king's lands he has in Austerfield, the other of the closes which he has of Mr. Morton in Martin lordship. He consigns the care of his four children, who were all under age, to 'my good neighbour Mr. Richardson, of Bawtry,' William Downes, of Scrooby, and Mr. Silvester, of Alkley. We may fairly infer from this that the Bradfords were in good repute and association with the more prosperous of their neighbours, for, next to the Mortons

Mr. Richardson was the most considerable person then living at Bawtry; Mr. Downes was a subsidy-man at Scrooby, while Mr. Silvester, the third of the guardians of Robert Bradford's children, was a divine at Alkley, possessed of a fair estate, and, what perhaps had some influence on the intellectual growth of the future governor of Plymouth Colony, was possessed also of a library of English and Latin books at a time when in the rural parts of England books were costly and few As a quaint illustration of the times, it may be mentioned that this good divine of Alkley, by his will, made in 1615, gave to the poor scholars of the grammar school at Rossington his *Cooper's Dictionary*, to be chained to a stall in the church, and used by them as long as it will last.[1]

Such, with their local and social surroundings in early life, were the two men William Brewster and William Bradford, who were to impress their own individuality so powerfully upon the religious life of the American people. The friendship which sprang up between them amid the tranquil surroundings of the North Midlands of their native land was to be deepened by common labours and aspirations, and by common hardships and sufferings endured side by side both in the Old World and the New. Through all the discipline of coming years they were to be trained by Him who leads men in a way they know not, for service the issues of which they see not. The honour of helping humanity forward towards its great consummation can only thus be won by those who are willing to bear the cross to the steep of Calvary, to go through sorrow and self-sacrifice with meekness and magnanimous patience:

> We know the arduous strife, the eternal laws
> To which the triumph of all good is given.
> High sacrifices, and labour without pause,
> Even to the death:—else wherefore should the eye
> Of man converse with immortality?

[1] Hunter's *Collections*, pp. 103-109.

SCROOBY MANOR HOUSE.
(From a sketch by CHARLES WHYMPER.*)*

THE BRIDGE, GAINSBOROUGH.
(*From a sketch by* CHARLES WHYMPER.)

III.

BEGINNINGS OF CHURCH LIFE.

WHEN the Pilgrim Fathers of New England founded Plymouth Colony, they did so as a federal body bound together by solemn, social compact, and not as separate emigrants drawn by mere accident to the same settlement. This special character of the colony, which had important political results in after time, may be explained by the fact that its founders had first been in fellowship in the same Christian community in the Old World before they were colonists together in the New. The Covenant of Citizenship signed on board the Mayflower, in 1620, really had its origin in that 'Covenant of the Lord' which, 'as the Lord's free people,' the members of the Church, first at Gainsborough, and then at Scrooby, solemnly made, 'to walk together in all His ways made known, or to be made known to them, according to their best endeavours, whatsoever it should cost them, the Lord assisting them.'

The church thus founded by covenant, unlike the other Separatist churches we have already met with in London, or in provincial cities like Norwich, took its rise in a scattered rural district, remote from the great centres of population. What is also remarkable is that this church took its rise in a region where, a generation or two before, the people had risen in revolt against Protestantism and in favour of retaining Roman Catholicism as the religion of the National Church. It was only some forty miles from Scrooby, as the crow flies, and only about thirty years before William Brewster was born, that the insurrection known as the 'Pilgrimage of Grace' took its rise. For it was on October 2, 1536, that the Ecclesiastical Commissioners for the Suppression of Monasteries were to hold their visitation at Louth, and it was then the people of Lincolnshire rose in armed rebellion against them. As one of the commissioners rode into the town the alarm bell pealed out from Louth Tower, and the inhabitants swarmed into the streets with bills and staves, 'the stir and noise arising hideous.' The commissioner, alarmed for his safety, fled into the church for sanctuary, but was soon brought out into the market-place, and with a sword held at his breast was made to swear to be true to the Commons upon pain of death. There were risings, too, at Caistor and at Horncastle, where the bishop's chancellor was murdered in the street; at Lincoln also, where the bishop's palace was attacked and plundered. Before the week was out all the countryside was in movement, beacons blazing, alarm bells ringing, and whole parishes rising to demand that the suppressed monasteries should be restored, and the new Protestant bishops deprived and punished. From the Lincolnshire side of Scrooby the rising spread to the Yorkshire side also, taking even more serious shape. It was at Scrooby that on October 21, the Earl of Shrewsbury, Lord Steward of the King's Household and Lieutenant-General from the Trent northward, was in anxious consultation with the Earls of Rutland and Huntingdon concerning this Catholic rebellion, and it was from Scrooby that same day they sent Thomas Myller, Lancaster Herald, as he himself tells us, 'with a proclamation to be read amongst the traitors and rebellious persons assembled at Pomfret, contrary to the King's laws.'[1]

The intense feeling of hostility thus manifested against the Reformation, in the district of which Scrooby may be roughly regarded as the centre, was doubtless largely owing to the numerous monasteries the district contained. All the more conspicuous monastic orders had their representatives within a comparatively short distance of the village where William Brewster was born. There were Cistercians at Rufford, Gilbertines at Mattersey, Carthusians in the Isle of Axholm, Benedictine monks at Blythe, Benedictine nuns at Wallingwells, Augustinians at Worksop, and Premonstratensians at Welbeck—the chief house of that order in the country—so that together they seemed to form a circle round that part of he Basset-Lawe Hundred to which Scrooby belonged. The influence of these great religious houses remained after they themselves were suppressed, and goes far to explain why, long after the Reformation, so many of the county families of the neighbourhood, the Molineuxes and Markhams, the Cliftons and Mortons, the Countess of Shrewsbury at Rufford, and her sister Frances Lady

[1] *State Papers.* Henry VIII. Part II., p. 462, sq. 1536.

Pierrepoint at Thoresby, held tenaciously to the Church of Rome, and in Elizabeth's reign were ready, many of them, to face dangers and endure hardship in its service.

In the second half of the sixteenth century, however, other influences had been at work in a contrary direction. Many of the ministers introduced to the parish churches of the district were of a strongly marked Puritan type. Bradford, in his *History of Plymouth Plantation*, distinctly traces the rise of the Scrooby church, of which he was himself one of the foremost members, to the religious influence exercised by the Puritan clergy. He tells us that it was 'by the travail and diligence of some godly and zealous preachers and God's blessing on their labours, as in some other places of the land, so in the north parts, many became enlightened by the Word of God, and had their ignorance and sins discovered unto them, and began by His grace to reform their lives and make conscience of their ways.' The movement, therefore, was from the first distinctly spiritual in its character, proceeding from earnest men with a deep sense of the infinite, and feeling the gravity and grandeur of eternal things. The craving for the new life thus created by the truth and the Spirit of truth, also kindled in them a spirit of holy indignation against the abuse of sacred things they saw going on around them. The free spirit of Englishmen was stirred within them as they saw what they described as 'base and beggarly ceremonies' retained in the Church, and enforced both upon clergy and laity by 'the lordly and tyrannous power of the prelates, which ought not to be submitted unto.' They protested that it was 'contrary to the freedom of the Gospel so to load and burden men's consciences, and by their compulsive power to make a prophane mixture of persons and things in the worship of God.' They maintained that these ecclesiastical 'offices and callings, courts and canons were unlawful and un-

Christian, and had no warrant in the Word of God.' 'So many, therefore, of these professors as saw the evil of these things in these parts, and whose hearts the Lord had touched with heavenly zeal for His truth, shook off this yoke of anti-Christian bondage, and as the Lord's free people joined themselves, by a covenant of the Lord, into a church estate, in the fellowship of the Gospel.'

We are able to recall to our minds some at least of the godly and zealous preachers whose travail and diligence in that region produced such enduring results. Between six and seven miles due south of Scrooby was the village of Babworth, close to Retford. It had for its rector in those days Richard Clyfton, described by Bradford as 'a grave and reverend preacher, who by his pains and diligence had done much good.' He was instituted to the rectory of Babworth on July 11, 1586, and was probably set aside from his cure about the time of Bancroft's enforcement of the canons of 1603. Long years afterwards, when he was growing an old man himself in his New England home, William Bradford recalled the name and memory of this good man, whom in his youth he walked some nine miles from Austerfield on Sunday mornings to hear. There is a touch of filial affection in the way he speaks of him. He says: 'He was a grave and fatherly old man when he came first into Holland, having a great white beard; and pity it is that such a reverend old man should be forced to leave his country and at those years to go into exile. But it was his lot, and he bore it patiently. Much good had he done in the country where he lived, and converted many to God by his faithful and painful ministry, both in preaching and catechizing.'

Even Richard Bernard, his clerical neighbour at Worksop, though in after years they took divers ways, could not help saying that Richard Clyfton was one whom he truly and entirely loved as a man devoted to

God, and every way worthy of love for his irreprovable life and conversation. This venerable man, who seems to have been the spiritual father of many of those who formed the Scrooby church, became their first pastor, and in 1608, as we shall see, went with them into exile to Amsterdam.[1]

We have already mentioned Clyfton's clerical neighbour Richard Bernard, the vicar of Worksop, who was one of the notable men of the Basset-Lawe Hundred, and who, as living only some eight miles south-east of Scrooby, came to be well known to the brethren there. Judging from a rather fine portrait of him which has come down to us, he was a noticeable man to meet in a country road or to listen to from the pulpit of a country church. After graduating at Cambridge he was, in 1598, presented to the living of Epworth in Lincolnshire, the birthplace of John Wesley and Alexander Kilham, where he began his literary career by publishing a quaint translation of *Terence*, and on June 19, 1601, he was instituted to the vicarage of Worksop. He is interesting to us as the man in controversy with whom John Robinson wrote the greatest work of his life, and interesting for his own sake, too, as a writer of more than ordinary versatility and genius. His book, entitled *The Isle of Man, or the Legall Proceeding in Man-shire against Sin*, shows him to have been an original allegorist long before John Bunyan took up his pen. Indeed, it is not possible to compare this work with Bunyan's *Holy War, or the Losing and Taking again of Mansoul*, without coming to the conclusion that the Great Dreamer had read the book and received many suggestions from it. Bernard, for example, tells us that in travelling through the Isle of Man he came to the 'county

---

[1] He was later the author of *A Plea for Infants and Elder People concerning their Baptism*. Printed at Amsterdam, by Giles Thorp, 1610; also of *An Advertisement concerning a Book lately published by C. Lawne and others against the English Exiled Church at Amsterdam*. 1612.

RICHARD BERNARD.
(From an old print.)

towne called Soule.' This Soule's-towne is a place of great resort, a thorowfare never without travellers, and has four great streets: Sense Street, Thought Street, Word Street, and Deed Street, along which that pestilent thief Sin, with his Copemates, may often be found wandering. There is also a Common Inne in the place kept by Mistress Heart, who lives there with one Old Man. This Inne is a well-accustomed house, for many pests, which are Satan's suggestions, take up their lodgings there. It has five doors, the five senses, for the guests to come in at, and these guests are well-waited upon, for Mistress Heart hath the eleven passions for her maids, and her man Will hath at his command the feet, the hands, and the tongue, who act as hostler, tapster, and chamberlaine. The book is in two parts; the first setting forth the search for, the attacking and imprisoning of Sin, the second narrating the trial, before the bar of Conscience, and a jury of the Virtues, of Old Man, Mistress Heart, Covetousness, and Idolatry. There is considerable resemblance between this second part and the trial of the Diabolonians, Atheism, Hard-heart, False-peace, No-truth, and Pitiless, decribed by Bunyan as taking place in Mansoul; and Bernard is almost as happy in hitting off some of his names as Bunyan himself.

Curiously enough, in this book he not only anticipated one Bedfordshire worthy, but also another who did honour to its county town—John Howard, the prison philanthropist. In the Epistle to the Reader, Bernard pleads on behalf of an 'unbegun worke' in the interest of the prisoners in the gaols of the kingdom. He says that the state of these prisoners is well known, and how their souls' safety is neglected; he urges, therefore, the appointment of prison chaplains. He pleads also for prison labour against the then existing system of wasteful and destructive idleness: 'If there should be means to set them on worke they might get somewhat for food and raiment.

They might so prevent the miserable fruits of sloth; their minds would be imployed, their bodies be preserved in health, and not pine away.' Enforced labour would, he thinks, 'terrifie loose vagrants, lazie wanderers, and the idle route from turning theeves.' The prison is now, he says, 'a very picture of Hell, and (more is the pity), as the case now stands, is no less than a preparation thereto;' whereas if prisoners were treated as he suggests, they would, on their release, 'become through God's mercie more profitable members in the Common-Weale afterwards; whereas now they become twice more the children of Belial than they were before.'

The man who could say this a hundred and fifty years before John Howard published his *Survey of the State of Prisons*, was no commonplace observer, but one who looked at things with his own eyes and could think his own thoughts. That he was an earnest preacher of Christ's Gospel, as well as a social reformer before the days of social reform, may be gathered from another book of his entitled, *The Faithfull Shepeard, or the Shepeard's Faithfulnesse*. It is an appeal for an earnest ministry as the need of the times, and also serves as a study in Homiletics. He is severe on those among the gentry who think the ministry of the Gospel beneath the notice of their sons: 'Some of our states and gentric wish their children anything; worldly lawyers, fraudulent merchants, killing physicians, bloody captains, idle, loose livers, swearing ruffians, walkers on Shooter's Hill, and coursers on Salisburie Plains, to maintain their riot, rather than as they call them—priests. And yet this state is magnified of God and man.' In charging young preachers he advises them not to venture into regions too high for them: 'Controversies require sharpness of wit and some cunning to find out Satan's sophistries. Young cockerills that begin but to crowe may not set upon the great cocks of the

BEGINNINGS OF CHURCH LIFE. 83

game.' Beginners in the work of preaching sometimes 'want seemly gesture' from two opposite causes : first, from rash boldness or an inconsiderate zeal, 'they have moved them to violent motions, as casting abroad of their armes, smiting on the pulpit, lifting themselves up and againe suddenly stamping downe.' On the other hand, they fall into undesirable ways through 'too great feare and bashfulness, which causeth hemmings, spittings, rubbing the browes, lifting up of the shoulders, nodding of the head, taking often hold of the cloake or gowne, fidling with the fingers upon the breast buttons, stroaking of the beard and such-like toies.'

This vivid piece of literature is dated 'Worksop, June 16, 1607,' and therefore saw the light the very year the Scrooby church was worshipping at the old manor house before going into exile, and its author must have been a familiar presence to Brewster and Bradford at the time it was written. The truth is, that Richard Bernard was at one time so entirely in sympathy with the views on church life held by the Scrooby brethren that they expected him to become a Separatist with them. He went so far as to set up a Congregational church within the walls of his parish church, 'did separate from the rest' of the parishioners 'a hundred voluntary professors into covenant with the Lord, sealed up with the Lord's Supper, to forsake all known sin, to hear no wicked or dumb ministers.' This is what John Robinson[1] tells us of him, and his neighbour John Smyth of Gainsborough 'Took notice of his forwardness in leading to a reformation by public proclamation in several pulpits, as if he had meant contrary to the king's mind to have carried all the people of the country after him against the ceremonies and subscription.'[2]

[1] *Works*, II., 101.
[2] *Paralleles, Censures, Observations.* A Letter to Mr. Ric. Bernard. 1609.

After the passing of the canons of 1603, Bernard did indeed for a while refuse subscription or conformity, but on being silenced by the Archbishop of York he began to reconsider his ways. The new light thrown upon his opinions by this action of the archbishop gave him pause, and led him to say: 'Time is an instructor to a diligent searcher; I see now what then I saw not . . . Through ignorance, which taketh for light that which is darkness, I was tossed by the present tempest sometime to a favouring but otherwhile to a great dislike. . . . I confess I was much moved with fair show of Scripture, but I was not removed.' When danger threatened he faced about and kept his place; and, what is perhaps not unusual with men of his class, from the time of his own retreat he began to assail those with whom he had formerly agreed. It was this which led John Robinson to say to him in solemn searching way: 'A speech of your own uttered to myself (ever to be remembered with fear and trembling) cannot I forget, when after conference between Mr. H[elwisse] and me you uttered these words: "Well, I will return home and preach as I have done, and I must say as Naaman did, The Lord be merciful to me in this thing."'[1]

Besides Richard Clyfton, who went forward even to exile, and Richard Bernard, who drew back, there were other Puritan ministers in the neighbourhood, such as Thomas Toller, of Sheffield, who was presented before the Ecclesiastical Court at York in 1607, and of whom the records say: 'Did not appear in the Visitation, is said to be a Precisian, if not a Brownist; he is no observer of the Book of Common Prayer, nor any way conformable to order.' Robert Gifford, also of Laughton-en-le-Northen, though he did not go the length of actual separation, was one of those ministers who 'seemed weary of the ceremonies,' and whom Bradford describes as being 'hotly

[1] *Works*, II., 8.

BEGINNINGS OF CHURCH LIFE. 85

pursued by the prelates.' There was yet another clergyman of the neighbourhood, Hugh Bromhead, who shared these convictions so strongly as to give up his living and go into exile. In a letter to his cousin, William Hamerton, who remonstrated with him on the step he had taken, he expresses his convictions strongly and clearly. Among other reasons he gives for his separation from the National Church, he emphasises two, on which stress was laid by the early Congregationalists. He left, he says, 'For that the profane, ungodly multitude, without exception of any one person, are with them received into and retained in the bosom of the Church'; also, 'for that these churches are ruled by and remain in subjection unto an antichristian and ungodly government, clean contrary to the institution of our Saviour Christ.'[1]

Besides these brethren on the Nottinghamshire side of the Trent, averse to what they regarded as Romish concessions in the Church, there were Puritan ministers also across the river in Lincolnshire, who in 1605 published an abridgment of the points at issue between themselves and the conformable clergy. In this pamphlet they state that they can join with the Church in her doctrines and sacraments, but cannot declare their approbation of the ceremonies. These men, as more scrupulous than some of their brethren, were yet not favourers of the Presbyterian discipline, and were therefore called 'the brethren of the Second Separation.'[2]

The Puritan feeling thus fostered by many of the clergy themselves on both sides the Trent finally took actual shape in the formation of a Separatist community, first of all in the town of Gainsborough, in the year 1602. This town, where the northern Separatists first entered into organised Christian fellowship, was one of the most ancient

[1] *Harl. MSS.* 360, fol. 70.
[2] Lathbury's *History of Episcopacy*, p. 74. 1836.

in the kingdom. On the site of the quaint old hall still standing by the banks of the Trent, once stood the palace in which King Alfred was married, and where Canute, the son of Sweyn, was born. It was here also that Canute was proclaimed King of England by the captains of his navy, and where, as tradition says, he rebuked his courtiers by commanding the onward rushing *eagre* in the stream of the Trent to stand still. In the old hall itself Henry VIII. held his court in 1541, after spending the night at Scrooby manor house on his way to receive their submission and peace-offerings from the Yorkshire malcontents. A native of Gainsborough, of Oriel fame, has told us that in his time it was the most foreign-looking town he knew in England. It seemed to him that the red-fluted tiles, the yellow-ochre doorsteps, the green outside shutters, the frequent appearance of the jawbones of whales, utilised as garden gate-posts, and, above all, the masts and spars suddenly appearing high over cornfields, took one quite out of every-day England. With the enthusiasm of a man recalling the days of his youth, he tells how he and his brothers used to climb Pringle Hill, from the top of which they could see the western towers of the great minster of Lincoln, eighteen miles away, a glorious vision standing out in the sky, clear of the horizon. To him, too, in these boyish days the region across the Trent, looking westward towards Scrooby, with its comfortable towns and villages, its thriving homesteads, its vast fields of wheat, its mansions great and small, and its tall church-towers, seemed like a man-made paradise, the first stage into England and the world for him.[1]

This town, then, of ancient fame, and with associations both rural and marine, was the meeting-place of the first Separatist church in the north of which we have any

[1] *Reminiscences chiefly of Towns, and Villages, and Schools.* By Rev. T. Mozley, M.A., formerly Fellow of Oriel.

BEGINNINGS OF CHURCH LIFE. 87

definite account. Two things, in addition to the Puritan feeling of the district, may have contributed to this. First, the town was remote from great cities, and from it in times of persecution flight to the Continent was comparatively easy; and next, it is tolerably certain that the lord of the manor, William Hickman, who had purchased the manor of Gainsborough from Lord Burgh in 1596, was in sympathy with the Puritans of the time. We know that his parents, Anthony and Rose Hickman, had suffered for their strong Protestant sympathy in the previous generation. His venerable mother, in the year 1620, when in her eighty-fifth year, and probably in the old hall itself wrote for the benefit of her children the story of her life during the persecuting days of Queen Mary. She came of a true Protestant lineage. She remembered hearing her father, Sir William Locke, say that when he was a young merchant, and went beyond sea, Ann Boleyn caused him to get her the Gospels and Epistles written on parchment in French, together with the Psalms. Then when she herself became the young wife of Anthony Hickman, her husband was not unmindful to use and employ his substance to the glory of God and good of His Church, as he daily manifested by giving entertainment to Bishop Hooper, John Foxe, the martyrologist, John Knox, the Scottish Reformer, and divers other godly preachers, of which some did afterwards suffer martyrdom in Queen Mary's days. They also held conventicles in their house, with divers godly and well-disposed Christians, 'and we and they did table together [*i.e.*, observe the Lord's Supper] in a chamber, keeping the door close shut for fear of the promoters, as we read in the Gospel the disciples of Christ did for fear of the Jews.' For such practices as these, and for not conforming themselves to Popery according to the Queen's Injunctions, her husband and her brother were called before the Court of High Commission and sent close prisoners to the Fleet. On her husband's release she went to Antwerp into exile with him, for, said she, 'I accounted all nothing in comparison to liberty of conscience for the profession of Christ.' Recalling the rough experiences of those bygone times, she piously says: 'For all our blessings and deliverances sent to me from my good God, I most humbly beseech His Majesty that I and mine may never forget to be thankful.' She has written this narrative, she says, in the hope that her children 'may stand fast in that faith and service of God into which their father and mother do stand so firmly, and manifest such zeal and affection as in this little treatise appeareth.'[1]

The lord of the manor of Gainsborough from 1596 to 1625, was one of the children of this venerable lady for whom this pious wish was expressed. That he had some devout feeling himself would seem to be indicated by the motto he placed with his initials on the sundial of the west wing of the old hall:—*Deus mi—ut umbra sic vita.* Is it improbable that a lord of the manor so trained and so expressing himself would be favourable and friendly to such earnest Christian men as those who founded the church at Gainsborough in 1602? Is it beyond the bounds of possibility that he in whose father's house conventicles had been held in Mary's days, should favour them in or near his own house in the days of Elizabeth and James? May it not even be permitted to us to believe that both he and the godly mother who reared him were sometimes found worshipping with Brewster and Bradford, perhaps in the old hall itself, 'accounting all nothing,' as she said, in comparison to liberty of conscience for the profession of Christ?

The pastor of this Gainsborough church was John

---

[1] 'Certaine Old Stories recorded by an aged Gentlewoman. Written by her with her owne hand, 1620.' Stark's *History of Gainsborough*, pp. 126-139. 1817.

THE OLD HALL, GAINSBOROUGH.
(*From sketches by* CHARLES WHYMPER.)

BEGINNINGS OF CHURCH LIFE.

Smyth, M.A., of Christ's College, Cambridge, where he graduated 1575-6, and where he had Francis Johnson for tutor, a man of whom we shall hear more hereafter. In 1585, he preached a sermon at Cambridge on Sabbath-keeping, for which he was cited before the vice-chancellor. William Bradford tells us that he was an eminent man in his time and a good preacher and of other good parts. In a work of his entitled *Paralleles, Censures, Observations, &c.*, he states that before separating from the National Church he passed through several months of anxious doubt and inquiry, and at one time held a conference at Coventry as to the duty of withdrawing from churches in which the ministry and the worship have become corrupted. He is said to have been beneficed at Gainsborough before becoming pastor of the separated church in that town. This is scarcely probable, inasmuch as the following list covers the period: John Jackson, vicar, 1589; Henry Clifford, 1608; Francis Spiers, 1610. Moreover he appears to have been labouring at Lincoln previous to coming to Gainsborough.

A few years ago, Professor Whitsitt, of Amsterdam, found in the library of Emmanuel College, Cambridge, a little book of his entitled: '*The bright morning starre, or the resolution and exposition of the 22 Psalme.* Preached publicly in foure sermons at Lincoln by John Smith, preacher of this Citie. Printed 1603.' The book seems to have been printed after he left Lincoln, otherwise the date of the foundation of the Gainsborough church would be a year later than is usually supposed. He was a man of fervent soul, following truth wherever it seemed to lead him, but somewhat extreme and unstable. In some respects he reminds us of Richard Baxter, and perhaps most of all in this, that towards the close of his life he published as 'the last book of John Smyth,' what he called *The retraction of his errors*, a copy of which has been preserved in the library of York Minster. This shows that in the nearing prospect of that 'all-reconciling world where Luther and Zuinglius are well agreed,' he came to lay more stress on the true essentials of the Christian life and less upon mere outside questions. His desire, he said, was to end controversies among Christians rather than to make and maintain them, especially in matters of the outward Church and ceremonies. It is the grief of his heart that he has so long cumbered himself and spent his time therein. Henceforth difference in judgment in matters of circumstance shall not cause him to refuse the brotherhood of any penitent and faithful Christian whatsoever. More than in the past he will spend his time in the main matters wherein consisteth salvation.

When driven from Gainsborough into exile Smyth practised as a physician in Amsterdam, usually, however, taking nothing of the poorer sort. A kind-hearted man, who gave away his own gown to make clothes for one slenderly apparelled, 'he was well-beloved of most men, and hated of none save a few of our English nation, who had nothing against him but that he differed from them in some points of religion.' This was the man who from 1602 to 1606 was pastor of the Gainsborough Church. The members of that church gathered to its services for miles from the country round. All the way from Austerfield and Scrooby, ten or twelve miles distant, William Bradford came with William Brewster and the rest of the brethren and sisters from Scrooby, having Sabbath day converse about the things of the kingdom as they journeyed past Scaftworth, Everton and Gringley-on-the-Hill to the ferry-boat on the Trent. This went on for three or four years, till at length 'these people became two distinct bodies or churches, and in regard of distance of place did congregate severally; for they were of sundry towns and villages,' where the three counties border nearest together. From this time forward therefore the brethren nearest to Scrooby met at Scrooby, forming that church in the old manor house which has become historic and with which henceforth we are solely concerned. This second community, Bradford tells us, 'ordinarily met at William Brewster's house on the Lord's day, and with great love he entertained them when they came, making provision for them, to his great charge.' For years past, ever since he had returned from the court to the manor house he had taken a foremost part in promoting the spiritual welfare of the district. That the preachers in the churches round were the earnest men they were seems to have been largely owing to him. 'He did much good in the country where he lived in promoting and furthering religion, not only by his practice and example and provoking and encouraging of others, but by procuring good preachers to the places thereabout, and drawing on of others to assist and help forward in such a work, he himself most commonly deepest in the charge, and sometimes above his ability.'

So things went on from 1590, when he came back to Scrooby, till the end of the century, 'he doing the best good he could, and walking according to the light he saw till the Lord revealed further unto him.' Shrewd Englishman as he was, with his Bible in his hand and his eyes open, it is scarcely wonderful that he began to come to conclusions not favourable to the cruel and intolerant system pursued so relentlessly by Archbishop Whitgift and those who acted with him. 'In the end, by the tyranny of the bishops against godly preachers and people, in silencing the one and persecuting the other, he and many more in those times began to look further into things.' The further he looked the less he liked what he saw, and in the event he and they who saw with him 'shook off this yoke of antichristian bondage, and as the Lord's free people joined themselves,' as we have seen, 'by a covenant of the Lord into a church estate.' 'After they were joined together in communion he was a special stay and help unto them.' And when again still later the one church at Gainsborough became two, that at Scrooby found shelter beneath his roof, and so, as one of the ironies of history, the house where Archbishops of York had found a home for centuries, where Wolsey had lodged, and from which Bishop Bonner had dated his letters, became for the Separatist church the house of God and the gate of heaven.

Here the good and venerable man Richard Clyfton became their pastor by free choice of the people, and joined with him as teacher was another man of the strength and nobleness of whose Christian character, and the breadth and enlightenment of whose mind, two continents were to hear more and more as the centuries passed on. This was John Robinson, a man whose name is fragrant and memorable in Free Church story. Before he came to Scrooby he had been a preacher of Christ's Gospel in the county of Norfolk, and there had won men's hearts to himself as well as to the truth. Henry Ainsworth, who knew him well, tells us that 'certain citizens of Norwich were excommunicated for resorting unto and praying with Mr. Robinson, a man utterly reverenced of all the city for the grace of God in him.' None of his contemporaries have given us a connected story of this good man's life. Joseph Hall, afterwards Bishop of Norwich, says that 'Lincolnshire was his county,' a statement borne out by the following entry in the register of Corpus Christi College, Cambridge : 'John Robinson. F. Lincsh. admitted 1592. Fell. 1598.' As to where in Lincolnshire his birthplace was, still remains uncertain. Gainsborough claims him, and there is this much to be said for that claim, that among the benefactors who have left money to the town may be found the names of Nathaniel Robinson and John Robinson. This, however, in the case of a name so

BEGINNINGS OF CHURCH LIFE. 95

common does not count for much in the way of evidence. So far as dates are concerned, John Robinson, D.D., Archdeacon of Lincoln and Precentor of Lincoln Cathedral, may very well have been his father. He was of Pembroke College, Cambridge. In Bishop Kennett's Collections it is recorded that May 31, 1574, 'he was installed Archdeacon of Bedford, in the place, as it seems, of William Rodd, and about 1576 he succeeded John Aylmer in the Archdeaconry of Lincoln, of which church he was about that time made chauntor. Obiit 1597.'[1] He would seem to have been made precentor before he became archdeacon, for in the Lincoln register there is the following entry: 'Collated to the Precentory, Aug. 3, 1572, John Robinson, M.A.' If there is anything in this conjecture, John Robinson of Scrooby and Leyden was born in the precentory at Lincoln in 1575, some three years after his father became precentor. A mere youth of seventeen he entered the University when Cambridge was keenly alive to the religious movements of the time. That eminent Puritan William Perkins was public catechist of Robinson's own college, where it was his duty to read a lecture every Thursday during term time on some useful subject of divinity. He was also afternoon lecturer at St. Andrew's Church, where he attracted great numbers of Cambridge men by his earnest spirit-stirring addresses; and as Robinson states that his 'personal conversion' was brought about in the Church of England, it is probable that it was under this man's influence, all the more probable, inasmuch as in later years Robinson published a catechism as an *Appendix to Mr. Perkins' Six Principles of the Christian Religion.*

On leaving college Robinson began life as a Christian minister somewhere in the county of Norfolk, but from the first seems to have been troubled with scruples about the

[1] *Lansdowne MSS.* 982. *Kennett's Collections*, Vol. xlviii., 24.

vestments and ceremonies insisted upon in the Church. Long and anxious were his searchings of heart as to conformity. He was held back, he tells us, for a long time by the example of many who did conform, 'blushing in myself to have a thought of pressing one hairbreadth before them in this thing, behind whom I knew myself to come so many miles in all other things; yea, and even of late times, when I had entered into a more serious consideration of these things, and, according to the measure of grace received, searched the Scriptures whether they were so or no . . . had not the truth been in my heart as a burning fire shut up in my bones, Jer. xx. 9. I had never broken those bonds of flesh and blood wherein I was so straitly tied, but had suffered the light of God to have been put out in mine own unthankful heart by other men's darkness.'[1] Scruples leading to suspension of clerical functions and suspension to separation, Robinson became pastor of a Congregational church in the city of Norwich. This must have been subsequent to 1600, for in that year the pastor of this church was a Mr. Hunt, as we learn from an incidental reference in George Johnson's *Account of the Troubles at Amsterdam.* As both Robinson and many in his Norwich congregation were harassed by fines and imprisonment, he eventually found it necessary to seek asylum and service elsewhere. This accounts for his appearance in the north as the colleague of Richard Clyfton in the church at Scrooby. Though he had left Norwich and the people of his charge in that city, he often turned back to them with affectionate regard. In a preface *To my Christian Friends in Norwich and thereabouts,* penned a dozen years after he had left them, he says that 'that loving and thankful remembrance in which I always have you, my Christian friends, provoketh me as continually to commend unto God your welfare.'

[1] *Works*, II., 52.

BEGINNINGS OF CHURCH LIFE. 97

It would seem from Bradford's narrative that Robinson did not return into Lincolnshire till after the separation of the Scrooby brethren from the Gainsborough Church, and their being independently constituted. After speaking of the separation and referring to the newly organised community at Scrooby, he says, 'In this other church, which must be the subject of our discourse, besides other worthy men was Mr. Richard Clifton, a grave and reverend preacher . . . and also that famous and worthy man Mr. John Robinson, who afterwards was their pastor for many years, till the Lord took him away by death.' Though 'they ordinarily met at William Brewster's house, on the Lord's day (which was a manor of the bishops), and with great love he entertained them when they came,' the stress of persecution sometimes compelled them to move elsewhere to avoid observation and arrest. Bradford says that 'they kept their meetings every Sabbath in one place or other, exercising the worship of God among themselves.' The manhood of these men was wrought to truest temper in the fire of the times. 'They could not long continue in any peaceable condition, but were hunted and persecuted on every side. Some were taken and clapt up in prison, others had their houses beset and watched night and day, and hardly escaped their hands; and the most were fain to fly and leave their houses and habitations and the means of their livelihood.' These quietly suggestive words of William Bradford are fully borne out and sustained by the records of the Ecclesiastical Court at York, in which we come upon the following entries: 'Office against Gervase Nevyle of Scrowbie, dio: Ebor.' It is stated that the said Gervase was one of the sect of Barrowists, or Brownists, holding and maintaining erroneous opinions and doctrines, and for his schismatical obstinacy an attachment was awarded to William Blanchard, messenger, to apprehend him. On his appearance he refused to take oath and make answer, or to recognise the authority of the archbishop; he, therefore, 'as a very dangerous schismatical Separatist, Brownist, and irreligious subject,' was delivered by strait warrant 'to the hands, ward, and safe custody of the Keeper of His Majesty's Castle of York; not permitting him to have any liberty or conference with any without special license.'

'Gervase Nevile, of York Castle, Brownist or Separatist. He appeared and made answer March 22, 1607-8.'

On September 15, 1607, an attachment was awarded to William Blanchard 'to apprehend Richard Jackson and William Brewster, of Scrooby, gentlemen, for Brownism, but he certifieth that he cannot find them, nor understand where they are.' We shall see reason hereafter for supposing that if William Blanchard had gone to Boston he would have found them safely locked up in the dungeons under the Guildhall. Again, on the first of the following December, after Jackson and Brewster had been liberated at the autumn Assize, we find the law once more set in motion against them at York.

'December 1, 1607. Office against Richard Jackson, of Scrooby, for his disobedience in matters of religion. A process was served upon him by the pursuivant, and he gives his word to appear, and is find £20, and a warrant sent out for his apprehension.'

'December 1, 1607. William Brewster, of Scrooby, gentleman. Information is given that he is a Brownist, and disobedient in matters of religion.'

In the spring of 1608 the following return was made to the Exchequer by the Archbishop of York:

'Richard Jackson, William Brewster, and Robert Rochester, of Scrooby in the county of Nottingham, Brownists or Separatists; for a fine or amercement of £20 apiece, set and imposed upon every one of them by Robert Abbot and Robert Snowdon, Doctors of Divinity, and Matthew

Dodworth, Bachelor of Law, commissioners for causes ecclesiastical within the province of York, for not appearing before them upon lawful summons at the collegiate church of Southwell, 22nd day of April.'

Thus remorselessly hunted down by the legal representatives of Christ's Gospel of love, and seeing how little hope there was of peaceable living in their own land, the brethren at last, by joint consent, resolved to cross the sea to Holland, where they heard there was freedom of religion for all men. Others had preceded them. The persecuted brethren in London and their former neighbours and fellow-worshippers at Gainsborough had already found peaceable settlement at Amsterdam, and the number of exiles for conscience' sake was continually being increased by arrivals from most of the counties of England. In the autumn of 1607 they therefore resolved to go over into the Low Countries as best they could. Bradford tells us that they felt the decision to be fateful and momentous. It was much, and thought marvellous by many that they should leave their native soil and country, their lands and livings, and all their friends and familiar acquaintances, to go into a country they only knew by hearsay, where they would have to learn a new language and get their living they knew not how, and that, too, in a land too often desolated by the miseries of war; this was by many thought an adventure almost desperate, a case intolerable, and a misery worse than death. The necessity was all the harder, inasmuch as they had only been accustomed to a plain country life and the innocent occupation of husbandry, and were entirely unacquainted with such trade and traffic as that by which the land to which they were going did mainly subsist. But though these things did trouble them they did not dismay them, for their desires were set on the ways of God and the enjoyment of His ordinances, they therefore rested on His providence and knew whom they had believed.

> Their altars they forego, their homes they quit,
> Fields which they love, and paths they daily trod,
> And cast the future upon Providence,
> As men the dictate of whose inward sense
> Outweighs the world.

But here was the perplexity of their position. It was as unlawful to flee from their native land as to remain in it without conforming. Emigration without license was prohibited by an ancient statute of 13 Richard II. Ports and havens would therefore be closed against them, and if they got away at all it would have to be by stealth, by secret means of conveyance, by bribing the captains of vessels, and by paying exorbitant rates of passage. They made many attempts to get away in separate parties, and were as often betrayed, and both they and their goods intercepted and surprised. But there were two occasions of more memorable sort which Bradford never forgot.

The first of these was in the autumn of 1607, probably about the month of September, for, as we have seen, on the 15th of that month, William Blanchard certified to the Ecclesiastical Court at York that he cannot find Richard Jackson or William Brewster, of Scrooby, nor understand where they are. On the 30th of the same month also, the first payment was made to Brewster's successor as postmaster of Scrooby. Besides Brewster, his neighbour Thomas Helwisse was one of the foremost promoters of the movement. 'He above all, either guides or others, furthered this passage into strange countries; if any brought oars, he brought sails.'[1] On July 26 his wife Joan was brought from York Castle to appear before the Ecclesiastical Court, and sent back thither, along with John Drewe and Thomas Jessop, for refusing to take an oath according to law. Persecution thus coming close home to his own door made him the more anxious to find asylum in a land where Blanchard's warrants and pursuivants had no power to

[1] Robinson's *Works*, III., 159.

run. On the occasion referred to these voyagers in search of freedom resolved to move as a body, and not in detached companies, and to make Boston, on the Lincolnshire coast, their point of departure. They therefore hired a vessel wholly to themselves, making agreement with the captain to be ready at a certain day to take them and their goods at a convenient place where they would meet him. Meantime the deceitful scoundrel had privately arranged their betrayal, and no sooner had they stepped on board than the officers and searchers were at hand to arrest them. Put back into open boats, the minions of the law 'rifled and ransacked them, searching them to their shirts for money, yea, even the women further than became modesty, and then carried them back into the town, and made them a spectacle and wonder to the multitude who came flocking on all sides to behold them. Being thus first by the catchpole[1] officers rifled and stripped of their money, books, and much other goods, they were presented to the magistrates, and messengers were sent to inform the Lords of the Council of them ; and so they were committed to ward.'

Boston, in which these unfortunate prisoners found themselves after their arrest, one of the most curious old towns in England, had long been declining from the good old days when in the reign of Edward III. it sent seventeen ships and three hundred and sixty men for the invasion of Brittany. Its ancient buildings : .the quaint old house in Wormgate, the old building in Spain Lane, the Grammar School, the Hussey Tower, the Guildhall in South Street, and most of all the great Church of St. Botolph, with its magnificent tower, seen as a landmark far off at sea, and known all the world over as Boston Stump ; these all

[1] *Catchpole*, from Central Old French *chacepol;* Med. Latin, *chassipullus* (Du Cauge), lit. chasefowl, one who hunts or chases fowls ; later, a petty officer of justice.

bespeak the antiquity and former importance of this eastern port on the Lincolnshire coast. It was in the old court-room on the first floor of the Guildhall that William Brewster and his companions were presented to the magistrates, and it was to the old cells, still to be seen on the ground floor, they were remitted back 'till order came from the Council Table.' These cells had been in use at that time for about sixty years, for 'in 1552 it was ordered that the kitchen under the town hall and the chambers over them should be prepared for a prison and a dwelling-house for one of the sergeants.'[1] There must have been more cells formerly, but there are now only two of these gruesome chambers remaining, and these, with the increasing growth of humane feeling, have ceased to be used. They are entered by a high step rising some thirty inches, are some six feet broad by seven feet long, and in lieu of doors are made secure by a five-barred, whitewashed iron gate. A quaint winding stair to the right of the cells, terminating at a trap-door in the old court-room, was the way by which prisoners ascended to the Palace of Justice till the new sessions house was built in 1843. In this chamber, with its wagon roof, its arch beams, and its wainscoted walls, and with the Boston coat-of-arms and the list of Boston mayors since the charter of 1545 displayed to view, the would-be exiles were brought up, charged with the high crime and misdemeanour of trying to escape from their native land.

The magistrates were not unfavourable to them, for Puritanism was too rife in Boston itself for them to think ill of those who went that way. When, a quarter of a century later, nine hundred Puritan colonists sailed for Massachusetts with John Winthrop, many of the leading townsmen of Boston were among the number: Richard Bellingham, recorder of the town from 1625 to 1633, Atherton Hough,

[1] Thompson's *History of Boston*, p. 235.

THE GUILDHALL, BOSTON.

1. Cells in which the Pilgrims were confined.
2. Passage and stairs leading to cells.
3. Guildhall, front view.

mayor of the borough in 1628, and Thomas Leverett, an alderman; Thomas Dudley, Richard Bellingham, and John Leverett were afterwards governors of Massachusetts, and William Coddington, father and governor of Rhode Island; while John Cotton, the Puritan preacher of Boston Church for twenty years, became one of the leading religious forces of New England life. It was because this Lincolnshire town sent so large a contingent of Puritan townsmen to America between 1620 and 1630 that at a Court of Assistants held at Charlestown, September 7, 1630, it was 'ordered that Trimountain shall be called Boston.' Thus from the Eastern Lincolnshire town in which Brewster's company were prisoners in 1607, came the name of the greater Boston of the Far West.[1]

The seeds of all this movement were therefore in the town at the time these prisoners were there. This was probably why that, as Bradford tells us, 'the magistrates used them courteously and showed them what favour. they could, though they could not deliver them till order came from the Council Table.' What was done in the matter by the Lords of the Council we do not know. Unfortunately the Privy Council Register for that year happened to be one of the volumes carried over to Whitehall for reference, and consumed in the fire which wrought such havoc in the palace in 1618. Nor are there any local references in the town records of Boston itself; again unfortunately the leaves for that year, happening to come at the beginning of a volume, are missing. After detaining them for a month, and possibly receiving instructions to that effect from the Privy Council, the magistrates dismissed the main body of the prisoners, sending them back to their homes at Scrooby or elsewhere, and keeping seven of the leaders still in prison. These, after a further period of detention, they bound over to appear at the Assizes. One of these seven,

[1] *Young's Chronicles*, Massachusetts, pp. 48, 49.

Bradford tells us, was William Brewster, who 'was chief of those that were taken at Boston, and suffered the greatest loss.'

What happened at the Assizes there are no records to show, but the failure of this attempt in the autumn of 1608 did not prevent the making of other endeavours to get away in the course of the following spring. This time they resolved to try the port of Hull as the point of departure, and meeting with a Dutchman who had a ship of his own, belonging to Zealand, they made a bargain with him to carry them over, hoping to find him more reliable than they had found their own countryman on the former occasion. He assured them there was no fear of him, and that all would go well. The agreement was that he was to take them on board at a lonely point on the coast between Grimsby and Hull, where was a large common, a good way distant from any town. The women and children, with what goods they were taking with them, went by boat by way of Gainsborough and the Trent, while the men travelled across country, a journey of some forty miles from Scrooby. It so happened that both parties arrived at the place appointed before the ship appeared, and had to wait. Meantime, the sea being rough and the women suffering, they prevailed upon the men in charge of the boat to run it into a creek, where it might lie aground at low water. So that next morning, when the Dutchman came with his ship, they were fast, and could not stir till high water, which would not be till about noon. The captain therefore thought the best thing to do under the circumstances was to take the men into the ship, whom he saw ready, walking to and fro on the shore. He had already brought one boat-full on board, and was starting for a second, when, to his dismay, he saw in the distance, in full pursuit, 'a great company, both horse and foot, with bills and guns and other weapons;

for the country was raised to take them.' The Dutchman, feeling that his first duty was to take care of himself, 'swore his country's oath—*sacramente*,' and having the wind fair, weighed anchor, hoisted sail, and away. Thus that first boat-load received on board found themselves in evil case indeed. True, they had escaped the soldiers sent in pursuit, but they had nothing with them but the clothes upon their backs; their wives and children, their money and their goods, were all in the boat stuck fast in the creek, and therefore at the mercy of men who had no mercy for them. The tears, we are told, came to their eyes, and they wished themselves back on shore again, that they might share the fortunes of those they were leaving behind. To make their evil case worse, no sooner were they out upon the North Sea than a terrific storm swept down upon them, driving them out of their course, till they found themselves not far from the coast of Norway. Fourteen long days they were tossed hither and thither, during seven of the fourteen seeing neither sun, nor moon, nor stars. The sailors themselves abandoned all hope, and once even sent up shrieks and cries, thinking their ship to be foundering. They did, however, reach land at last, the captain and crew being welcomed ashore by eager friends, who at one time never expected to see them again.

Scarcely less pitiful was the plight of those who had been left behind on the English coast. Some of the men tarried with the women and children at the boat, for their assistance, the rest made good their escape before the troops arrived. As we may well suppose, the women were broken-hearted; some of them weeping and crying for their husbands carried away in the Dutchman's ship; others distracted as to what would become of themselves and their little ones; and yet others again, looking with tearful eyes into the faces of helpless children, who were clinging about them, crying for fear and quaking with cold.

The arresting party, coming with bills and guns and other weapons, soon found this defenceless company entirely at their mercy. But then came the question, what were they to do with weeping women and children, now they were in their power? Hurrying them from one place to another, and from one justice to another, they were at length almost as weary of the enterprise as the prisoners themselves. For no magistrate was eager to incur the public odium of sending women to prison for no other crime than that of wanting to go with their husbands, and they could not be sent back to their homes, for homes they had none to go to, having either sold or otherwise disposed of their houses and livings. Their very necessity was the defence of these hapless prisoners, and at last those who had seized them were only too glad to be rid of them. What became of them in the interval between their arrest and their final departure we are not told. Probably they took divers ways, and were received to various homes by kind-hearted country-folk. The poor are often wonderfully kind to each other in times of trouble. They would not inquire too curiously into the nature of the offence committed against the laws of the realm, and they could not be made to see that the claims of ecclesiastical uniformity are paramount to the claims of humanity.

The later and detailed story of the wanderings and travels of these exiles, both by land and sea, has not been told. We only know that they rallied together somewhere, that John Robinson and William Brewster, and other principal members, including, of course, the venerable pastor, Richard Clyfton, 'were of the last, and stayed to help the weakest over before them,' that, 'notwithstanding all these storms of opposition they all got over at length, some at one time and some at another, some in one place and some in another,' and that on a happier shore they 'met together again according to their desires with no small rejoicing.'

After all there is a soul of good in things evil. The historian of this simple seventeenth-century epic has left it on record that not merely in after generations, but even then, the sufferings of these resolute people were fruitful of good. Through their so-public troubles in so many eminent places their cause became famous. Men began to inquire into the nature of the principles for which they were willing to suffer so much. Their very enemies dragged them into fame, and 'their godly carriage and Christian behaviour was such as left a deep impression on the minds of many.' It was the old story repeated of the blood of the martyrs becoming the seed of the Church. 'Though some few shrank at these first conflicts and sharp beginnings (as it was no marvel), yet many more came on with fresh courage, and greatly animated others.' Thus ever, the generations one after another pass on the torch of truth, win for themselves and their children the realm of a larger, nobler freedom, and prove by victorious suffering how

> Unbounded is the might
> Of martyrdom, and fortitude and right.

IV.

THE EXILES IN HOLLAND.

THROUGH storms o'er land and sea these wanderers in search of freedom had reached a resting-place at last. They arrived in Holland at a time of pause and expectancy. An armistice had just been concluded for the purpose of negotiating a truce with Spain after a war which had lasted for five-and-twenty years. A few months before their arrival, and in the midst of the severest winter that had been known for many years, Prince Maurice, attended by a distinguished retinue, had left the Hague on the last day of January to meet the Marquis Spinola, who had travelled from Spain with a long train of carriages, horses, lackeys, cooks, and secretaries, for the purpose of negotiating terms of peace. Meantime armed men were still marching and counter-marching, and all the paraphernalia of war met the view of the English exiles on their arrival. There was the usual diplomacy, involving the usual delays, and it was not till April 9, 1609, that the States General signed that truce with the Spanish king which was to last for twelve years to come. Thus the fugitives from Scrooby arrived in Holland just as the Five-and-Twenty Years' War had spent itself; they departed in 1620, when the Thirty Years' War was bursting into flame.

The city of Amsterdam was the place they made for at first, and that for obvious reasons. It was the city which

THE STABLE OF SCROOBY MANOR HOUSE (PROBABLE PLACE OF MEETING IN 1607).
(*From sketches by* CHARLES WHYMPER.)

had stood for Protestantism, for liberty of speech and thought through that long and desperate struggle with Spain which had ended in the foundation of the Netherlands Republic in 1579, and in the Declaration of Independence on July 26, 1581. On the fifth of that month the knights, nobles, and cities of Holland and Zealand had called upon William the Silent to accept entire authority as sovereign and chief of the land, directing him 'to maintain the exercise only of the Reformed Evangelical religion, without, however, permitting that inquiries should be made into any man's belief or conscience, or that any injury or hindrance should be offered to any man on account of his religion.' Thus Amsterdam became the asylum of liberty, and as such drew to itself, from many lands, those who valued their freedom, whether civil or religious. As a consequence, it drew to itself also the elements of national prosperity. The men driven from their own land by the narrow-minded bigotry of their rulers were often the very flower of the nation's life— earnest-minded, skilled and thrifty, and they helped to enrich the nation which gave them welcome.

Workers in iron, paper, silk, linen, and lace, the makers of brocade, tapestry, and satin, as well as of all coarser fabrics, found their way from oppression to this land of liberty. Historians tell us that never in the history of civilisation had there been a more rapid development of human industry than in Holland during these years of bloodiest warfare. The towns were filled to overflowing. Amsterdam grew in wealth and population. 'It is the epoch to which the greatest expansion of municipal architecture is traced. Warehouses, palaces, docks, arsenals, fortifications, dykes, splendid streets and suburbs, were constructed on every side, and still there was not room for the constantly increasing population.'[1]

[1] Motley's *United Netherlands*, III., 25.

As far back as 1593 English Separatists had begun to come to Amsterdam in search of liberty, and this by the advice of one of the martyrs whose memory was dear to them. Shortly after the execution of Barrowe and Greenwood at Tyburn, John Penry, the Welsh martyr, was led forth to the gibbet a mile or two out of London on the Old Kent Road. A few days before his death he sent a farewell address to his brethren of the Separatist Church in London, advising them, since there was no hope of religious freedom at home, to prepare themselves to go into exile abroad, and to keep together. He is sure they will yet find days of peace and rest, if only they will be faithful. This stamping and treading of them under feet, this subverting of their cause in right and judgment, is permitted to the end that they may search and try their ways; but the Lord will yet maintain the cause of their souls and redeem their lives. He further touchingly beseeches them that wherever they go into exile, they would take his poor and desolate widow and his fatherless and friendless orphans with them. His advice was taken and his request carried out. As many of the secret Church as could made their way to Amsterdam. For the present at least some could not go. Francis Johnson, the pastor, and his brother George, were in prison, the one in the Clink and the other in the Fleet; Settle, another of the members, was in the Gatehouse, and Daniel Studley in Newgate. It was not till 1597 that these were able to join their brethren, but in that year they also made their way to Amsterdam, Francis Johnson and Daniel Studley hiring a house in the Reguliers-poort in that city.[1] They seem also to have carried out Penry's wish about his widow and

---

[1] *A Discourse of some Troubles in the Banished English Church at Amsterdam.* Printed at Amsterdam, 1603. The only known copy of this book is in the Library of Trinity College, Cambridge [VI., 7, 18].

fatherless children, for in the list of marriages recorded as taking place among the English in Amsterdam we find from the Puibocken, or city register, that Deliverance Penry, aged twenty-one years, from Northamptonshire, was married May 14, 1611, to Samuel Whitaker, bombazine-worker, from Somersetshire, aged twenty-three.

There were thus two Separatist communities already in Amsterdam when the exiles from Scrooby arrived, the one from London, of which Francis Johnson was pastor, and that from Gainsborough, under the care of John Smyth. Francis Johnson was a man of some individuality and force of character. The son of a former mayor of Richmond in Yorkshire, he was also a graduate and fellow of Christ's College, Cambridge. In 1588, when only twenty-six, he preached a sermon in the University Church in favour of the Presbyterian system, the want of which, he said, accounted for the prevailing ignorance and impiety of the time. It was a daring thing to do, and for doing it he was committed to prison, and refusing to make public recantation was expelled the University. He subsequently became the minister of the church of the English merchants at Middleburgh in Zealand, and while there, in 1591, he discovered that one of Barrowe and Greenwood's prison books was being printed by stealth at Dort. The Separatists at that time being the objects of his strong aversion, he at once communicated with the English ambassador, and received authority to intercept the book at the press and see all the copies burnt. All were burnt but two, which he saved from the fire for himself and a friend. Having burnt the rest, he then sat down in his study to read the one he had kept. Perhaps it would have been more rational to read first, and then, if needful, burn after; but he reversed the process, and that after-reading changed all his after-life. The farther he read the more the book laid hold of him. He began hating the Separatists and all their works, he ended resolved to join them. Making his way back at once to London, he sought out Barrowe and Greenwood, the writers of the books in the Fleet prison, entered into earnest conference with them, and eventually joined the London brotherhood with which they were associated. So deeply did he regret his former animosity and the destruction of the books he had burnt, that fourteen years later, in 1605, he had another edition printed at his own expense.

Chosen pastor of the brotherhood he had joined, he with John Greenwood was arrested at the house of Edward Boyes, on Ludgate Hill, and committed to prison. He in the Clink and his brother George in the Fleet, they remained prisoners till the year 1597, when hearing there was a project on foot for an expedition to Canada, they craved permission to join it. Under date March 25, 1597, there is an entry in the Privy Council Register to the effect that Abraham Van Hardwick and Stephen Van Hardwick, merchant strangers, and Charles Leigh, merchant of London, have undertaken a voyage of fishing and discovery unto the Bay of Canada, and to plant themselves in the Island of Rainea or thereabouts. It is further said: 'Forasmuch as they have made humble suit unto Her Majesty to transport out of this realm divers artificers and other persons that are noted to be sectaries, whose minds are continually in an ecclesiastical ferment, whereof four shall at this present sail thither in those ships that go this present voyage. You will therefore understand that Her Majesty is pleased they shall carry with them the aforesaid persons.'

The four thus chosen to go to plant themselves on the Island of Rainea to be the first Pilgrim Fathers before the Pilgrim Fathers' time, were Francis and George Johnson, Daniel Studley, an elder of the Church, and John Clark. This first voyage of the Separatists across the Atlantic ended in failure. They met with rough weather and disastrous fortune. Off the coast of Newfoundland one of the vessels went on to the rocks; they were captured by Frenchmen and pillaged, and finally, after a variety of adventures, had to make their way back to Southampton as best they could. One good thing, however, came out of this ill-fated enterprise. They were now free of the Fleet after five years' imprisonment, and were therefore able to join the rest of their brethren in Amsterdam, where Francis Johnson was again chosen pastor, with Daniel Studley, Stanshall Mercer, George Knyveton, and Christopher Bowman as elders. This story of shipwreck and disaster at sea the brethren from Scrooby may have heard from the shipwrecked men's own lips, and remembered it with misgiving hearts in after days, when thinking of crossing the Atlantic themselves.

In the Church of Amsterdam there was associated with Francis Johnson as teacher, Henry Ainsworth, a man altogether too memorable to be passed without notice. Bradford says that he originally came 'out of Ireland with other poor,' was 'a single young man and very studious'; and Roger Williams tells us that he lived on ninepence a week, and subsisted on boiled roots. We may assume that as time went on his finances improved, for in the Puiboeken we read that on March 29, 1607, Henry Ainsworth, who is described as a teacher, thirty-six years of age, and residing on the Singel by the Heipoort, was married to Margaret Haley, of Ipswich. He was, says Bradford, a man of a thousand, and in the opinion of members of the University 'had not his better for the Hebrew tongue in the University, nor scarce in Europe.' His Annotations on the Pentateuch, the Psalms, and other portions of Scripture, were long held in esteem for the healthy spirit of exegesis by which they were pervaded, and as setting aside the allegorising system of interpretation then too prevalent.

This first Church of Amsterdam of which, as we have

seen, Francis Johnson was pastor and Henry Ainsworth teacher, was composed of exiles who had come from almost all parts of England in search of freedom of worship. Dr. Hoop Scheffer, of the Mennonite College in that city, has given from the Puiboeken, to which reference has already been made, a list of one hundred and eighteen marriages celebrated among these English exiles between 1598 and 1517. The place of their previous domicile is always given, from which we find that they came from no fewer than twenty-nine English counties, and in addition from the Welsh county of Caermarthen. Northumberland and Yorkshire are represented as well as Sussex and Kent, Cornwall and Devon along with Norfolk and Suffolk; the North and South Midlands as well as Lancashire and Lincoln.[1] The Church seems to have been at the height of its prosperity about the time the brethren from Scrooby arrived in the city.

Pleasant were the reminiscences which William Bradford called up in after days of the Christian fellowship enjoyed in this place of refuge, and quaint the pictures of church life as it existed among them. 'Truly,' says he, 'there were many worthy men; and if you had seen them in their beauty and order, as we have done, you would have been much affected thereby. At Amsterdam, before their division and breach, they were about three hundred communicants, and they had for their pastor and teacher those two eminent men before named, and in our time four grave men for ruling elders, three able and godly men for deacons, and one ancient widow for a deaconess, who did them service many years, though she was sixty years of age when she was chosen.' Quaint and old-worldlike is the picture of this venerable lady he goes on to paint for us: 'She honoured her place, and was an orna-

[1] *Proceedings of the Koninklijke Akademie van Wetenschappen*, 1880-1. Bijlage I., pp. 384-392.

THE EXILES IN HOLLAND. 119

ment to the congregation. She usually sat in a convenient place in the congregation, with a little birchen rod in her hand, and kept little children in great awe from disturbing the congregation. She did frequently visit the sick and weak, especially women, and as there was need, called out maids and young women to watch and do them other helps as their necessity did require; and if they were poor she would gather relief for them of those that were able, or acquaint the deacons; and she was obeyed as a mother in Israel and an officer of Christ.'[1] Many churches have been, and all churches would be, the better for having such saintly, Christ-like souls as this 'Mother in Israel and officer of Christ,' whose memory William Bradford has preserved for us.

It would seem that the Church which went out from Gainsborough about 1606 retained under its pastor, John Smyth, an existence separate from that under Francis Johnson. This may have been necessitated by the lack of a building sufficiently large to accommodate the two communities together, or it may have been occasioned by the fact that 'the anciente church' under Johnson's care was more presbyterian than popular in its government. The later comers, again, from Scrooby, also worshipped separately, having their own pastor, Richard Clyfton, and their own teacher, John Robinson. Considerations of space and convenience may have determined this partly, but there were also other considerations. Smyth's views underwent a change in the matter of doctrine first and of baptism afterwards, and in Johnson's church some internal matters of discipline had altered his views of church government generally. He now came to the conclusion that it ought to be vested in elders chosen by the congregation, while Robinson and Ainsworth were of opinion that it should be vested in the Church of which

[1] Bradford's *Dialogues*, p. 455.

the elders were a part. They contended that bishops or elders were ordinary governors, and not lords over God's heritage, as if 'the Church could not *be* without them.' It is given to ministers, they said, to feed, guide, and govern the Church, but *not themselves to be the Church*, and to challenge the power of the same in things pertaining to the kingdom of God. They pointed out that it was through yielding in this matter that a priestly hierarchy rose to power in the Church, with all the evils ensuing, which, had the people made a stand against at the outset, and practised the Gospel in the order set by Christ, would never have prevailed. They could not yield on this point. 'If,' said they, 'we should let the true practice of the Gospel go, posterity after us, being brought into bondage, might justly blame and curse us that we did not stand for the rights of the people in that which we acknowledge to be their due.'

Seeing storms gathering, after being about a year at Amsterdam, Robinson and the brethren from Scrooby resolved peaceably to withdraw and start church life afresh at Leyden, though, as Bradford says, 'they well knew that it would be much to the prejudice of their outward estate both in the present and in the future, as indeed it proved to be.' Having thus resolved, Robinson and his people made formal application to the authorities of Leyden for leave to come and reside in that city. This application is recorded in the *Gerechts dags boeken*, or Court Register of the City, preserved among the archives in the *Stad-huis*, and was first printed in 1848 by Professor Kist.[1] It runs as follows:—

'To the Honorable the Burgomasters and Court of the city of Leyden: With due submission and respect, *Jan Robarthse*, minister of the Divine Word, and some of the members of the Christian Reformed Religion, born

[1] *Nederlandsch Archief voor Kerkelijke Geschiedenis*, vol. viii.

in the kingdom of Great Britain, to the number of one hundred persons, or thereabouts, men and women, represent that they are desirous of coming to live in this city, by the first of May next, and to have the freedom thereof in carrying on their trades, without being a burden in the least to any one. They therefore address themselves to your Honors, humbly praying that your Honors will be pleased to grant them free consent to betake themselves as aforesaid.'

The application itself bears neither date nor signature, but the reply of the authorities has the date upon the margin, and is as follows :—

'The Court, in making a disposition of this present memorial, declare that they refuse no honest persons free ingress to come and have their residence in this city, provided that such persons behave themselves, and submit to the laws and ordinances; and therefore the coming of the memorialists will be agreeable and welcome.

'Thus done in their session at the Council House, 12 February, 1609.

'Signed, I. VAN HOUT.'

Leyden, now reduced to one-half of its former population, was then a city of 100,000 inhabitants, and had to a large extent recovered itself from the disastrous effects of the memorable siege of thirty years before. Bradford speaks lovingly of their new home as a fair and beautiful city and of a sweet situation. And, indeed, with the return of peace and the development of commerce there had come back something also of the city's former splendour. For long the residence of the Counts of Holland, it was and still remains the seat of the Rynland Syndicate for the control of the waters in a region specially exposed to their ravages. The great cathedral church of St. Peter, a vast basilica with five naves, dating from the early part of the fourteenth century, had fortunately escaped the destruction which had overtaken so many of the other buildings during the war. The Hôtel de Ville, many times burnt with fire, had been rebuilt as we see it now, after the designs of the great Flemish architect, Lievin de Key. Great municipal and military services and important commercial corporations had taken possession of such religious edifices, cloisters, and chapels as had been left without use by the Reformation; the Drapers' Company, for example, the most influential of the local industries, held their gatherings in the chapel of the Hospital of St. Jacques. On all sides were signs of growing wealth and prosperity. In the main streets and upon the quays of the Breedstraat, the Oude Singel, the Rapenburgh and the Langeburg, rose the habitations of the burghers, some of them presenting examples of the ancient national style, and others inspired by the art of the Renaissance then rising into favour.

But while the Leydenese were proud of the architectural adornments of their city, they were especially proud of it as a rising seat of learning. William of Orange, wishing to recognise the splendid services rendered to the Commonwealth by the citizens during the great siege, granted the charter of foundation for the University of Leyden. Created by a decree of February 9, 1575, and largely endowed, it was first established in the ancient cloister of St. Barbe, from which it was transferred to the Chapel of the Jacobins, where it still remains. It rapidly rose to fame, and gathered to itself some of the most distinguished scholars of the time. Though at the period with which we are dealing it had been in existence little more than a quarter of a century, students were drawn to it from all parts of Europe, attracted by the fame of such men as Francis Junius, who had been its professor of theology; Justus Lipsius, who held its chair of history; the younger Scaliger, Vossius, Saumaise, Daniel Heinsius, and Philip Marnix St. Aldegonde, famous both as scholar and diplomatist. The eminent controversialists, Gomar and Arminius, were joint professors of theology at the time the exiles came to Leyden, though the latter died on October 19, 1609, and therefore shortly after their arrival. And if one may for a moment leave the University and stray from great names already achieved in literature to a name yet unknown, but destined to become great in art, it may not be uninteresting to note that, during John Robinson's life at Leyden, young Rembrandt was growing up from childhood to early manhood in his father's house on the ramparts at the western extremity of the city. Here, at the point where the branches of the Rhine reunite, Rembrandt's father, Harmen Gerritsz, owned the greater part of a mill on the Pelican Quay, near the White Gate ; and there is nothing improbable in the thought that Robinson in his walks may have seen the bright-faced lad at his games, and in later years passed him as a student on the University stairs. It sets one musing and looking wistfully forward, to remember that John Robinson, the pastor of a church so profoundly concerned in laying the foundations of democracy across the Atlantic, should for sixteen years of his life have lived side by side with the young artist of whom it has been said that he concentrated in himself the life of many generations of Dutch artisans and peasants, and felt the full influence of the democratic movement which had been going on all over Europe for two centuries past. It has been said that if any one wishes to know what it was the common people in Holland and Germany did actually believe in the 16th century concerning the Gospel of Jesus Christ, he must not go to the Synod of Dort, or to the writings of Lutheran and Calvinistic divines, or even to the biographies of saints, but to the works of Rembrandt, in which nothing is more manifest than that to him the Gospel of Jesus Christ was the Gospel of the poor, his creations being a wonderful testimony to the truth that that Gospel corresponds exactly to humanity's needs.[1]

[1] Richard Heath.

On their arrival in the city of Leyden, which was to be their home for some years to come, the exiles from Scrooby seem naturally to have lived very much together, a community within a community dwelling among a people of strange language. It was not, however, till 1611 that they acquired a place they could call their own. In that year John Robinson, in conjunction with William Jepson, Henry Wood and Randall Thickins, his brother-in-law, purchased for 8000 guilders a house and garden in the Kloksteeg, which may be anglicized as Bell Lane, where the Pesyns Hof now stands. This property stood on the ground nearly opposite the belfry built in the rear of St. Peter's Church. It was conveyed 'from John de Lalaing to Jan Robinson, Minister of God's Word of the English congregation in this city,' by a transport brief or deed made on the 5th of May, 1611, and is thus described: 'a house and ground with a garden situated on the west side thereof, standing and being in this city on the south side of the Pieter Kirckhoff near the belfry formerly called the Groene poort [Green Gate], bounded and having situated on one side eastwardly a certain small room which the comparant [the grantor] reserves to himself, being over the door of the house hereby sold; next thereto is Willem Simonsz van der Wilde, and next to him the residence of the Commanderije; and on the other side westwardly having the widow and heirs of Huyck van Alckemade, and next to him the comparant himself, and next to him is the Donckere graft [the Dark Canal], which is also situated on the west of the aforesaid garden, and next to it is the Falide Bagynhoff [the Veiled Nuns' Cloister], extending from the street of the Kirckhoff aforesaid to the rear of the Falide Bagynhoff.'[1] The garden ran back to the extent of 125 feet, and at the end of it was the wall enclosing the land on which stood the old chapel of the Falide Bagynhoff, the upper story of which

[1] Hon. Henry C. Murphy, U.S. Minister at the Hague, *Hist. Mag.* 1859, iii., p. 330.

was used as the university library, one of the lower being occupied by the English Presbyterian Church, founded in the year Robinson came to Leyden, and of which Robert Durie was minister till his death in 1616.

The Pilgrims probably worshipped in some part of the buildings connected with this house of Robinson's during their life in Leyden. There is no record of any other place of meeting, or anything to indicate that any public building was granted to them by the authorities for their use, as was the case with the English Presbyterian congregation just referred to. Further it appears from Brodhead (i. 101) it was the custom of the Dutch government to restrict new and unusual sects to worship in private houses, which were frequently as spacious as the churches themselves. To the same effect Cardinal Bentivoglio in his *Relazione di Fiandra* says, that in the cities of the Netherlands public exercises of religion were not permitted to any sect but the Calvinists, presumably of the Reformed Churches of the Continent. The exercises of all others, he says, 'are permitted in private houses, which are in fact as if public, the places of preaching being spacious and of sufficient size for any assembly.' John Robinson's house was apparently of this character, for in after years Edward Winslow, speaking of the leave-taking of those who were going to New England, says, ' they that stayed at Leyden feasted us that were to goe, at our pastor's house, being large.' Further, Dr. Dexter, in the course of his loving and painstaking researches in Leyden, discovered that in the great garden of this house William Jessop built twenty-one small tenements, which were probably intended as dwellings for the poorer members of the congregation. Upon the front of the present modern building facing the cathedral there was placed in recent years by consent of the owners a marble slab with the inscription:—' On this spot lived, taught, and died, John Robinson. 1611-1625.'

His people appear to have found life harder at Leyden than at Amsterdam, there being less traffic by sea, and therefore less opportunity of obtaining employment. But, as Bradford says: 'Being now here pitched, they fell to such trades and employments as they best could, valuing peace and their spiritual comfort above any other riches whatever. And at length they came to raise a competent and comfortable living, but with hard and continued labour.' Some of them became baize-weavers and serge-workers, while others were hat-makers, wool-carders, twine-manufacturers, masons and carpenters. In the Church at Leyden, as well as in that at Amsterdam, there were bombazine-workers, cabinet-makers, wool-combers and stocking-weavers, engravers, trunk-makers, goldsmiths, bellsmiths and the like. William Bradford, as we find from his marriage register in the Puiboeken at Amsterdam, was a *vastijnwerker*, or fustian-worker. The full entry of this interesting event in the life of the man who was after-ward Governor Bradford is as follows: '1613. Nov. 9. William Bradford of Austerfield, fustian-worker, 23 years; living at Leyden, where the banns of marriage were laid; it was declared that he had no elders [*i.e.*, parents]; and Dorothea May, 16 years, of Wisbeach. The attesting witness is Henry Mayr.' We may mention, by the way, that four years earlier Dorothy May's sister, Jacomyne May, also of Wisbeach in Cambridgeshire, was married to Jean de l'Ecluse, a book printer from Rouen, who was an elder of the 'ancient church,' at Amsterdam, having come over from the French Church for 'known evils' existing among them.

While Bradford and the rest of the exiles were thus occupied in humbler callings, William Brewster, as a Cambridge man, and therefore of scholarly tastes, earned his living at first by giving lessons in English to students of the University anxious to acquire the language. We are told that he drew up rules for them 'to learn it by, after the Latin manner,' so that 'many gentlemen, both Danes and Germans, resorted to him, some of them being great men's sons,' until 'his outward condition was mended, and he lived well and plentifully.' By and by he drifted into other employment more immediately connected with the furtherance of the principles for which he and his brethren went into exile. In concert with Thomas Brewer, in the city famed for the beautiful productions of the Elzevir press, he set up a printing establishment in the Choor-steeg (*in vico Chorale*), mainly for the purpose of producing books in defence of their church principles, such as were not allowed to be printed in England. Other books also of a less controversial kind were sent forth by him, some of which, as specimens of his work, are preserved in Pilgrim Hall, and in the library of the Pilgrim Society at Plymouth.

While thus occupied in their every-day callings, their Sabbath services and their church gatherings for fellowship were the solace of their pilgrimage. With the beginning of their life at Leyden, John Robinson became the sole pastor of the community, having William Brewster as his principal elder. For Richard Clyfton, their pastor hitherto, remained behind at Amsterdam, partly because at his time of life he was unwilling to change his abode again, and partly also because he had come to sympathize with Francis Johnson's views in favour of a less popular form of church government. So that henceforth, from 1609 till his death in 1625, we are to think of John Robinson as the pastor, friend, and guide of the Leyden brotherhood. In that capacity and to an eminent degree he seems to have lived in their confidence and love. Bradford gives an ideal picture of the relations existing between them. He says it was hard to judge whether he delighted more in having such a people, or they in having such a pastor. Besides his singular ability in Divine things, wherein he excelled, he was also wise to give directions in civil affairs, so that he was helpful to their outward estates, and was in every way a common father to them. The people, on their part, also had ever a reverent regard unto him, and had him in precious estimation, and though they esteemed him highly while he lived and laboured among them, yet much more after his death they came to realise how much they had lost, to the grief of their hearts and wounding of their souls.

With an unwavering belief this pastor held to the principle that a Christian Church should be composed of Christian men, and that, being Christian men, and therefore possessed of the indwelling of the Holy Spirit, they were, under that illumination, capable of self-government. No other power, either civil or ecclesiastical, ought to supersede the exercise of the right on which such sacred duties were made to depend. Holding such views, Robinson regarded the call of God to service as coming to him through the Christian brotherhood. He says: 'I was ordained publicly upon the solemn call of the Church in which I serve both in respect of the ordainers and the ordained.'[1] Even in each separate community he held that the officers of a Church are not, by themselves, the Church. They may confer and arrange affairs privately in their consistory, 'so also (and that specially) publicly and in the face of the congregation they execute the same.' While there are many things in the settled and well-ordered state of the Church which he would willingly leave to the administration of the officers thereof, he maintained at the same time 'that they are or can be rightly and orderly done but with the people's privity and consent.' Having thus wisely directed self-government, the Church under his care enjoyed steady and healthy growth until it

[1] *Works*, I., 463.

THE EXILES IN HOLLAND.

numbered nearly three hundred communicants, besides adherents.

Governor Bradford cherished grateful remembrances of those Leyden days, and that true church life. He says: 'They continued many years in a comfortable condition, enjoying much sweet and delightful society and spiritual comfort together in the ways of God. So as they grew in knowledge and other gifts and graces of the Spirit of God, and lived together in peace and love and holiness, many came unto them from divers parts of England, so that they grew a great congregation. If at any time differences arose, as differences will arise, they were so met with and nipt in the head betimes, or otherwise so well composed that love, peace, and communion were still continued. I know not but it may be spoken to the honour of God, and without prejudice to any, that such was the true piety, the humble zeal and fervent love of this people towards God and His ways, and the single-heartedness and sincere affection one towards another, that they came as near the primitive pattern of the first Churches as any other Church of these later times have done according to their rank and quality.'[1] In his later *Dialogues*[2] he returns to these earlier memories: 'For the Church at Leyden they were sometimes not much fewer in number [than the Church at Amsterdam] nor at all inferior in able men, though they had not so many officers as the others; for they had but one ruling elder with their pastor [William Brewster], a man well approved and of great integrity; also they had three able men for deacons. And that which was a crown unto them, they lived together in love and peace all their days without any considerable difference or any disturbance that grew thereby, but such as was easily healed in love; and so they continued until with mutual consent they

[1] *History of Plymouth Plantation*, pp. 17-19.
[2] Young's *Chronicles*, p. 456.

removed into New England. . . . . Many worthy and able men there were among them who lived and died in obscurity in respect of the world, as private Christians, yet were they precious in the eyes of the Lord, and also in the eyes of such as knew them.'

Robinson himself bears similar testimony. Their former neighbour, Richard Bernard, of Worksop, had published a book, just as they were leaving Scrooby in 1608, entitled *Christian Advertisements and Counsels of Peace*, in which he had spoken of popular self-government in the Church by Christian men very much in the style of Mrs. Oliphant and other novelists of our time, whereupon in reply John Robinson solemnly protests against this 'contemptuous upbraiding of God's people with inconstancy, instability, pride, contention and the like evils, and specially this scurrilous and profane spirit, in which you nickname them Symon the Saddler, Tomkin the Tailor, Billy the Bellows-maker.' He reminds Bernard that not thus doth God's Spirit speak of God's people, and that as to what he had said about Christian men being incapable of self-government, it must not be forgotten that the leaders of the Church had more often gone wrong than the people ; that in the days of Queen Mary, for example, when all went back to Popery, many prelates and priests were the ringleaders in the reaction. ' For ourselves,' he adds, speaking of his own Church at Leyden, 'I tell you that if ever I saw the beauty of Sion and the glory of the Lord filling His tabernacle, it hath been in the manifestation of the divers graces of God in the Church, in that heavenly harmony and comely order wherein by the grace of God we are set and walk, wherein if your eyes had but seen the brethren's sober and modest carriage one towards another, their humble and willing submission unto their guides in the Lord, their tender compassion towards the weak, their fervent zeal against scandalous offenders and their long-suffering towards all, you would, I am persuaded, change your mind, and be compelled, like Balaam, to take up your parable, and bless where you purposed to curse.'[1]

This testimony was borne out by others who must be regarded as impartial witnesses. For example, Edward Winslow, an able and educated young English gentleman from Droitwich, being on his travels, happened to come to Leyden in 1617, and was so struck with the Christian life of this brotherhood that he cast in his lot with them, and not only became a member of the fellowship, but went with them afterwards to New England, his name standing third among those who signed the compact on board the Mayflower. Writing a quarter of a century later, he says: 'I persuade myself never people upon earth lived more lovingly together and parted more sweetly than we the Church at Leyden did; parting not rashly in a distracted humour, but upon joint and serious deliberation, often seeking the mind of God by fasting and prayer, whose gracious presence was not only found with us, but His blessing upon us from that time until now.'[2]

Among other principal men who joined them, as Edward Winslow did, on beholding their order, were Thomas Brewer, a wealthy Puritan from Kent, John Carver, an early deacon of the Church and leader of the first migrating colony, and Robert Cushman, who was associated with Carver in effecting the migration. Miles Standish, one of the many English gentlemen who sought military service in the Netherlands, was in friendly relations with the Church at Leyden; he also went with them in the Mayflower and became the soldier of the colony; but whether he was ever a member of the Church, or whether, like the rest of his family at Duxbury Hall, in Lancashire, he was a Roman Catholic, seems not so clear.

[1] *Works*, II., 223.
[2] Young's *Chronicles*, p. 380.

Their Dutch neighbours also seem to have had good opinion of these Christian people from England planted in their midst: 'Though many of them were poor, yet there was none so poor but if they were known to be of that congregation, the Dutch (either bakers or others) would trust them in any reasonable matter when they wanted money. Because they had found by experience how careful they were to keep their word, and saw them so painful and diligent in their callings; yea, they would strive to get their custom, and to employ them above others in their work for their honesty and diligence.'[1] The Dutch officials were of the same mind as the Dutch people in their estimate of the strangers. Bradford mentions also that 'the magistrates of the city, about the time of their coming away or a little before, in the public place of justice gave this commendable testimony of them in the reproof of the Walloons who were of the French in that city, "These English," said they, "have lived among us now these twelve years, and yet we never had any suit or accusation come against any of them; but your strifes and quarrels are continual."'[2]

The intellectual eminence of John Robinson, the pastor of these people, was also honourably recognised by the University authorities, with the consent of the magistrates, by his being received as an honorary member of the University September 5, 1615. This distinction carried with it not only literary privileges, but also certain substantial civil advantages. He thus became free from the liability to which ordinary citizens were subject of having soldiers billeted upon them in case of siege or other military emergency, also from the requirement of having to take turn in the night-watch, and having to pay contributions to public works and fortifications. There was also the further privilege of being allowed to purchase a certain quantity of

[1] *Bradford*, pp. 19, 20.   [2] Ibid.

wine or beer without payment of duty to city or state.
The following is a copy of the record on the University
roll :—

 1615
 Sept. 5° Joannes Robintsonus.   Anglus.
 Coss. permissu.   Ann. xxxix.
            Stud. Theol. alit Familiam.

During those Leyden days the controversy between Calvinist and Arminian was stirring hot blood on both sides. Lectures by Polyander and counter-lectures by Episcopius were being delivered in the University itself, John Robinson listening and deeply pondering. He was even prevailed upon—though after much hesitation—by Polyander, Festus Hommius, and other professors, to enter the lists himself against Episcopius in public discussion. This discussion lasted three days; and Bradford, who probably was present, and perhaps not altogether impartial, says that the Lord did so help this pastor of his 'to defend the truth and foil his adversary, as he put him to an apparent non-plus in this great and public audience. This so famous victory procured him much honour and respect from those learned men and others who loved the truth.'

The question at issue between Robinson and Episcopius was more vital and far-reaching than these quiet words of Bradford might lead us to suppose, and we shall not feel to the full the pulsations of life in the midst of which the exiles were living at Leyden unless we realize what these deeper issues were. The controversy of that time between the followers of Arminius and of Gomarus, between Remonstrant and Contra-Remonstrant, was no mere academical question, no merely intellectual tournament. The question of predestination and free-will had become more than a doctrinal question among theologians. It had widened out into far broader issues, and become the watchword of political party and national strife. The Remonstrants were not merely the followers of Arminius and Grotius in the matter of doctrine ; they were on the side of John of Barneveld, and therefore in favour of a National Church, controlled, in Erastian fashion, by the magistracy, and in favour also of the unpopular truce with Spain, the national foe. The Contra-Remonstrants, on the other hand, were not merely the followers of Calvin and Gomarus in the matter of predestination unto life, politically also they were on the side of Prince Maurice, the Stadholder, against Barneveld, the advocate, and therefore in favour of a Free Church in a Free State, and in favour, also, of still carrying on the war with Spain, their ancient and implacable foe.

Here, indeed, was burning material enough to set many cities on fire. This controversy ran through the whole community, as did the Arian controversy at Constantinople and Alexandria, centuries before. Speaking of the latter, Eusebius says that bishop rose against bishop, district against district, only to be compared to the Symplegades dashed against each other on a stormy day ; and Gregory of Nyssa adds to this that every corner, every alley of Constantinople was full of these discussions—the streets, the market-places, the drapers, the money-changers. Scarcely less absorbing came to be the question between Remonstrant and Contra-Remonstrant during much of the time the Scrooby brethren found a home in Leyden. In burghers' mansions and peasants' cottages, in shops, counting-houses, farmyards, and guard-rooms ; in blacksmiths' shops on land and in fishermen's barques at sea, the controversy went on its way, men losing themselves in high converse on fate, free-will, and foreknowledge absolute. Not seldom the tumult round the churches, even on Sundays, ended in open fight with knives, bludgeons, or brickbats. The conflict for supremacy between the civil and military elements, as embodied in Barneveld on the one hand and Prince Maurice on the other, was coming to a death-grapple. In 1617 the prince took military possession of some of the principal cities, and one morning the people from Scrooby, along with the rest of the citizens, saw the beautiful townhall of Leyden enclosed by a solid palisade of oaken planks, strengthened by iron bars with barbed prongs, saw cannon planted along the work, and companies of Waartgelders, armed from head to foot, drawn up in line. The conviction spread through Zealand, Friesland, Gröningen, and Guelderland, that the Arminian party was dangerous to the State, that the danger should be met by a common act of the confederacy, and that to this end a national synod should be called. This was the origin of the great Synod of Dort, which held its hundred and eighty sessions between November, 1618, and the following May, and which ended in pronouncing the followers of Arminius to be heretics and schismatics, and declaring them incapable of holding either clerical or academical post. So for the moment the storm passed off till a greater storm should come, and Europe, in a Thirty Years' War, be deluged with blood.

BOSTON STUMP AND MARKET PLACE.
(*From a sketch by* CHARLES WHYMPER.)

V.

THE WRITINGS OF JOHN ROBINSON.

THE pastor of the Pilgrim Fathers wielded so powerful an influence over the minds of the men who were the earliest founders of New England, that it may be worth while to see what he was, not only as the pastor of the Leyden Church, but also as a worker in the fields of literature. There are three volumes of his collected works,[1] and a further little tractate which has come to light in recent years.[2] As we might expect from the circumstances of the time, his writings are mainly controversial, but defensive rather than offensive. He was the trusted leader of a little

[1] *The Works of John Robinson: with Memoir and Annotations by Robert Ashton.* Three vols. London, 1851.
[2] *A Manumission to a Manuduction.* By John Robinson. 1615.

band of Separatists who were assailed from many sides, and he felt it to be his duty to go forth again and again into the field as their champion. They had no occasion ever to be ashamed of their leader. If his thrusts are penetrating, his temper is Christian. He seldom speaks bitterly, only, indeed, when he feels more keenly than usual the cruel injustice of the time which keeps them in exile from the land he loves.

The non-controversial writings of John Robinson consist of sixty-two essays on various religious and moral subjects, which had occupied mind and pen during different periods of his life, but which did not see the light till after his death. He describes them as *New Essays; or, Observations Divine and Moral*, and in framing them he says he had respect first of all to the Scriptures, next to the memorable sayings of wise and learned men, which he had carefully stored up as a precious treasure ; and, lastly, to the great book of human life in its many phases, the volume of men's manners, which he had diligently observed during the days of his pilgrimage, having had special opportunity of conversing with men of divers nations, estates, and dispositions in great variety. During his stormy and troubled life this kind of study and meditation had been to him full, sweet, and delightful, and had often refreshed his spirit amidst many sad and sorrowful thoughts unto which God had called him. These essays show the varied range of his reading as well as the reflective character of his mind. We find him quoting Plato, Aristotle, Herodotus, Thales, Cicero, Terence, Pliny, Plutarch, Seneca, Epictetus, and Suetonius; among the Fathers, Ignatius, Tertullian, Cyprian, Ambrose, Augustine, Gregory Nazianzen, Lactantius, Jerome, Basil, and Eusebius; while from among the writers of later times we find quotations from Bernard, Anselm, Scaliger, Beza, Erasmus, and Melanchthon, as well as from his own contemporaries.

The subjects dealt with in these essays are too many and too varied for anything like orderly analysis, but we may recall a few of the many sententious and sagacious sayings scattered through these pages and worthy of remembrance. For example, to good men we must do good, he says, because they do deserve it; to strangers because they may deserve it and do stand in need of it; to all men because God deserves it at our hands for them. Then, too, we ought to accept kindness as well as give it, for to refuse a kindness offered is to shame it, as a ball ill-sent and let fall to the ground. It is dangerous in religion, he thinks, to fall forward by overmuch zeal, yet not so dangerous as to fall backward by an unfaithful heart. The former may injure his face and lose his comfort, but the latter is in danger utterly to break the neck of his conscience, as old Eli by falling backward brake his neck bodily and died. A man hath in truth so much religion as he hath between the Lord and himself in secret, and no more. At the same time God is not partial, as men are; nor regards that church and chamber religion towards Him which is not accompanied in the house and streets with loving-kindness and mercy and all goodness towards men. He that strives for error strives for Satan against God; he that strives for victory strives for himself against other men; but he that strives for truth against error helps the Lord against God's and his own enemy, Satan, the father of lies. Talking of fickleness, while there is wantonness in finding and following new fashions of apparel, it were well if this vanity and newfangledness were to be seen only on people's backs. He has known divers that have more lightly and licentiously changed their religion, and that in no small points, than a sober man would the fashion of his coat, and who if it might but have gained or saved them twelve pence would have held their former religion still.

Speaking on other matters, he says that love is the loadstone of love, and the most ready and compendious way to be beloved of others is to love them first. While it is an ancient and received saying that heresy ariseth from want of faith, and schism from want of love, yet men are often accounted heretics, with greater sin, through want of charity in the judges, than through defect of faith in the judged. 'Of old some have been branded for heretics for believing in the existence of the antipodes ; others for holding the original of the soul by traduction ; others for thinking that Mary the mother of Christ had other children by her husband Joseph: the first being a certain fact, the second a philosophical doubt, and the third, even if it were an error, one neither against foundation nor post of the Scripture building.' As for schism, the Scriptures note it as sometimes made *from* the Church but most commonly *in* it. In the matter of truth and falsehood, he holds that nothing true in right reason and sound philosophy is, or can be, false in divinity. Though the truth be uttered by the devil himself, yet is it originally of God. Our Lord Christ called Himself truth, not custom, neither is falsehood, error, or heresy convinced by novelty, but by truth. 'This truth is always the same whilst the God of truth is in heaven, what entertainment soever it find with men upon earth ; it is always praiseworthy, though no man praise it ; and hath no just cause to be ashamed, though it often goes with a scratched face. They that fight against truth are like the floods beating upon the strong rocks, which are so much the more miserably dashed in pieces by how much they are the more violently carried.' He is of opinion that while want of wisdom makes some men too forward in speaking, over-much wisdom makes other men too backward. 'As the bird often flies away whilst the fowler still seeks to get nearer and nearer her, so doth golden opportunity many times, whilst we wait too long for better and fitter passage for our speech.' 'As a woman over-curiously trimmed is to be suspected, so is a speech. And, indeed, he that goes about by eloquence, without firm ground of reason, to persuade goes about to deceive. As some are large in speech out of abundance of matter and upon due consideration, so the most multiply words either from weakness or vanity. Some excuse their tediousness, saying that they cannot speak shorter, which is all one as if they said that they have unbridled tongues and inordinate passions setting them a-work. I have been many times drawn so dry, that I could not well speak any longer for want of matter: but I could ever speak as short as I would.'

Speaking of society and friendship, he notes that the woman in the Gospels who lost her piece of money lit the candle, swept the house, and sought diligently, and this she did alone, but when she had found it she called in her friends and neighbours to rejoice with her; upon which he observes that it is best mourning alone, and best rejoicing in company. Some friends, he thinks, are rather to be used than trusted, others rather to be trusted than used. So the proverb fitteth—'Rich men's purses and poor men's hearts.' Wealth makes many friends, and poverty tries them; as the wind shows which clouds have rain in them and which not. There are in pride, he thinks, many strange touches. Some men are proud of not being proud, nor lofty in carriage, apparel, or contempt of inferiors; and of being called rather good-man than master, and rather master than Sir Knight. Then, again, many will go on tiptoes, though barefoot, being proud of no man knows what, either within or without them; and none more than they. Speaking in the closing essay of death, he points out that natural death stands in the separation of the soul from the body; spiritual, of the soul and the whole man from God, in respect of grace; eternal in respect both of grace and glory, with the sense of the contrary evils. The first death is a natural evil, the second a spiritual, the third both. We have also such aphorisms as these: 'Young folk may die shortly, but the aged cannot live long. The green apple may be plucked off or shaken down by violence, but the ripe will fall of itself. Precious in the sight of the Lord is the death of his saints, as the gold melting and dissolving in the furnace is as much esteemed by the goldsmith as any in his shop or purse. If he put their tears in his bottle, he will not neglect their blood, nor easily suffer it to be shed; neither doth death, when it comes, part him and them, though it part man and man, yea man and wife, yea man in himself, his soul and body.' 'We are not to mourn for the death of our Christian friends as they who are without hope, either in regard of them or of ourselves. . . . . But we should take occasion by their deaths to love this world the less out of which they are taken; and heaven the more whither they are gone before us, and where we shall ever enjoy them.'

Possibly in many of the wise sayings scattered through these two and sixty essays we have unspent echoes of some of the sermons to which the Pilgrims listened during their Leyden days. And as we catch up these echoes again we feel that Governor Bradford spake truly when he tells us that this revered pastor of theirs was a man not easily paralleled for all things; was learned and of a solid judgment, and of a quick and sharp wit, was of a tender conscience, and very sincere in all his ways; was never satisfied in himself until he had searched any cause or argument he had to deal in thoroughly and to the bottom; and that he was very profitable in his ministry and comfortable to his people.

The rest of his Works were necessarily, from the stress of the times, as we have said, mainly controversial. The Separatists had to defend their principles of church government by the Christian people under the headship of Christ from Episcopalians and Presbyterians alike. In this way it came to pass that it was in the field of controversy that Robinson made his first appearance as an author. In the year 1609, the year of migration from Amsterdam to Leyden, he published a reply to Joseph Hall, the vicar of Halstead, in Essex, better known as the Bishop of Norwich of a later time. Hall had sent forth what Robinson called 'a censorious epistle,' which was addressed to John Smyth and himself, whom the writer described as 'ringleaders of the late separation at Amsterdam,' and whom he blames for their separation from the Church of England. She may have her faults: this were cause enough for them to lament her, to pray for her, to labour for her redress, not to avoid her. This unnaturalness is shameful. If they had only loved peace half so well as truth, this breach had never been, and they who were yet brethren had been still companions. Is the Church of England Babylon? If so, where are the main buildings of that accursed city— infallibility, dispensings of sin, deposition of princes and the like? Where her rotten heaps of corrupt errors— transubstantiation, image worship, indulgences and pilgrimages? Where her deep vaults of penances and purgatories? Are they not all razed and buried in the dust? He thinks they may find too late that it would have been a thousand times better to swallow a ceremony than to rend a Church; yea, that even whoredoms and murders shall abide an easier answer than separation.

To this Robinson makes answer that separation is not the odious thing his opponent seems to think it, for separation from the world, and so from whatsoever is contrary to God, is the first step to our communion with God and angels and good men, as the first step to a ladder is to leave the earth. As to his being 'a ringleader,' if a thing be good, it is good and commendable to be forward in it. Let it be shown that it is wrong, and if he have fled away on foot he will return on horseback. Hall charges him with unnaturalness towards their mother, the Church of England; but we must not so cleave to Holy Mother Church as to neglect our Heavenly Father and His commandments. She may be our mother and yet not the Lord's wife. Were not Luther, Zwinglius, Cranmer, Latimer and the rest begotten of the Lord in the womb of the Romish Church, and yet did they not forsake her, and that justly for her fornications? Though they have forsaken England for Holland, yet have they not ceased to love and desire to live in their native land. The commonwealth and kingdom of England they honour above all states of the world, and if with a free conscience they might live there, they would thankfully embrace the meanest corner in the land, at the extremest conditions of any people in the kingdom.

Robinson's next book, *A Justification of Separation from the Church of England*, was a more elaborate production on the same theme, and was also a reply to a remonstrance from the other side. In 1608, the year the exiles left Scrooby for Amsterdam, their former neighbour, Richard Bernard, of Worksop, sent forth a little book entitled, *Christian Advertisements and Counsels of Peace. Also Dissuasions from the Separatists' Schism, commonly called Brownism*. To this Robinson makes reply in a justification of his separation, which is the longest and most elaborate work we have from his pen.[1] He would much rather, he says, have built up himself and that poor flock over which the Holy Ghost has set him in holy peace, as becometh the house of God, than enter the lists of contention; but feeling that he must defend the truth, he will endeavour in a good conscience before God so to bear himself as not to be

[1] *A Justification of Separation from the Church of England, against Mr. Richard Bernard: his Invective.* Entitled the Separatists' Schisme. By John Robinson, 1610.

contentious in contention. He cannot admire the manner of those who commend peace that they may smother truth and plead for Cæsar's due that they may detain from God His due. It is an easier thing, he is aware, to tie knots than to loose them, and a simple man may cast a stone into a ditch which a wise man cannot get out again, still the questions at issue between him and the minister of Worksop are, after all, not so dark and doubtful that a man needs take so long a journey as the Queen of Sheba did for resolution. For himself so dearly does he love preaching the Gospel that he would count himself happy if with the exchange of half the days of his life he might freely publish it in his own nation. Still even for so good a work he dare not by a bait draw his conscience, as a bird into a snare, into most fearful entanglements. He is aware that against separation good men have spoken strongly; indeed, he has to confess that a long time before he entered this way himself he took some taste of the truth in it by some treatises published in justification of it, which the Lord knoweth were sweet as honey to his mouth, and the only thing which kept him back then was the over-valuation which he made of the learning and holiness of these men, he being afraid to press one hairsbreadth in this thing before men, behind whom he knew himself to come so many miles in all things. Indeed, since then, having searched the Scriptures and found much light, had not the truth been in his heart as a burning fire shut up in his bones he had never broken those bonds of flesh and blood wherein he was so straitly tied; but had suffered the light of God to have been put out in his own unthankful heart by other men's darkness.

Bernard had defended the mixed communion of all the persons in a parish, whatever their spiritual condition, by having recourse as usual to the parable of the tares and the wheat, interpreting the field to be the visible Church and the tares scandalous offenders. If this be the right interpretation, Robinson replies, then the power which Christ gave to His Church to root out obstinate offenders is not only weakened, but disannulled. Moreover, if offenders be not to be cast out, how dare the prelates of England take this forbidden weed-hook and uproot the Separatists? If any tares be to be plucked up, why not all? And if all be to be let alone, why meddle they with any? If they execute their own canons, perhaps they would not be so much plucking up the tares from among the wheat as the wheat from among the tares. But if the Lord Jesus, who knew His own meaning, calls the field not the Church but the world, as He does, why should we admit any other interpretation? This mixture of all sorts, godly and ungodly, in a parish is of the very essence of a National Church; but what husbandman is either so foolish or so careless as to sow his field with tares and wheat together? Yet this fair field of England, of whose beauty all the Christian world is enamoured, is so sown, this pleasant orchard so planted, this flourishing Church so gathered!

Passing to the executive authority in the State Church, Robinson shows that it is neither in the people nor the principal members. The truth is that in the parish church of Worksop, and also in all the other parish churches in the land, there is only one member that hath power, and that under the ordinary, namely, the parish priest. But for the exercising of the censures, that belongs not to the whole body or to any member thereof, principal or less principal, but to the bishop and his substitute, who are foreigners and strangers. The minister's only portion in the censure is to do the executioner's office when the official has played the judge; and even if he should be so bold as to refuse, he would be punished for his contumacy and the church door would do his office, for the bill of excommunication hanged up there by the sumner binds the offenders both in heaven and earth.

Robinson contends that the company of faithful people even without the officers are the Church. For if not, if Mr. Bernard, for example, should leave his vicarage for a better, then the church of Worksop would be dischurched and remain a church no longer. Thus an assembly might be churched and unchurched and churched again every week during a time of persecution or plague, by having and losing and recovering again her officers. Referring to the size of a church, he maintains that two or three gathered in the name of Christ have the same right with two or three hundred; neither the smallness of the number nor the meanness of the persons can prejudice their right. He goes on to show that a true ecclesiastical polity doth comprehend within itself whatsoever is excellent in all other bodies political. Thus wise men writing on this subject have approved as good and lawful three kinds of politics— monarchical, aristocratical, and democratical—and all these three forms have their place in the Church of Christ. In respect of Christ the head it is a monarchy, in respect of its officers it is an aristocracy, and in respect of the body a popular state. The governors of the Church must be in and of the Church they govern, but they are not the Church. In the apostles' time, as we learn from the Acts of the Apostles, preaching was carried on to and fro, turning and joining of multitudes to the Lord when neither apostles nor officers were present; for this is too gross to affirm that during all the apostles' days nothing was begun but by them. And what if the Lord should now raise up a company of faithful men and women in Barbary or America by the reading of the Scriptures or by the writings, conferences, or sufferings of some godly men? Must they not join themselves to the Lord in the fellowship of the Gospel, nor have any communion together for their mutual edification and comfort, till some vagrant priest from Rome or England be sent unto them to begin their church matters with his service-book? And yet he, from his unknown tongue, might be a barbarian to them, and they barbarians unto him.

Dealing with the well-known passage, Matthew xviii. 17, 'Tell it unto the Church,' he thinks it is as clear as the sun that the Church there means the assembly whereof the offender is a member. Whomsoever the Lord Jesus meant by 'the Church' He certainly never meant that the Archbishop of York, the Archdeacon of Nottingham, and the official of Southwell were the Church of Worksop. So far are they from being the Church of Worksop that they are not so much as members of it, nor of any other particular church in the kingdom; they are neither the pastors so called nor under the pastors of any particular church, but with their transcendent jurisdiction in their provincial and diocesan churches take their scope without orb or order.

Robinson contends that to maintain that government suffers by being in the hands of the people, and to deprive them of their rights in consequence, is to act in the spirit of those who enclose the commons of their poorer neighbours on the plea that common things are commonly neglected, and that by enclosing one acre of ground they can make it worth two acres left in common. He further disapproves of the choice of a minister for a congregation being left to a patron, and asks, if the patron stand in the room of the people to choose for them, who set him there? If some one man in a parish had entailed to him and his heirs for ever the power of appointing husbands to all the women in the parish, it would be an intolerable civil bondage, and it is an intolerable spiritual bondage for parish assemblies to be under the imperious presentations of those lord patrons whose clerks they must submit unto whether they will or no. Great is the sin of the people who lose this liberty, greater that of the patrons who engross it. The bond between the minister and the people he holds to be one of the closest and most sacred kind, and is therefore not one to be entered upon but with mutual consent. This mutual relation has many advantages: it incites the minister himself to all diligence and faithfulness ; it is a source of comfort to him under all the trials and temptation incident to the minister's life, and it much furthers the love of the people to the person of their minister.

Such is the main drift, briefly summarised, of John Robinson's main venture into the field of authorship. The year following its publication letters passed between him and William Ames, then at the Hague, on the question of communion among believers. This correspondence led Robinson to issue in 1614 a treatise of some extent on *Religious Communion, Private and Public*. Comparing the book of 1614 with the letters of 1611, his opinions seem to have undergone some modification, are certainly softened in expression. Referring to those in England who point to the dissensions which sometimes arise in free Christian communities, he reminds them that they only who enjoy liberty know how hard it is to enjoy it aright. Two prisoners being chained and manacled together, feet and hands, may wonder that other men at liberty do not walk closer together. Passing from this point to his main purpose he maintains that he with those who are with him, ' who profess a separation from the English national, provincial, diocesan, and parochial church and churches in the whole formal state and order thereof, may, notwithstanding, lawfully communicate in private prayer and other the like holy exercises (not performed in their Church communion, nor by their Church power and ministry) with the godly amongst them, though remaining members of the Church.' With the large tolerance of mind and feeling with which his name is associated, Robinson says :

'For myself thus I believe with my heart before God, and profess with my tongue, and that before the world, that I have one and the same faith, hope, spirit, baptism, and Lord which I had in the Church of England, and none other; that I esteem so many in that Church, of what state or order soever, as are truly partakers of that faith, as I account many thousands to be, for my Christian brethren, and myself, a fellow-member with them of that one mystical body of Christ scattered far and wide throughout the world ; that I have always in spirit and affection all Christian fellowship and communion with them, and am most ready in all outward actions and exercises of religion, lawful and lawfully done, to express the same ;' saving only 'that I cannot communicate with or submit unto the said Church order and ordinances there established, either in state or act, without being condemned of mine own heart, and therein provoking God, who is greater than my heart, to condemn me much more.'

To meet this state of mind William Ames sent forth *A Manuduction for Mr. Robinson and such as consort with him in private communion to lead them on to publick.*[1] He tries by certain queries to break down, as he says, the middle wall of partition between private communion and public conformity. Moreover, he intimates that to his knowledge Robinson has often been at services where Mr. Perkins's service-book appeared, and once also came to listen to the sermon of Mr. Perkins's successor, and that since his professed separation. To this Robinson replied in a little pamphlet entitled, *A Manumission to a Manuduction.*[2] He contends there is an important difference

---

[1] 'Briefly comprised in a letter written to Mr. R. W., at Dort. Printed by George Waters. And are to be sould at his shop at the Signe of the Snuffers, on the Fishmarket. 1614.'

[2] *A Manumission to a Manuduction; or answer to a Letter inferring Publique Communion in the parish assemblies upon private with godly persons there.* By John Robinson. Anno Domini, 1615.

between private communion with good men and public conformity to a system which ignores the rights of the Christian commonalty. 'The Church of England,' he says, 'doth acknowledge no such calling as is chiefly grounded upon the people's choice, but only that which is grounded upon the bishop's ordination, and that not to the ministry of some one church, but to the ministry at large; and determinately either upon the bishop's license, or upon the patron's presentation, the bishop's institution, and archdeacon's induction, confirmed by the public laws of the same Church, both ecclesiastical and civil. The mere fact that the people accept and submit to a ministry when they have no alternative does not alter the essential character of the procedure. The parish ministry is a branch of the prelacy, as receiving power from it by which it doth administer; and therefore to be avoided by God's people.' In reply to what Ames says as to his inconsistency in being present at certain services, he gives us a piece of autobiography not without interest. It is true, he says, that during the time he was debating the question of separation in his mind, and disputing for it with others, but had not otherwise professed it, he had been present at the services of the National Church. As to what took place later, on the occasion referred to by Ames, he will state the facts, and leave him to gain what advantage he can out of them: 'Coming to Cambridge (as to other places where I hoped most to find satisfaction to my troubled heart), I went the forenoon to Mr. Cha[derton] his exercise; who upon the relation which Mary made to the

---

This reply to Ames is not found in the collected edition of Robinson's Works, having come to light since 1851. The first copy known in recent years came into the possession of Charles Deane, LL.D., Vice-President of the Massachusetts Historical Society, and was reprinted in the Collections of that Society. 4th Series; Vol. i. A second copy of the original edition was obtained by the British Museum, through Dr. R. W. Dale, of Birmingham, April, 1894.

disciples of the resurrection of Christ, delivered in effect this doctrine, that the things which concerned the whole Church were to be declared publicly to the whole Church, and not to some part only, bringing for instance and proof the words of Christ, Matt. xviii. 17, confirming therein one main ground of our difference from the Church of England, which is that Christ hath given his power for excommunication to the whole Church gathered together in His name, as 1 Cor. v., the officers as governors and the people as governed in the use thereof, unto which Church his servants are commanded to bring their necessary complaints. And I would desire mine opposite either to show me how and where this Church is having this power in the parish assemblies, or else by what warrant of God's word, I (knowing what Christ the Lord commanded herein) may with good conscience remain a member of a church without this power, much less where the contrary is advanced, and so go on in the known transgression of that his commandment—"Tell it to the Church."'

'In the afternoon I went to hear Mr. B[aynes], the successor of Mr. Perkins, who from Eph. v. 7 or 11 showed the unlawfulness of familiar conversation between the servants of God and the wicked, upon these grounds or most of them : That the former are light and the other darkness, between which God hath separated ; the godly hereby are endangered to be leavened with the others' wickedness ; that the wicked are hereby hardened in receiving such approbation from the godly ; and that others are thereby offended and occasioned to think they are all alike, and as birds of a feather. Whom afterwards, privately, I desired, as I do also others, to consider whether these very reasons make not as effectually and much more against the spiritual communion of God's people, especially where there wants the means of reformation, with the apparently wicked, to whom they are as light to darkness.'

Ames had remarked on the fact that Robinson did not refuse public communion with the Reformed Churches of the Continent, though they, like the English Church, used a form of prayer; to which he replied that he should not refuse all public communion with a true church because of the use of set forms of prayer; but there was a difference in his opinion between their use in the Reformed Churches and in the unreformed Church of England; a difference not only in the matter and sundry orders thereof, but more especially in the manner of imposing it, which in the Reformed Churches is not by compulsion, nor as in the Church of England, where the reading of it is preferred before and above the preaching of the Gospel. In the latter Church more ministers (and those of the best sort) have been deprived of their ministry in a few months for the not reading and observing it in manner and form, than have been ever since the Pope was expelled, not only for not preaching (for which no man is censured), but for all other wickedness of what kind soever, though abounding in the ministry there. By which that their set service is advanced above all that is called God, and made the very idol to which both great and small are compelled to bow down and it to honour.

In 1618 Robinson published *The People's Plea for the exercise of Prophecy*, a defence of lay-preaching in reply to John Yates, B.D., minister of St. Andrew's Church, Norwich, who had written against *Persons Prophesying out of Office*. This reply was dedicated by Robinson to his Christian friends at Norwich and thereabouts, to whom he had ministered in former years, and of whom, he says, he has always loving and thankful remembrance. Joseph Hall had about the same time published his *Apology of the Church of England*, and Robinson says, if it be asked why he did not reply to this rather than to the smaller work by Yates, he answers that truth requires that not persons but things be answered, and things there are none in Hall's book which have not been already answered in his reply to Bernard. Moreover, he puts as great a difference between Hall and Yates as between a word-wise orator better able to feed his readers with leaves of words and flowers of rhetoric than with fruits of knowledge, and a man sincerely zealous for the truth, as Mr. Yates.

Mr. Yates argued that from the commission of Christ, given John xx. 21-23, all prophecy in public is to remit and retain sins, and that Christ grants this power to none but such as He sends and ordains thereunto. Robinson assents to the position that all prophecy in public is for the remitting and retaining of sins, but not to the assertion that Christ grants this power to none but such as He sends and ordains by the commission given in the passage in question, for in that case He would have granted to none but apostles. His answer would have been more effective had he noticed that when our Lord gave the commission recorded by John He gave it to all who were present in the room where the disciples were met with locked doors for fear of the Jews, and that others besides the apostles were present. It is evident that the gathering on the first Easter Sunday evening mentioned by John is the same as that recorded by Luke (xxiv. 33). If so, there were certainly other disciples present besides the apostles. For, as Luke tells us, when the two disciples returned to Jerusalem from Emmaus, they found the eleven gathered together, *and them that were with them*. These two disciples themselves, one of whom was named Cleopas, had joined the company before Jesus appeared, and were certainly not apostles. The disciples, not merely the apostles, were glad when they saw the Lord, and it was upon the whole body of those in Jerusalem thus gathered together that Jesus breathed, and to whom He said: 'Receive ye the Holy Ghost; whosoever sins ye forgive, they are forgiven unto them ; whosoever sins ye retain, they are retained.'

Robinson having said that the woman of Samaria carried the truth about Christ to her countrymen, Yates exclaims : 'O simplicity which cannot see between preaching of the Gospel and carrying tidings of a man that told her all things that ever she did.' Robinson rejoins : 'It is indeed my simplicity to think that the Gospel, as the word importeth, is nothing else but glad tidings, and that to preach the Gospel is nothing else but to carry or bring glad tidings of Christ, before promised, then come into the world. Through her many of the Samaritans believed on Christ, therefore she preached the word as truly and effectually as ever did minister to his parishioners, though she went not up into a pulpit to do it.' After other arguments in defence of his position, Robinson concludes by saying that in Leyden, where he is living, it is not only permitted as lawful, but required as necessary that men not in office and not ordained should preach, that such as have bent their thoughts towards the ministry should beforehand use their gifts publicly in the church. Intolerable bondage, he says, it would be thought by them to be, if they had to have pastors ordained for them, as all there are unto the places in which they are to minister, of whose ability in teaching they had had no opportunity of taking former experience. Finally he trusts that the Lord will give courage unto His people to stand for this liberty of lay-preaching among the rest of the liberties wherewith Christ hath made them free.

It was not till 1624, and therefore nearly at the close of his life, that Robinson published his *Just and Necessary Apology of certain Christians no less contumeliously than commonly called Brownists or Barrowists.* In this he says he agrees with Jerome that the crime of heresy none ought patiently to endure ; but if he and his people are charged with being heretics they have this consolation, that they have with them their gracious Lord and Saviour, by whose judgment alone, notwithstanding all men's prejudices, they shall stand or fall for ever. If any in this world have need to get this divine comfort deeply printed in their hearts, he and those with him have, since their profession gives occasion to many, and their condition liberty to all, to spare no severity of censure upon them. Four sorts of heavy friends they have found and felt in sorrowful experience, wherever they have gone: the unhallowed multitude walking perversely; those who are enamoured of the Romish hierarchy as of a stately and potent lady, who are servilely in bondage, themselves and their consciences, either to the edicts of certain princes, or to the determination of certain doctors, or both these together, who think nothing well done in case of religion which either these teach not or command not, and on the other hand regard almost anything warranted which is commended by the one or commanded by the other; and finally they have suffered from those who through credulity and lightness of belief have their minds open to false and feigned suggestions of slanderous tongues. He maintains that the Separatists are not, as is alleged, unduly contentious. So far from that, he says:

'We account the Reformed Churches true Churches of Jesus Christ, and here in Holland both profess and practise communion with them in the holy things of God; their sermons such of ours frequent as understand the Dutch tongue; the sacraments we do administer unto their known members, if by occasion any of them be present with us; and we do desire from the Lord their holy and firm peace.' Having declared and defended the principles and practice of the Leyden Church, he most willingly admits that in the Church of England lively faith and true piety are both begotten and nourished in the hearts of many by the preaching of the Gospel within her borders. 'God forbid,' he cries, 'that we should not acknowledge that, and withal that infinite thanks for the same are due to God's great power and goodness!'

What, in spite of all his Christian charity, he must and will affirm is that the parish assemblies, with their motley gatherings of all sorts of characters at the Lord's table, are not in any real and scriptural sense Churches of Christ.

'That so it stands with the Church of England, no man to whom England is known can be ignorant, seeing that all the natives there and subjects of the kingdom, although never such strangers from the show of true piety and goodness, and fraught never so full with many most heinous impieties and vices, are without difference compelled and enforced by most severe laws, civil and ecclesiastical, into the body of that Church. And of this confused heap a few, compared with the rest, godly persons mingled among is that national church, commonly called the Church of England, collected and framed. Such is the material constitution of that church. It is constituted only by their parish perambulation and the standing of the houses in which they dwell. Every subject of the kingdom dwelling in this or that parish, whether in city or country, whether in his own or other man's house, is thereby, *ipso facto*, made legally a member of the same parish in which that house is situated, and bound, will he nill he, fit or unfit, as with iron bonds, and all his with him, to participate in all holy things, and some unholy also, in that same parish church.'

To the Christian reader he makes his final appeal. If he and his are in error, let them be advertised brotherly. 'Err we may, alas! too easily; but heretics by the grace of God we will not be.' If, however, men be either forestalled by prejudice, or by prosperity made secure, 'this alone remaineth that we turn our faces and mouths unto Thee, O most powerful Lord and gracious Father, humbly imploring help from God towards those who are by men left desolate. There is with Thee no respect of persons, neither are men less regarders of Thee, if regarders of Thee, for the world's disregarding them. They who truly fear Thee and work righteousness, although constrained to live by leave in a foreign land, exiled from country, spoiled of goods, destitute of friends, few in number and mean in condition, are for all that unto Thee (O gracious God) nothing the less acceptable. Thou numberest all their wanderings and puttest their tears into Thy bottles. Are they not written in Thy book? Towards Thee, O Lord, are our eyes; confirm our hearts, and bend Thine ear, and suffer not our feet to slip or our face to be ashamed, O Thou just and Merciful God!'

VI.

WHERE LIES THE LAND?

Where lies the land to which the ship would go?
Far, far ahead, is all her seamen know.—*A. H. Clough.*

WATCHING the birds in field and woodland as the time for migration draws near, you note a strange restlessness coming over them which they seem unable to resist. He who guides their wondrous flight across the sea also implants within them the longing to go. Some such longing, also divinely implanted, came over the hearts of the exiles in Leyden, after years of sojourn among strangers. Human reasons there were on the surface sufficient to make them wish to go, but the real reason lay deeper, in the very heart of the Divine purpose. That God who is the beginning and the author of nations was calling them as surely as He called Abraham from east to west, saying :
 Get thee out of thy country into a land which I will show thee.' Like Abraham, they heard a voice calling them away from the city where they dwelt ; like him, they went forth in faith, not knowing whither they went ; and like him, too, they went to found a great nation and become a multitude of people. They, even as we, found themselves in a world in which they were not to rest content, except in the contentment of advance.

The human reasons for leaving Leyden which lay near at hand on the surface were many and forcible. For the conditions of life where they lived were stern and hard, so that few from the mother country cared to come and join them, even preferring the prisons in England to liberty in

Holland under such conditions ; others who did come soon spent their estate, and were forced to return to England, shrinking from great labour and hard fare. They loved the persons of their brethren in Leyden, approved their cause and honoured their sufferings, yet were forced to leave them ; regretfully they left, as Orpah left Naomi, apologetically, as the Romans left Cato, saying they could not all be Catos. Then, too, what touched the hearts of the exiles keenly was that some of their own children began to sink under the hardships of their lot ; their minds were free and willing enough to share their parents' burdens, but their bodies bowed under the weight of the same, so that they became decrepit even in early youth, and the vigour of nature seemed to be consumed in the bud. While this was true of the more gracious of their children, others less amenable were drawn aside by the temptations of the city, and were led by evil example into extravagant and dangerous courses. Some of their sons enlisted into the armies of the Netherlands, others took service as sailors in the Dutch merchantmen, while others again fell into dissolute ways, 'to the great grief of their parents and dishonour of God.' Then, again, there was the fact that the twelve years' truce with Spain would soon come to an end by mere lapse of time, and if they still remained in the country, they might then find themselves in the stress and straits of another Leyden siege. Even if it should not come to this, some of them were distressed by the fact that they could not, in the circumstances in which they found themselves, give to their children such education as they had themselves received ; and they were pained, too, by the open profanation of the Sabbath day prevalent among the Dutch. So rife was this evil that even the Dutch ministers themselves deplored their inability to keep their people away from Sunday sports and labour ; and the clergy sent over by King James to represent

England at the Synod of Dort felt called upon to move the Synod to make strong representations to the local magistracy on the subject. Further, these exiles were still Englishmen in heart and soul. The spirit of nationality and the love of self-government were too strong within them to permit them to think with equanimity of the possibility of their descendants becoming absorbed into the Dutch nation. Then, to quote Bradford's own words: 'Lastly (and which was not the least) a great hope and inward zeal they had of laying some good foundation, or at least to make some way thereunto, for the propagating and advancing the Gospel of the Kingdom of Christ in those remote parts of the world; yea, though they should be but even as stepping-stones unto others for the performing of so great a work.'

Another reason had probably some weight with them, though not mentioned either by Bradford or Winslow. Even in Leyden they were not altogether beyond the reach of harassment from King James. The States of Holland, anxious to retain him as their ally against Spain, were afraid to offend him, and permitted him at times still to disturb those of his subjects who had sought asylum among them. The correspondence of Sir Dudley Carleton, at that time English ambassador at the Hague, furnishes us with a case in point. Among the brethren in the Leyden Church was a Kentish man of the name of Thomas Brewer, whom Carleton, writing to Secretary Naunton, in London, describes as 'a gentleman of a good house, both of land and living, which none of his profession in these parts are; though through the reveries of his religion (he being, as I advertised your honour, a profest Brownist) he hath mortgaged and consumed a great part of his estate.'[1] In conjunction with William Brewster, Brewer had, as we

---

[1] *Letters from and to Sir Dudley Carleton, Knt.*, during his Embassy in Holland from 1615-16 to December, 1620, p. 406.

have seen, set up a printing-office in the Choorsteeg, for the purpose of producing such English books explanatory of their principles as were forbidden to be printed at home. Carleton, reporting to Naunton, says: 'This Brewer, and Brewster, whom he hath set to work, having kept no open shop nor printed many books fit for public sale in these provinces, their practice was to print prohibited books, to be vented underhand in His Majesty's kingdoms.' Two books printed in the Netherlands, though as it turned out not by them, had excited the wrath of James, who sent instructions to Carleton to take action in the matter. Acting upon these instructions, Carleton writes to Secretary Naunton under date July 22, 1619, and says, 'I believe I have discovered the printer of *De Regimine Ecclesiae Scoticanae*, which His Majesty was informed to be done in Middleburgh, and that is one William Brewster, a Brownist, who hath been for some years an inhabitant and printer at Leyden, but is now within this three weeks removed from thence and gone back to dwell in London, where he may be found out and examined not only of this book but likewise of the *Perth Assembly*, of which, if he was not the printer himself, he assuredly knows both printer and author; for, as I am informed, he hath had, whilst he remained here, his hand in all such books as have been sent over into England and Scotland, as, particularly, a book in folio, entitled *A Confutation of the Rhemish translation*, anno 1618.'[1]

A month later (Aug. 20) Carleton tells Naunton, 'I have made good inquiry after William Brewster at Leyden, and am well assured that he is not returned thither, neither is it likely he will, having removed from thence his family and his goods.'[2] Meantime, while Sir Dudley was keeping a sharp look-out for Brewster in Holland, we catch a glimpse of what was going on in relation to him in Eng-

[1] *Carleton Letters*, p. 380. [2] Ibid., p. 386.

land. Among the State papers there has been preserved a single sheet, consisting of brief extracts of some letters from Naunton to the Duke of Buckingham [?] in this same month of August, 1619. Under date, August 1, is the following abstract :—' Brewster frighted back into the Low Countries by the bishop's pursuivants. Sir Rob. Naunton will follow him with his letters to Sir Dudley Carleton.' Two days later Naunton writes again to the duke :— ' Brewster's son, of his father's sect, within this half-year now comes to church. Sir Rob. Naunton hath received a note from him to his son, and committed the deliverer close until he discovers where the father is.'[1] From which broken hints we gather, that on Brewster's coming to London, not so much, as we know now, to escape the attentions of Sir Dudley Carleton, as to carry on negotiations with shipmasters and others in reference to a voyage to the West, he finds himself the object of hot pursuit on the part of the Bishop of London's pursuivants. Further, we gather that his son, still remaining in England, having quailed before the storm, has conformed and come to church, and that the messenger bringing a letter from father to son has been arrested and locked up close till he reveals Brewster's hiding-place, which, apparently, he has persistently refused to do.

Meanwhile the English minister on the other side the sea was still eagerly in pursuit, and indeed, at one time, congratulated himself that he had secured the fugitive. He even sent word to Naunton that he had caught Brewster at last. But he was mistaken ; his stupid official had laid hold of the wrong man, had seized Brewer instead of Brewster. Brewer, however, being arrested, was detained, for it was discovered that he was quite as deeply implicated in the printing of the surreptitious books as Brewster himself. In September, Carleton writes : 'In my last I

[1] *State Papers, Domestic.* James I. Vol. cx. : Aug. 1619.

advertised your honour that Brewster was taken at Leyden, which proved an error, in that the *schout* [the bailiff] who was employed by the magistrates for his apprehension being a dull, drunken fellow, took one man for another. But Brewer, who set him on work, and being a man of means, bare the charge of his printing, is fast in the university's prison; and his printing letters, which were found in his house, in a garret where he had hid them, and his books and papers, are all seized and sealed up. I expect to-morrow to receive his voluntary confession of such books as he hath caused to be printed by Brewster for this year and a half or two years past; and then I intend to send some one expressly to visit his books and papers, and to examine him particularly touching *Perth Assembly*, the discourse *De Regimine*, and other Puritan pamphlets which I have newly recovered.'[1] A few days later Carleton further informs Naunton that he had sent an advocate of Leyden, who understands English, to examine Brewer's books and papers, and, his answers not being satisfactory, he has used the Prince of Orange's authority, who has himself spoken to the rector of the university not to give the prisoner his liberty until the pleasure of the King of England is known concerning him. The rector has promised this, although the whole company of the Brownists offer security for Brewer; and he being a university man, the students are urged by the Brownists to plead privilege in the case where security is offered. Carleton requests that the rector and M. Brookhoven, the deputy of the town of Leyden in the Council of Holland, may know the king's pleasure as soon as possible, so as to prevent any disorder, which otherwise might arise out of this matter in that tumultuous town. Meantime M. Brookhoven, when he goes to Leyden next Monday for two or three days, will give orders to have Brewer further examined.

[1] *Carleton Letters*, p. 389.

The matter proved not so easy to deal with as was expected. Brewer stood upon his rights, and showed little regard for the ambassador's authority. Moreover, it was a complicated case of combined jurisdiction between Town and Gown, Brewer having been arrested by the town *escoulete*, but detained as a university man in the university prison. Carleton feels he must move cautiously, and must work upon the curators and rector of the university beforehand ; and also upon the magistrates of the town, through their deputy Brookhoven. He will also seek private interviews with the Prince of Orange. On the 22nd of October he reports progress. He has seen two of the curators of the university, the rector and his two assessors, and also the town deputy, who all came to him in one company. They were very polite, made large professions of due respect to the King of England, but could not follow up their fine words by sending Brewer to England as a prisoner, which was what Carleton asked them to do ; for, as a member of the university, Brewer might, they said, insist on his privilege of being tried without removal to another jurisdiction. Their university, consisting chiefly, as it did, of students from other countries, would be seriously injured if, in a matter of so much consequence, their privileges were not preserved ; in fact, the foreign students might leave in a body. Moreover, there was a precedent they could not forget. Some time ago a member of the university, one Cluverus, a German, had published a book against the Emperor Rudolph, and a demand was made that he should be sent to Prague to be punished. To this demand the university made absolute refusal, on the ground that it could not be granted without a breach of their privileges. In the face of such a precedent what could they do? On the other hand, Carleton pleaded that for as long a period as three years past Brewer had gone on printing prohibited books and pamphlets, not for the university or the Dutch provinces, but to His Majesty's disservice and the trouble of his kingdom.

In the midst of such complications Brewer himself, in the most chivalrous manner, came to the rescue of these belated diplomatists. To save the Leyden authorities from coming into open conflict with King James, which they were very unwilling to do, Brewer offered to go to England of his own accord, and submit to examination on certain conditions. The conditions were : that he should be assured in writing that it was His Majesty's pleasure that he should come; that he should go as a free man, and not as a prisoner ; that he should not be punished during his abode in England, either in body or goods ; that he should be allowed to return in competent time ; and, finally, that he should not be expected to make the journey at his own charges. His offer was accepted, and he prepared to go, though much against the will of John Robinson, his pastor, and his fellow-members in the Leyden Church. Carleton wrote to England, expressing the hope that Brewer would be well treated, inasmuch as he had taken his resolution of presenting himself unto His Majesty against the minds of some stiffnecked men in Leyden, who did all they could to dissuade him from going.

On the 3rd November, attended simply by the beadle and one other officer of the university, Brewer set out for Rotterdam, and was delivered to Sir William Zouch, who was travelling to England in a private capacity. The following day they set forward on their journey by way of Zealand, and on reaching Middleburgh the people there proved to be of the same mind as the brethren at Leyden, and were strongly opposed to Brewer placing himself in the power of the King of England. Sir William Zouch, writing to Carleton, says Brewer 'hath many friends in Middleboro, and those exceeding earnest in his cause, as, the treasurer-general, his brother the chief of the reckon-chamber, and his other brother, a minister (their name is Teebake); and one Mr. Vosberg, chief reckon-master, who was on the way towards Holland to speak to his excellency on Mr. Brewer's behalf, and to have advised him to have challenged the privileges of the university and of the town, by which he would have had his trial there. I was, on Monday was seven-night, invited to dinner by them, when they did expostulate in the business.'

In spite of remonstrance and expostulation, however, Thomas Brewer remained faithful to his compact with the English and Leyden authorities. On reaching Flushing, where they were to embark, they found the wind against them, as it remained for weeks, so that they were unable to cross to England. Fierce storms prevailed: 'No day,' writes Sir William, 'hath passed without a storm; the streets run with salt water that hath scaled the walls, made pools and lakes, and kept the people within their doors.' During these weeks of waiting and wild tempests they seem not to have been without social enjoyment, for Carleton tells us, with smile and shrug of satisfaction, that Brewer's fellow-Brownists at Leyden are somewhat scandalised, because they hear that Sir William Zouch has taught him to drink healths.

Some time about the beginning of December the two travellers reached London, where Brewer's guarantee of safe-conduct seems to have been duly respected. Whether his explanation of the work carried on in the printing-office in the Choorsteeg by Brewster and himself was satisfactory or not, the English Government were bound to observe the compact entered into by the English ambassador on their behalf. On the 29th January Sir Dudley Carleton acknowledges the receipt of a letter of the 14th, by way of Antwerp, from Secretary Naunton, and says he has acquainted the curators of the university with the good treatment Brewer has received in England—

WHERE LIES THE LAND? 167

far, indeed, beyond his deservings—and with his delivery, for which they render His Majesty their humble thanks. When he returns to Leyden, unless he undertakes to do his utmost to find out where Brewster is, he is not like to be at liberty long, the suspicion whereof, Carleton thinks, keeps him away from Holland, for as yet he appears not in those parts.

We know nothing more of Brewer till the following June, when we hear of him in a letter from John Robinson to John Carver, in connection with the negotiations going on by way of preparation for the voyage to the West. He appears to have remained with Robinson and the rest of the Leyden Church after the sailing of the Mayflower for New England. It is stated that soon after John Robinson's death—if we may so far anticipate our story—Brewer sold his property in Leyden and returned to England, where he came under the ban of the authorities for his separatist principles, and was cast into prison. All that we know of him afterwards we learn from the state papers and the journals of parliament. In 1626 James Martin gave information respecting Thomas Brewer and other Puritans and Brownists in Kent, in the course of which he tells the Government 'that Thomas Brewer, coming not long since from Amsterdam, where he became a perfect Brownist, and being a man of good estate, is a general patron of the Kentish Brownists, who by his means daily and dangerously increase; the said Brewer hath provided a most pestilent book beyond the seas. One Turner, of Sutton Valence in Kent, seems to be a chaplain of his, and preaches in houses, barns, and woods. He hath many followers, and is maintained principally by the said Thomas Brewer.'[1]

The result was that this former colleague of ͵Elder Brewster in Leyden, this zealous member of the brother-

[1] *State Papers, Domestic.* Charles I. Vol. xxxv., 110: Sept. 17, 1626.

hood to which the Pilgrim Fathers once belonged, became a prisoner for conscience' sake for the next fourteen years of his life. He came forth from durance only when the Long Parliament had begun its memorable work, and Laud and Strafford had reached the end of their lease of power. In the Journal of the House of Commons, under date November 28, 1640, there is this entry: 'The humble petition of Thomas Brewer, gentleman, close prisoner in the King's Bench, was read and referred to the Committee for Dr. Leighton's petition; and he to have the same favour and privilege in all points as Dr. Leighton has.' The Journal of the House of Lords of the same day (iv. 100) gives further particulars: 'The Earl of Dover reported to the House, "that the Lords' Committee appointed by this Honourable House have considered of the petition of Thomas Brewer, gentleman, who hath been imprisoned in the King's Bench and other prisons fourteen years, whereof five years close prisoner, and do desire that he might be released," whereupon it was ordered: "That the said Thomas Brewer shall forthwith be discharged of his imprisonment, giving his own word for his forthcoming and to abide their Lordships' order."' To show what a changed world had come about, the same day the Lords discharged Thomas Brewer, 'It was ordered by the Lords Spiritual and Temporal in the High Court of Parliament assembled: "That the Earl of Strafford should put in his answer unto this Court to the impeachment made against him by the House of Commons by Tuesday next come seven-night, viz., December 8, 1640, and sooner if he can."'

After this digression, which throws light on a matter which must have much exercised the minds of the Pilgrim Fathers in their Leyden days, we return to the consultations of the Church as to their own movements. The thought which was gradually taking shape in their minds was that of founding a Puritan Colony, where they might

WHERE LIES THE LAND?

enjoy liberty of worship and at the same time remain Englishmen. The idea of founding a colony in the interests of religious freedom was not altogether new. It is curious to note a document among the State papers bearing date as far back as 1572, and endorsed by Lord Burleigh as 'sent from Thomas Cecil to me, written by Mr. Carleton,' which, after several military suggestions for the safety of the kingdom, proposes, as a peaceable way of settling the Puritan question, 'to suffer the precise sort to inhabit Ireland.' This contemporary document, which throws interesting light upon the strength of the Puritan movement at the time Separatism took its rise, runs as follows: 'This realm hath a great people daily increasing which are professors of the Gospel towards sincerity, and as they hate all heresy and popery, so they cannot be persuaded to bear liking of the Queen's proceedings in religion by reason that our Church here is not reformed. This people consist of all degrees, from the nobility to the lowest, and so hot is the desire of God's truth in them that they will not frame themselves to favour any of the laws or ordinances set forth by the Queen in God's matters but such as are void of all offence and reformed according to sincerity. This people, as they do not like the course of our Church, so they do and will practise assemblies of brethren in all parts of this realm and have their own churches in companies, contrary to the proceedings which will and may offend Her Majesty, and yet not be punished for the same because they are the Queen's own bowels, her dearest subjects, servants of God, and such as do tread the straight path of the Lord's salvation. So that either the Church of England must be framed to their appetite, or else they must be suffered without blame to proceed as they begin.'

There are three courses open, the writer says, whereby 'to satisfy those griefs and relieve this people': (1) to allow as many of them as choose to depart the realm; or, (2) to let them remain to congregate in companies together and have their own churches; or, (3) 'to bestow upon them a portion of the country of Ireland to inherit, and there, as concerning religion, to live according to the reformation of the best churches.' The first and second modes of dealing with this question are not to be thought of, for the first would weaken the realm, and as for the second, since our country is best governed by one king or queen, so both civil and ecclesiastical affairs ought to be directed by one course of law. But the third course he holds to be feasible. 'English gentlemen of religion and value may be found to take this enterprise in hand, and in this way deliver this realm of all the precise ministers and greatest part of the people that follow them, to the number of three thousand men, enter Ireland, inhabit the same, and there live under the Queen's subjection according to the faith of good subjects and laws of this realm, the Church's constitution only excepted.' The part of Ireland he would select for the experiment is the north, 'because the country of Ulster is the Irish piece of most danger to this State by reason it borders upon the Scot, the same is the soil in which I would have this people planted.'[1]

This ingenious idea of getting rid of Puritans by shipping them off in a body to Ireland seems not to have caught hold of the imagination either of the Queen or the Lord Treasurer. Half a century later it was too late in the world's history to found a new settlement in any part of Europe. The Leyden Church must therefore go farther afield, and carry out such a migration as that of the Greeks to Massilia, or the Syrians to Carthage. Years before it took practical shape John Robinson, as the pastor of the Church, seems to have thought of some such migration, and

[1] *State Papers, Domestic.* Addenda. Elizabeth. Vol. xxi., 121: 1572. Discourse on the present state of the realm of England.

to have spoken of it to his Dutch neighbours. In the archives of the Presbyterian Church at Amsterdam there is a document, signed by Antonius Walæus and Festus Hommius, theological professors at Leyden, stating that they had often heard Robinson say that, finding so many difficulties where they were, he had resolved his removal with a good part of his congregation to the West Indies, where he did not doubt to effectuate his design of founding a free religious settlement. Bradford, in his History, bears this out when he says that when they began to consult as to the place to which they should go if they did migrate, 'some (and none of the meanest) had thoughts and were earnest for Guiana, or some of those fertile places in those hot climates.' Those in favour of Guiana having heard that Sir Walter Raleigh had in 1595 described it as the true Eldorado, and having evidently met with Robert Harcourt's relation of his voyage thither, published in 1614, alleged that the country was rich, fruitful, and blessed with perpetual spring ; that vigorous nature brought forth all things in abundance and plenty without any great labour or art of man. It might be so, said others of the brethren, shaking their heads doubtfully, but tropical lands have dangerous diseases, and the dreadful Spaniard would be too near a neighbour. Half a century had scarcely gone by since the wholesale massacre of the Huguenots in Florida by the French, and the Spaniards might turn upon them in the same relentless fashion, and they would have but little strength to resist so potent an enemy.

The project of proceeding to the West Indies being thus disposed of, Virginia was next thought of as a place of settlement. As early as 1606 some London merchants had received from King James a patent constituting them the Virginia Company. It consisted of two branches, commonly spoken of as the London and Plymouth Companies. The former having its headquarters in London, and known as the Virginia Company, had jurisdiction from 34° to 38° north latitude; the latter, the Northern Company, having its seat of management in Plymouth, had jurisdiction from 45° down to 41°, the intervening territory between 38° and 41° to go to whichever of the two companies should first plant a self-supporting colony. The Southern or Virginia Company was to be governed by a council resident in the colony, which was, however, to be under the control of a superior council established in England and nominated by the king. On this superior council, consisting of twenty-five persons, was Sir Ferdinando Gorges, a name for many years prominent in American history, and also Sir Edwin Sandys, a Scrooby friend of William Brewster, and in later days the ruling spirit of the Virginia Company.

The first emigrants, one hundred and forty-three in number, sailed from the Downs on New Year's Day, 1607, but did not fix upon a spot for settlement till the following May. They were not, however, of the sort likely to prove successful colonists abroad, for most of them had been idle, thriftless failures at home. For the first two years of its history the settlement proved a sore discouragement, and in the plays of the day Virginia came to be described as the Transatlantic Alsatia, the last refuge of the destitute and dishonest. Two years later a change was made for the better, and 1609 has been described as the date of the real beginning of English colonisation. A new charter of incorporation was granted, doing away with the system of dual government, defining more accurately the extent of the plantation, and remodelling the constitution of the colony, so as to vest all legislative power in the council, and giving to the company full sovereignty over all British subjects settling in Virginia; and that year five hundred new emigrants were sent out in a fleet of nine vessels. Unfortunately, these new-comers were no great improvement on the older settlers. Captain John Smith described them as 'unruly gallants packed thither by their friends to escape ill destinies;' and we hear of them in after years as spending their time in playing bowls in the streets of Jamestown while their houses were crumbling to pieces before their eyes. Governor succeeded to governor with varying fortunes and results until the year 1617, when Captain Argall was sent out, an able, resolute, but unscrupulous man, whose care for the colony has been described as no better than the charity of the cannibal who feeds up his prisoner before making a meal of him.

During Argall's administration the brethren in Leyden first began to think of negotiating with the Virginia Company, and therefore before the more enlightened and public-spirited policy inaugurated by the appointment of Sir Edwin Sandys to the treasurership of the company. It was reasonably objected by some of the brethren that if they simply put themselves as ordinary settlers under the Virginia Company, they might as well, so far as religious freedom was concerned, go back to England and take their chance of hardship and imprisonment there. Under a charter granted by King James conformity to the Church of England was insisted on as a matter of course, but even good churchmen might well wince under a regulation which required that, even upon working days, every man and woman duly twice a day, upon the first tolling of the bell, should repair unto the church to hear divine service, upon pain of losing his or her day's allowance for the first omission, for the second to be whipped, and for the third to be condemned to the galleys for six months. On Sundays the penalty of neglect was still more severe: 'Every man or woman shall repair in the morning to divine service and sermons, and in the afternoon to divine service and catechisms upon pain for the first fault to lose their provision and allowance for the whole week following; for the second, to lose the said allowance, and also to be whipped;

and for the third, *to suffer death.*' The clergy of the church were hedged round with double sanctity. Any colonist who should 'unworthily demean himself unto any preacher or minister of God's Word,' or fail 'to hold them in all reverent regard or dutiful entreaty' should be openly whipped three times, and after each whipping should publicly acknowledge his crime. All new-comers were to report themselves on their arrival to the clergyman, to be instructed and catechised. Any one refusing was to be brought before the governor, who should cause the offender for the first time of refusal to be whipped; for the second time, to be whipped twice, and to acknowledge his fault upon the Sabbath day before the congregation; and for the third time, to be whipped every day until he made the same acknowledgment, asked forgiveness, and repaired unto the minister to be further instructed. Rather than repair to a colony where church arrangements were carried out with something like martial law, the brethren in Leyden might as well go back to England and take their chance of Newgate, the Gatehouse, or the Fleet.

But was not some other arrangement possible?

They resolved to try and arrange such terms with the Company as would allow them to live as a distinct body by themselves, and enjoy religious freedom under the general government of Virginia; and they hoped that through the good offices of friends in England they might sue His Majesty that he would be pleased to grant them this freedom they desired. They were encouraged to hope that they might succeed in this 'by some great persons of good rank and quality that were made their friends.' With these expectations, two of the brethren, Robert Cushman and John Carver, were sent over into England to negotiate with the Virginia Company. It was a favourable time for their purpose. For of late things had not been going very well with the colony, and the company, anxious for emigrants of their stamp and quality, were not unwilling to come to terms, were even ready to grant them a patent with as ample privileges as it was in their power to give, and to render them all the assistance they could. Some of the leading members of the council went so far as to say that they had no doubt of obtaining their suit with the king for liberty in religion, and to have it confirmed under the king's broad seal in accordance with their desire.

To facilitate this arrangement the brethren in Leyden made a formal statement of their religious opinions and practices, which might be submitted to the king and council. This they did in a series of 'seven articles which the church at Leyden sent to the council of England, to be considered of in respect of their judgments occasioned about their going to Virginia.' This document, which is of considerable interest historically, has been preserved among the Colonial State Papers, and is endorsed as sent unto the Council of England by the Brownists of Leyden.[1] The Seven Articles are as follows :—

1. To the confession of faith published in the name of the Church of England, and to every article thereof, we do with the Reformed Churches where we live, and also elsewhere, assent wholly.

2. As we do acknowledge the doctrine of faith there taught, so do we the fruits and effects of the same doctrine to the begetting of saving faith in thousands in the land (conformists and reformists, as they are called), with whom also, as with our brethren, we do desire to keep spiritual communion in peace, and will practise on our parts all lawful things.

3. The King's Majesty we acknowledge for supreme governor in his dominion in all causes and over all persons, and that none may decline or appeal from his authority or

[1] *Colonial Papers.* America and the West Indies, 1574-1660. Vol. i., 43.

judgment in any cause whatsoever, but that in all things obedience is due unto him, either active, if the thing commanded be not against God's Word, or passive, if it be, except pardon can be obtained.

4. We judge it lawful for his Majesty to appoint bishops, civil overseers, or officers in authority under him, in the several provinces, dioceses, congregations or parishes, to oversee the churches and govern them civilly according to the laws of the land, unto whom they are in all things to give account, and by them to be ordered according to godliness.

5. The authority of the present bishops in the land we do acknowledge, so far forth as the same is indeed derived from his Majesty unto them and as they proceed in his name, whom we will also therein honour in all things and him in them.

6. We believe that no synod, class, convocation, or assembly of ecclesiastical officers has any power or authority at all, but as the same is by the magistrate given unto them.

7. Lastly, we desire to give unto all superiors due honour, to preserve the unity of the Spirit with all that fear God, to have peace with all men what in us lieth, and wherein we are to be instructed by any.

These Articles were signed by John Robinson as the pastor, and William Brewster as elder. They contain large concessions, but there are also careful qualifications. They accept the Articles of the Church of England, but in the sense in which they are accepted by the Reformed Churches of the Continent; they acknowledge obedience to the king's authority, but only 'if the thing commanded be not against God's Word'; as for the rest, it has been well said that we must look on these Seven Articles not so much as an exposition of faith, but as rather conditions of agreement. They were well received on the part of the council.

On the 12th of November, 1617, Sir Edwin Sandys writes to Robinson and Brewster, saying that they had given that good degree of satisfaction which had carried the council on with a resolution to set forward their desire in the best sort. Cushman and Carver having gone back to Leyden and given a report to the Church of their interview with the council, the Church acknowledged the courtesy with which their agents had been treated, and drew up a formal statement of their wishes in writing, which was subscribed, as the council requested, by the hands of the greatest part of the congregation. This statement was sent on to London by the hand of John Carver and one other gentleman of their company, and with it a letter dated December 15, 1617, and signed by Robinson and Brewster as before, setting forth certain reasons and inducements for the granting of their requests. These 'instances of inducement' were of a tender and pathetic sort, and are as follows :—

(1) We verily believe and trust the Lord is with us, unto whom and whose service we have given ourselves in many trials ; and that He will graciously prosper our endeavours according to the simplicity of our hearts therein. (2) We are well weaned from the delicate milk of our mother country, and enured to difficulties of a strange and hard land, which yet in a great part we have by patience overcome. (3) The people are for the body of them industrious and frugal, we think we may safely say, as any company of people in the world. (4) We are knit together as a body in a most strict and sacred bond and covenant of the Lord, of the violation whereof we make great conscience, and by virtue whereof we do hold ourselves straitly tied to all care of each other's good, and of the whole by every one, and so mutually. (5) Lastly, it is not with us as with other men whom small things can discourage, or small discontentments cause to wish themselves at home again.' They add that they are not likely to wish

to return ; most of them are too old for that, and, indeed, if they did, it would be to be worse off than before. They are grateful for the godly disposition and loving towards their despised persons of many in the council, they will not be further troublesome, but take their leaves committing the council to the guidance and direction of Almighty God.

It would appear that some members of the council of the Virginia Company desired further information. Three points especially were specified by Sir John Wolstenholme, one of the council, to whom they made reply, under date Leyden, January 27, 1617 [O.S.], enclosing two notes—a longer and a shorter, for him to show to the council—the one or the other as he thought best. In the shorter note they state that, as to the officers of the Church—pastors, elders, and deacons, and the sacraments, they do wholly and in all points agree with the French Reformed Churches, according to their public confession of faith. They further state that they are willing to take the Oath of Supremacy if it be required of them, and convenient satisfaction be not given by their taking the Oath of Allegiance. The longer note simply points out some trivial differences existing between them and the Reformed Churches, such as that they at Leyden prayed with uncovered heads, the French covered ; they required their elders to teach as well as to govern, the French did not ; their officers were chosen for life, those in the Reformed Churches for a term of years ; they administered discipline and excommunication before the whole Church, the French privately and in their consistories.

This letter and the enclosures were carried to Sir John Wolstenholme by Sabin Staresmore, a member of the Leyden Church, who stood by while they were opened and read. Sir John asked further about the ministers, as to who made them? Staresmore replied that the power of making was in the Church, to be ordained by the imposition of hands, by the fittest persons they had, adding that that power must either be in the Church or in the Pope, and that the Pope was Antichrist. But, said Sir John, if the Pope holds what is true, as for example the doctrine of the Trinity, we do well to assent also; but he would not argue the point. He said he would not show the letters, lest they should spoil all. He expected they would have been of the archbishop's mind as to the calling of ministers, but it seemed they were not. Their messenger further says that Sir John wished him to be at the Virginia Court the following Wednesday, after which he hoped to be able to report more definitely and certainly.

It is curious to note that during the months in which these negotiations were going forward for permission to set up Congregationalism in one part of the territory of the Virginia Company, Presbyterianism had actually been established in another—in the Bermudas or Summer Islands—the shareholders of the one company being for the most part shareholders also of the other. Under date May 19, 1617, Lewis Hughes writes to Sir Nathaniel Rich, describing the arrangements made for religious worship. He says: 'The ceremonies are in no request, nor the Book of Common Prayer, I use it not at all. I have by the help of God begun a Church government by ministers and elders. I made bold to choose four elders for the town publicly by lifting up of hands and calling upon God, when the governor was out of the town, in the main. At his return it pleased God to move his heart to like well and to allow of that we had done, and doth give to the elders all the grace and countenance that he can.' He hopes God 'will give His blessing to this poor and weak beginning to His own glory,' and he trusts 'that the service of God in these islands may be so established now as that hereafter there be no such bitter contention about it as in England.'[1]

[1] *MSS. of the Duke of Manchester*, No. 209.

A copy of the Directory of Worship for use in the Summer Islands was also sent over by him, and is preserved at Kimbolton Castle.[1] He also wrote under date December 15, 1618, to Sir Nathaniel Rich, giving his reasons for not using the Book of Common Prayer, and his opinion of the elders who had been chosen to serve the Church.[2] In trying to obtain permission for similar freedom of worship in Virginia the Congregationalists of Leyden secured the powerful influence of Sir Edwin Sandys, who prevailed upon Sir Robert Naunton to speak to the king privately, urging him to grant them this liberty of conscience under his gracious protection in America. While averse to Nonconformity in England, James seems not to have been equally averse to it as far away as Virginia. When Naunton said that these people would endeavour the advancement of his Majesty's dominions and the enlargement of the Gospel by all due means, he replied that this was a good and honest motion, and asked what source of profit they looked for in the part they intended? Naunton replied, 'From fishing.' 'So God have my soul,' said the king, ''tis an honest trade ; 'twas the apostles' own calling.' Thinking over the matter again, and fearing lest he had committed himself too hastily on what was a somewhat thorny ecclesiastical subject, the king afterwards told Naunton that these people had better confer with the Archbishop of Canterbury and the Bishop of London.[3] Winslow, after narrating this interview, adds : 'Whereupon we were advised to persist on his first approbation, and not to entangle ourselves with them.' He seems not to have been aware that the archbishop and other bishops were approached on the subject. Among the Kimbolton MSS. there is a note (No. 368) which was taken by Sir Nathaniel

---

[1] *MSS. of the Duke of Manchester*, No. 234.
[2] Ibid., No. 239.
[3] Winslow's *Hypocrisy Unmasked*, pp. 89, 90.

Rich of a conversation he had with Captain Bargrave about Sir Edwin Sandys. The purport is that Sir Edwin had moved the archbishop (unsuccessfully) to give leave to the Brownists and Separatists to go to Virginia, and designed to make a free popular state there, and himself and his assured friends to be the leaders. Bradford also says (p. 29) that the getting permission for the establishment of a colony in which they might enjoy religious freedom proved a harder piece of work than they took it for; for though many means were used to bring it about, yet it could not be effected; for there were divers of good worth laboured with the king to obtain it (amongst whom was one of his chief secretaries), and some other wrought with the archbishop to give way thereunto; but it proved all in vain. William Euring also, writing in 1619, says: 'Yet even for Virginia thus much,—when some of ours desired to have planted ourselves there with his Majesty's leave . . . the bishops did by all means oppose them and their friends therein.'[1]

It was clear after all these negotiations that no formal grant of liberty of worship could be obtained from either king or bishop; but reading between the lines it was equally clear that if these brethren went to Virginia as they proposed and conducted themselves peaceably, the king would connive at their proceedings and leave them unmolested. The leading men on the Virginia Company found it impossible to obtain for them public authority under the king's seal to set up religious freedom; nevertheless they advised them to go, feeling assured, they said, they would not be troubled. The agents having returned with this answer the Church at Leyden held conference on the matter. Some of the brethren were discouraged at the outlook. They did not like to unsettle themselves and venture their lives and fortunes on what might prove but a

[1] Hanbury's *Memorials*, p. 362.

sandy foundation. They even thought it would have been better to go to Virginia without asking for liberty than to ask and be thus rejected. The leaders, however, took a more hopeful view of the situation. They were of opinion that the king would look through his fingers, though he had reasons of his own for not confirming his goodwill by public act. Even if he granted permission under the Great Seal there might be no great security in that; for if afterwards there should be a purpose to wrong them, though they had a seal as broad as a house floor, it would not serve their turn, for there would be means enough found to recall or reverse it. They were of opinion that there was reasonable probability to go upon, and that for the rest they must trust themselves to God's providence in this matter, as they had done in other things.

They then laid the whole matter before the Lord afresh, arranging for a special day of humiliation, thanksgiving and prayer for the purpose. That day was solemnly observed, seeking Divine direction in the present position of affairs. John Robinson preached on the occasion, his text indicating clearly enough the bent of his mind. The verses he chose were 1 Sam. xxiii. 3, 4: 'And David's men said unto him, Behold, we be afraid here in Judah; how much more then if we come to Keilah against the armies of the Philistines? Then David inquired of the Lord yet again. And the Lord answered him and said, Arise, go down to Keilah; for I will deliver the Philistines into thine hand.'

The sermon ended, and many of the brethren, having, one after another, wrestled with God in prayer, pleading as men do plead in great crises and hours of fate, they fell to needful arrangement of business. It was decided first, that only part of the Church should go, the rest remaining at Leyden; that the youngest and strongest should lead the way, but that only those should go who should freely offer themselves for the purpose. If a majority of the Church should elect to depart, the pastor should go with them, but if only a minority, then their tried and trusted friend Elder Brewster should be the Great Heart of their pilgrimage. It was further agreed that if the enterprise turned out a failure, those remaining behind should welcome back the returning voyagers to heart and home ; but if it were successful, those going forth should afterwards endeavour to help over such as were poor and ancient and willing to go. These were the decisions arrived at. Night had already closed in upon that short February day ere those prayers and conferences had reached their end. The stars were shining serenely over Leyden city as the brethren left their place of meeting in the Klok-steeg. A new world was opening before them ; new hopes and new fears were stirring within them. 'And He brought him forth abroad, and said, Look now toward heaven, and tell the stars, if thou be able to number them : and He said unto him, So shall thy seed be. And he believed in the Lord ; and He counted it to him for righteousness.'

VII.

THE SAILING OF THE MAYFLOWER.

THE decision of the Leyden brethren to seek a home in the Far West was arrived at in the face of a series of discouragements. To begin with, at the very time they were debating the matter tidings reached them of the disastrous ending of a project similar to their own. In 1618 Francis Blackwell, an elder of the Amsterdam Church, had, with a party under his leadership, set sail for Virginia. Their means being limited their arrangements were defective. A hundred and eighty were stowed away in a vessel far too small for their number. Even before they left Gravesend the streets rang with complaints at the miserable arrangements made for them. Ill-starred from the first, nothing but disaster attended the expedition. Northwest winds drove them out of their course to the south; their fresh water failed; crowded unhealthily together, disease broke out among them, carrying off the captain and six of the crew; having no one left capable of managing the vessel, they drifted aimlessly to and fro, so that it was March, 1619, before they reached Virginia; when they did arrive Blackwell was dead as well as the captain, and altogether, out of one hundred and eighty who set out, one hundred and thirty perished by the way. Tidings of all this reached Leyden in the early summer, and were not inspiriting to intending emigrants.

Then, too, at the same time a serious crisis had arisen within the Virginia Company itself, which was divided into two hostile factions. The leaders on the one side, who supported Sir Thomas Smith, who had been treasurer of the company for the last twelve years, were the Earl of Warwick, Sir Nathaniel Rich, and Alderman Johnson; on the other side were the Earl of Southampton, Lord Cavendish, and Sir Edward Sackville, who succeeded in making Sir Edwin Sandys treasurer, and displacing Sir Thomas Smith.[1] While this intestine war was raging in the board, nothing, of course, was done to further the Leyden expedition to the West. Meantime, while matters were thus at a standstill in one direction, negotiations were commenced in another. The Dutch traders to Manhattan proposed to Robinson to transport the entire congregation to this trading-post, afterwards known as New York, providing cattle and furnishing protection as long as needed, and leaving the colony to self-government in all its internal affairs. On February 12, 1620, application was made to the Stadtholder, stating the conditions on which 'this English preacher at Leyden' and his people would consent to colonise that country. Their main stipulation was that they should be assured of the protection of the United Provinces; the Amsterdam merchants therefore prayed that such protection should be granted, and that two ships-of-war should be sent out to secure provisionally the lands to the Dutch Government. The matter thus referred to the States-General, after repeated deliberations, was rejected on April 11.[2] But we gather from a letter from Robinson to Carver (June 14, 1620), that, on the persuasion of one Thomas Weston, he and his associates had broken off negotiations with the merchants even before the rejection of their overtures by the States-General. Who Weston

[1] *The Colonial Papers* (ii., 20, 22, &c.) represent in the main the case of Sir E. Sandys; the MSS. in the Duke of Manchester's Collection at Kimbolton Castle represent, but far more in detail, the case of Sir Thomas Smith.
[2] Brodhead's *History of New York*, pp. 123-126.

was we are not told, but it is probable he had sympathy with the Pilgrims in their religious opinions, for Bradford says he 'was well acquainted with some of them, and had been a furtherer of them in their former proceedings.' He came over to Leyden and offered to find the necessary funds, along with their own means, if the Manhattan idea were dismissed. With this view he associated with himself some seventy English merchants and others, who, as a mercantile speculation, were prepared to take stock in this emigration scheme at £10 a share, on the understanding that at the end of seven years there should be a division between the shareholders and the inhabitants of all the colony's possessions and earnings. On this understanding articles were signed by both parties, and Carver and Cushman were at once sent over into England to receive the money subscribed by the Merchant Adventurers, as Weston's associates came to be called, and to make provision of shipping and all necessaries for the voyage. On their part also the brethren in Leyden who had arranged to emigrate prepared themselves with all speed, selling their goods and estates, putting their money into a common stock, and so making ready to depart when the word was given.

In 1620 the Plymouth Company, which, according to the original charter, had jurisdiction from 45° down to 41°, was revived. In its original form an ally of the Virginia Company, it now came to be a rival. The Merchant Adventurers, associated with the Pilgrims, thinking that New England with its fisheries might be a better field for their enterprise than Virginia, resolved to abandon the patent already obtained, and to get fresh powers from the Plymouth Company. Therefore, on February 12, 1620, the Wincob patent was superseded by one granted to John Pierce, one of the Adventurers, which conferred powers of self-government, and the right to a tract of land to be selected near the mouth of the Hudson by the planters themselves.

In addition to the emigrants from Leyden the expedition was to be joined by a contingent from England, and one of their number, Christopher Martin, an Essex man, was joined with Carver and Cushman in carrying out the arrangements as their representative. It was against Robinson's advice that Cushman was set over this matter, for, in his opinion, though a good man and of some ability, he was unfit to deal for other men by reason of his singularity, and as a man more facile in talk than fruitful in service. Events proved Robinson to be right in his judgment, for Cushman, on his own responsibility and without consulting with the rest, consented to a fundamental alteration in the terms agreed upon, for the purpose of meeting the views of the Merchant Adventurers. The original agreement was for a seven years' partnership, during which the labour of all the colonists was to be for the common benefit, except that each colonist might reserve two days in the week for his own purposes. By his subsequent private agreement with the Adventurers Cushman surrendered this reservation, so that the whole of the labour of the colonists was to go to the common fund, and he further consented that at the end of seven years everything, houses, lands and goods, should be equally divided between the settlers and the Adventurers. When these terms were made known at Leyden the brethren complained that Cushman had made conditions more fit for thieves and bond-slaves than honest men. On the other hand, he defended himself against their 'many quirimonies and complaints' by reminding them that it was one thing to settle matters among themselves at Leyden, and quite another to make terms with the other side in London. They had reckoned without their host. As to one of the clauses he had consented to alter, Sir George Farrer and his brother had withdrawn £500 from the scheme at the first sight of it, and if it had been insisted upon, the rest of the Adventurers, except Mr. Weston, would have withdrawn also; then where would they have been? As to the effect they stated the other clause would have in preventing the building of good houses, there would be, he thought, no great harm in that. His opinion was that for the present, and till the colony was further advanced, they had better only build such kind of houses as, if need be, they might with little grief set afire and run away by the light; that it would be better their riches should be not in pomp but in strength, for that a commonwealth is readier to ebb than to flow when once fine houses and gay clothes came up. If they had come to look upon him as the Jonas of the undertaking, he was quite willing to be cast off and left behind with nothing but the clothes upon his back. All that he asked for was that they might have quietness and no more of these clamours. Thus there was nothing for it but to yield the point and accept the terms, hard as they felt them to be.

When all was ready for the start a pilot came over to conduct the emigrants to England, bringing also a letter from Cushman, announcing that the Mayflower, a vessel of one hundred and eighty tons, Thomas Jones master, would start from London to Southampton in a week or two, bringing their English comrades to meet them in that port. Further, a sixty-ton pinnace, the Speedwell, had been bought for the Adventurers, and fitted out in Holland, which was to take the Leyden people to Southampton, and afterwards accompany the Mayflower across the Atlantic, remaining with the colony for a year.

Thus, after much travail and many debates—recounted by Bradford, as he says, 'that their children may see with what difficulties their fathers wrestled in going through these things in their first beginnings, and how God brought them along notwithstanding all their weaknesses and infirmities'—they were ready to set forth on their fateful voyage. Sore was the trial of parting between brethren who for so long had lived and laboured, sorrowed and rejoiced together. First, they joined in a day of solemn humiliation, when their pastor, John Robinson, preached the last sermon the departing Pilgrims were ever to hear from his lips. His text was the passage from the Book of Ezra (viii. 21) : 'I proclaimed a fast there at the river Ahava, that we might afflict ourselves before our God, to seek of Him a right way for us and for our little ones, and for all our substance ;' upon which, says Bradford, 'he spent a good part of the day very profitably and suitable to the present occasion.' How suitable, Edward Winslow, writing twenty-six years later, gives us the opportunity of judging for ourselves. 'At their departure from him to begin the great work of plantation in New England,' says Winslow, 'amongst other wholesome instructions and exhortations, he used these expressions, or to the same purpose :—

'We are now ere long to part asunder, and the Lord knoweth whether ever he should live to see our faces again ; but whether the Lord had appointed it or not, he charged us before God and His blessed angels to follow him no further than he followed Christ. And if God should reveal anything to us by any other instrument of His, to be as ready to receive it as ever we were to receive any truth by his ministry. For he was very confident the Lord had more truth and light yet to break forth out of His holy Word. He took occasion also miserably to bewail the state and condition of the Reformed Churches, who were come to a period in religion and would go no further than the instruments of their Reformation. As for example the Lutherans, they could not be drawn to go beyond what Luther saw ; for whatever part of God's will He had further imparted and revealed to Calvin, they will rather die than embrace it. And so also, saith he, you see the Calvinists, they stick where he left them, a misery much to be lamented. For though they were precious shining lights in their times, yet God hath not revealed His whole will to them; and were they now living, saith he, they would be as ready and willing to embrace further light as that they had received. Here also he put us in mind of our Church covenant (at least that part of it) whereby we promise and covenant with God and one with another to receive whatsoever light or truth shall be made known to us from His written Word. But withal exhorted us to take heed what we received for truth, and well to examine and compare and weigh it with other scriptures of truth, before we received it; for, saith he, it is not possible the Christian world should come so lately out of such thick anti-Christian darkness, and that full perfection of knowledge should break forth at once.

'Another thing he commended to us was, that we should use all means to avoid and shake off the name of "Brownist," being a mere nickname and brand to make religion odious and the professors of it to the Christian world. And to that end, said he, I should be glad if some godly ministers would go over with you, or come to you before my coming; for, said he, there will be no difference between the unconformable ministers and you when they come to the practice of the ordinances out of the kingdom. And so advised us by all means to endeavour to close with the godly party of the kingdom of England, and rather to study union than division, viz. how near we might possibly without sin close with them, than in the least measure to affect division or separation from them. And be not loath to take another pastor or teacher, saith he, for the flock that hath two shepherds is not endangered, but secured by it. Many other things there were of great and weighty consequence which he commended to us; but these things

I thought good to relate, at the request of some well-willers to the peace and good agreement of the godly (so distracted at present about the settling of church-government in the kingdom of England), that so both sides may truly see what this poor despised Church of Christ now at New Plymouth in New England, but formerly at Leyden in Holland, was and is; how far they were and still are from separation from the Churches of Christ, especially those that are Reformed.' [1]

Bradford tells us that the rest of the time 'was spent in pouring out prayers to the Lord with great fervency mixed with abundance of tears.' Looking back also upon Winslow's narrative, [2] it would seem that a second day was spent in farewells before leaving the city.

He says: 'When the ship was ready to carry us away, the brethren that stayed having again solemnly sought the Lord with us and for us, and we further engaging ourselves mutually as before, they, I say, that stayed at Leyden feasted us that were to go, at our pastor's house, being large, where we refreshed ourselves after our tears with singing of psalms, making joyful melody in our hearts as well as with the voice, there being many of the congregation very expert in music; and, indeed, it was the sweetest melody that ever mine ears heard.'

As the canal journey to Delfshaven would take from six to eight hours, the Pilgrims must have started early on that morning after the evening when, like showers and sunshine, these sorrowful tears and joyful melodies mingled together. The barges needed for the journey were most likely moored near the Nuns' Bridge which spans the Rapenburg immediately opposite the Klok-steeg, where Robinson's house was. This being their usual meeting-place would naturally be the place of rendezvous on the morning of departure.

[1] *A Brief Narration.* By Edward Winslow, 1646, pp. 98, 99.
[2] Pages 90, 91.

From thence it was but a stone's throw to the boats, and quickly after starting they would enter the Vliet, as the section of the canal between Leyden and Delft is named, and which for a little distance runs within the city bounds, its quays forming the streets. In those days the point where the canal leaves the city was guarded by a water-gate, which has long since been removed, as have also the town walls, the only remaining portions of which are the Morsch-gate and the Zyl-gate. So gliding along the quiet waters of the Vliet past the water-gate and looking up at the frowning turrets of the Cow-gate, 'they left that goodly and pleasant city which had been their resting-place near twelve years; but they knew that they were Pilgrims, and looked not much on those things, but lift up their eyes to the heavens, their dearest country, and quieted their spirits.'

It was a July day, and therefore summer was putting forth her quiet beauty as, accompanied by most of those who were to remain at Leyden, they sailed through the midst of the Dutch pastures and by the country-seats and gardens which line both sides of the canal from Leyden to Delft. Nine miles from Leyden a branch canal connects the Vliet with the Hague, and immediately beyond their junction a sharp turn is made to the left as the canal passes beneath the Hoorn-bridge; from this point, for the remaining five miles, the high road from the Hague to Delft, lined with noble trees, runs side by side with the canal. In our time the canal-boats make a circuit of the town to the right, but in those days the traffic went by canal through the heart of the city. The street formed by the banks on either side, and which is the fashionable quarter of residence, is called the Oud-Delft, and half-way through the city the travellers would pass the Old Kirk, with its lancet windows and tall, slender, leaning tower, and directly opposite to this would note with even painful interest the plain two-storied edifice with its red-tiled roof, which was formerly the mansion of William the Silent, and where, on another July morning, six-and-thirty years before, to the grief of all true men, he was assassinated by Balthazar Gérard. Passing out of the gates of Delft and leaving the town behind, they had still a good ten miles of canal journey before them ere they reached their vessel and came to the final parting. For, as Mr. Van Pelt has clearly shown, it is a mistake to confound Delft with Delfshaven as the point of embarkation in the Speedwell.[1] Below Delft the canal, which from Leyden thither is the Vliet, then becomes the Schie, and at the village of Overschie the travellers entered the Delfshaven Canal, which between perfectly straight dykes flows at a considerable height above the surrounding pastures. Then finally passing through one set of sluice gates after another the Pilgrims were lifted from the canal into a broad receptacle for vessels, then into the outer haven, and so to the side of the Speedwell as she lay at the quay waiting their arrival.

At Delfshaven the party was joined by other friends from Leyden who had come by road, and also by some from Amsterdam who wished to share in the leave-taking, and there, says Winslow, they feasted us again. That last night on shore was spent with little sleep by most, but with friendly entertainment and Christian discourse and other real expressions of true Christian love. There is some uncertainty as to the scene of the final farewell, Bradford making it to take place on the deck of the vessel, and Winslow on shore—'we only,' he says, that is the departing emigrants, 'going aboard.' They each wrote after an interval of more than a quarter of a century, when recollection on some points was growing hazy. Winslow touchingly tells us that 'after prayer performed by our

[1] *The Start from Delfshaven.* By the Rev. Daniel Van Pelt. *N. E. Mag.*, Nov. 1891.

pastor, when a flood of tears was poured out, they accompanied us to the ship, but were not able to speak one to another for the abundance of sorrow to part.' We may well let Bradford also describe the scene for us in his own pathetic old-world way. He says: 'The next day the wind being fair they went aboard, and their friends with them, when truly doleful was the sight of that sad and mournful parting: to see what sighs and sobs and prayers did sound amongst them, what tears did gush from every eye, and pithy speeches pierced each heart; that sundry of the Dutch strangers that stood on the quay as spectators could not refrain from tears. Yet comfortable and sweet it was to see such lively and true expressions of dear and unfeigned love. But the tide (which stays for no man) calling them away that were thus loath to depart, their reverend pastor falling down on his knees (and they all with him), with watery cheeks commended them, with most fervent prayers, to the Lord and His blessing. And then with mutual embraces and many tears they took their leaves one of another; which proved to be the last leave to many of them.' Winslow gives the final touch to this historic scene. As the Speedwell left the quay-side those on board fired a parting volley with their muskets, which was followed by the booming sound of shots from three of the ship's cannons, 'and so lifting up our hands to each other and our hearts for each other to the Lord our God, we departed, and found His presence with us, in the midst of our manifest straits He carried us through.' The memory of that time, he adds, the Dutch at Delfshaven preserve to this day.

It was about July 22 that, with a fair wind, they hoisted sail and had a prosperous run to Southampton. The Mayflower had already preceded them from London, carrying the English portion of the emigrants, and was riding at anchor, if we may trust local tradition, off the north end of the West Quay. Those who joined them at Southampton were partly labourers employed by the merchants, and partly godly Englishmen who sympathised with their religious opinions. Here also they found Mr. Weston, who had come to represent the merchants. He was angry at the discussion which arose about the change in the terms of the contract, so much so, that he went off leaving the contract unsigned and the arrangements so incomplete that the emigrants were forced to sell some of their not too-abundant provisions to meet necessary charges. On August 3 they wrote to the Merchant Adventurers explaining their position, and stating the reasons why they could not consent to the alterations made in the 5th and 9th articles of agreement. Still, as they had no wish to act selfishly in the matter, they were willing to agree that, if large profits were not realised within the seven years, the compact should continue for a longer period until further profits were made. They remind the Adventurers that they are in great straits, have had to sell some of their provisions to clear the haven, have scarce any butter, no oil, and not a sole to mend a shoe ; that they have not sufficient swords, muskets, or armour ; yet are they willing to expose themselves to such eminent dangers and trust to God's good providence, rather than that His name and truth should be evil spoken of through them. This document was signed by the leading men of the company.

While the Mayflower still lay at anchor off the West Quay two letters arrived from Leyden from their pastor, John Robinson, bearing date July 27, one of which was addressed to John Carver, the other to the whole company, expressive of his care and affection for them. In the letter to Carver, who was his brother-in-law, he repeats the assurance of his intention to join them on the other side of the Atlantic the first opportunity that presents itself.

The other letter was addressed to the whole company, who were called together to hear it read. It was eminently characteristic of the man. He is with them, he says, in best affection and most earnest longing, though constrained for a while to be bodily absent. Constrained he is, for God knows how willingly he would have borne his part with them in this first brunt, were he not held back for the present by strong necessity. They must think of him as a man divided in himself with great pain, and as having his better part with them.

He charges them first of all to seek heavenly peace with God and their own consciences by separation from sin; for 'sin being taken away by earnest repentance, and the pardon thereof from the Lord sealed up unto a man's conscience by His Spirit, great shall be his security and peace in all dangers; sweet his comfort in all distresses, with happy deliverance from all evil, whether in life or in death.' Then, being at peace with God and their own consciences, he charges them to be at peace with all men as far as in them lieth, and not be too ready to take offence, for, as far as his experience goes, the people most ready to give offence are those who most easily take it, and those who nourish this touchy humour have seldom proved sound and profitable members of the community. He points out that there may be need of watchfulness, because the Englishmen joining them at Southampton are comparative strangers, and their living together, having all things common, may minister continual occasion of offence, and be as fuel to the fire, except they diligently quench it with brotherly forbearance. And if we are to be careful not to take offence at one another, much more must we not take offence at God Himself, which we do so often as we murmur at His providence in our crosses, or bear impatiently such afflictions as He is pleased to visit us with. He would have them also cultivate common care for the common weal, avoiding as a deadly plague all retiredness of mind for mere personal advantage. As men are careful not to have a new house shaken with violence till it be well-settled and the parts firmly knit, so he would have them be careful that the house of God, which *they* are and are to be, be not shaken with unnecessary novelties or other oppositions at the first settling thereof. Finally, as they are become a body politic, setting up civil government, and are not furnished with any persons of special eminency above the rest to be chosen as governors, he trusts they will let their wisdom and godliness appear not only in choosing such persons as do entirely love and will promote the common good, but also in yielding unto them all due honour and obedience when they are chosen, not beholding in them the ordinariness of their persons, but God's ordinance for good, not being like the foolish multitude, who more honour the gay coat than either the virtuous mind of the man or the glorious ordinance of the Lord.

These and such-like things he commends to their care and conscience, joining therewith his daily incessant prayers unto the Lord that He who made the heavens and the earth, the sea and all rivers of waters, and whose providence is over all His works, especially over all His dear children for good, may so guard and guide them in all their ways, inwardly by His Spirit and outwardly by the hand of His power, as that they all may have cause to praise Him all the days of their lives. 'Fare you well in Him in whom you trust and in whom I rest'—so ends his letter, and so sends he them forth, well-willing them 'happy success in their hopeful voyage.'

This apostolic epistle, which 'had good acceptance with all and after-fruit with many,' having been read aloud, they then made final arrangements for the long voyage before them, choosing a governor and assistants for each vessel, and distributing the company as seemed best, ninety to the Mayflower and thirty to the Speedwell. Thus all being ready, on August 5, 1620, the two vessels dropped down Southampton Water, were soon past the cliffs of the Isle of Wight, and on into the English Channel. After this their progress was but slow. The delay at Southampton had lost them a favourable wind, and, what was worse, after beating about for three or four days, Reynolds, the captain of the Speedwell, reported that his vessel had sprung a dangerous leak, and they must put into Dartmouth for repairs. There she was overhauled from stem to stern, after which they put to sea again with good hopes that now all would go well. But these hopes also were doomed to early disappointment. The voyagers had only gone some three hundred miles beyond the Land's End when Reynolds again announced the Speedwell to be unseaworthy. She was still leaking, he said, and could only be kept afloat by the constant use of the pumps. Again there was nothing for it but to put back, and bear this time for Plymouth. Once there, it was finally determined to send the Speedwell back to London to the Adventurers, and with her eighteen of the passengers who had grown faint-hearted, among them being Cushman and his family. The remaining twelve were added to the already overcrowded passengers in the Mayflower. Out of all this came great discouragement and another sad parting, and thus, as Bradford notes by the way, 'like Gideon's army this small number was divided, as if the Lord by this work of His providence thought these few too many for the great work He had to do.'

At what date the returning ships arrived at Plymouth, or how long they stayed, is not known. Naturally, they would be impatient to be gone, for the season was advancing, and they knew they would soon have winter upon them. They seem, however, after landing at the Old Barbican, to have stayed long enough to receive hospitable kindness at the hands of the Plymouth people, of which they made grateful mention in after years. It was on the 6th September they once more turned their prow to the west. The wind was prosperous, and continued so for several days. Till they were half-way over the Atlantic, indeed, everything seemed in their favour. Then their good fortune appeared to have left them. The equinoctial gales came sweeping down upon them with terrific force, shaking the Mayflower from stem to stern, and so twisting one of her main beams out of its place that even the mariners began to be alarmed for her safety. Some of the leading men among the passengers seeing this, and noticing that the captain and crew were in close and anxious consultation, raised the question as to whether it would not be better even yet to try to return. But it was as far to go back as to go forward, and the captain assured them that he knew the ship to be strong and firm under water, and if they could only get the wrenched beam back to its place, all would yet go well. Fortunately it turned out that one of the passengers had brought a powerful screw with him, and by means of this the beam was brought back to its place again, and then supported by a strong post set firm on the lower deck. After setting this right, and caulking the opening seams to keep out the water, they once more committed themselves to the will of God, and resolved to proceed. But their course was still arduous and trying. Storm succeeded storm, with winds so fierce and seas so high that for days together not a sail could be spread, and the vessel went driving before the gale under bare poles. Crowded below for safety, their bedding and their clothing drenched with sea-water, as huge waves chased each other day and night over the vessel, these poor fugitives in search of liberty must have longed earnestly for their desired haven. One of their number, John Howland, venturing above the gratings, was washed overboard in a moment,

and had it not been that he caught hold of the coil of the
topsail-halyards, which, fortunately for him, had been
washed over and was trailing in the sea, he must have
perished. At some risk to the sailors, he was brought up
into the ship again, and so was saved. Thus day after day
fears came chasing each other over their hearts like the
waves over their ship. Still, through God's good mercy,
and in spite of close crowding and all the hardships of the
voyage, only one of the passengers, a servant of Samuel
Fuller, died by the way. Three days after his burial at
sea, on the 9th of November, and nine weeks after leaving
Plymouth Harbour, to the great joy of all, land was sighted.

It was a flat but well-wooded coast that rose to the view
of the brightening faces of the Pilgrims. The captain said
he thought it was the eastern side of the shore of Cape
Cod. He would probably have been more ingenuous had
he said at once that he knew it to be Cape Cod, and that
in fact he had been steering for it. Morton, in his *Memorial*,
plainly says that as the Dutch intended to have a plantation themselves at Manhattan, now known as New York,
they had fraudulently hired the captain of the Mayflower
to keep her away from that part of the coast. He says:
'Of this plot between the Dutch and Mr. Jones I have
had late and certain intelligence.' This, however, was not
suspected at the time, and the ship was headed round as if
to make for the Hudson, but after trying for half a day
they found themselves, as probably the captain intended
they should, among the shoals and currents off the elbow
of the cape. It was necessary therefore to make their way
back as best they could into clear water before night came
on. Then followed serious consultation. The southern
passage was evidently dangerous, the season was late, and
what was even worse, disease had begun to show itself
among the passengers; they therefore came to the conclusion that it would be better to abandon the journey to the

Hudson, and sailing round the crook of the cape put into Cape Cod Harbour, keeping the ship there until, by means of the shallop, they found a suitable place of settlement in the neighbourhood. With a sense of relief they came to this decision, and finding themselves once more safe in harbour, Bradford tells us, they fell upon their knees and blessed the God of heaven, who had brought them over the vast and furious ocean and delivered them from all its perils and miseries.

But now in these altered circumstances another question arose. The Virginia Company had no rights in New England, and therefore their patent could confer none, and there was no other recognised authority there. Under these circumstances it was found there was danger of disorder arising. Some of the company, probably the hired labourers, were putting forth the idea that as there was an end of all authority, every man might go his own way and do as he liked. The leaders saw the peril of this, and resolved to guard against it. If there was no other government over them, either of king or company, they would make a government for themselves. They therefore called the adult males into the cabin of the Mayflower, and there entered into that memorable compact which became the basis of the constitution for the infant colony. The original document is no longer in existence, but the following is a copy with the list of signatures appended:—

'In ye name of God, Amen. We whose names are underwritten, the loyall subjects of our dread soveraigne Lord, King James, by ye grace of God, of Great Britaine, Franc and Ireland King, defender of ye faith, &c., haveing undertaken, for ye glorie of God and advancemente of ye Christian faith, and honour of our King and countrie, a voyage to plant ye first colonie in ye Northerne parts of Virginia, doe by these presents solemnly and mutualy in ye presence of God, and of one another, covenant and combine our selves togeather into a civill body politick, for our better ordering and preservation and furtherance of y⁰ ends aforesaid; and by vertue hearof to enacte, constitute and frame such just and equall lawes, ordinances, acts, constitutions and offices from time to time, as shall be thought most meete and convenient for y⁰ generall good of y⁰ Colonie, unto which we promise all due submission and obedience. In Witnes wherof we have hereunder subscribed our names at Cap-Codd y⁰ 11 of November, in y⁰ year of y⁰ raigne of our soveraigne lord, King James of England, France and Ireland y⁰ eighteenth, and of Scotland y⁰ fiftie-fourth, Ano. Dom. 1620.'

JOHN CARVER.
WILLIAM BRADFORD.
EDWARD WINSLOW.
WILLIAM BREWSTER.
ISAAC ALLERTON.
MYLES STANDISH.
JOHN ALDEN.
SAMUEL FULLER.
CHRISTOPHER MARTIN.
WILLIAM MULLINS.
WILLIAM WHITE.
RICHARD WARREN.
JOHN HOWLAND.
STEPHEN HOPKINS.
EDWARD TILLEY.
JOHN TILLEY.
FRANCIS COOK.
THOMAS ROGERS.
THOMAS TINKER.
JOHN RIGDALE.
EDWARD FULLER.

JOHN TURNER.
FRANCIS EATON.
JAMES CHILTON.
JOHN CRACKSTON.
JOHN BILLINGTON.
MOSES FLETCHER.
JOHN GOODMAN.
DEGORY PRIEST.
THOMAS WILLIAMS.
GILBERT WINSLOW.
EDMUND MARGESON.
PETER BROWN.
RICHARD BRITTERIDGE.
GEORGE SOULE.
RICHARD CLARKE.
RICHARD GARDINER.
JOHN ALLERTON.
THOMAS ENGLISH.
EDWARD DOTEY.
EDWARD LISTER.

Bradford preserved the text of this compact in his

History, without giving the names of the signatories; these were furnished by Morton in his *Memorial*, apparently from some list in Bradford's papers to which he had access. Looking over these names, it may be noted that, in addition to captain and crew, 102 passengers in all left Plymouth, one died by the way, and a child was born, receiving from his birth-place the name of Oceanus Hopkins, so that they were still 102 when they reached their destination—seventy-three males and twenty-nine females. Of these the colony proper consisted of thirty-four adult males, eighteen of whom were accompanied by their wives and fourteen by children under twenty-one years of age, twenty boys and eight girls. Besides these there were nineteen men-servants and three maid-servants, sailors and craftsmen hired for temporary service. Of the thirty-four men who were the nucleus of the colony the great majority were from Leyden, only four of their number being certainly known to have joined them at Southampton. It may also be mentioned in advance that the last surviving signer of the far-famed compact was John Alden, who died in 1686 at the age of eighty-seven, and that of the passengers the one who lived longest was Mary, the daughter of Isaac Allerton, who died as late as 1699, at the age of ninety.

We shall best take in the whole situation if we remember that the compact was signed on November 11 (o.s.); that by this time the Mayflower had rounded the cape and found shelter in the quiet harbour within the crook on which now lies the village of Province Town, and that probably on the same day they chose John Carver as governor for the ensuing year. Here the vessel tarried at anchor while three explorations were made before the final settlement at Plymouth. They naturally looked round them with some curiosity at the new world in which they found themselves. The harbour itself was one in which a thousand sail of ships might safely ride, and the land, down even to the sea margin, was covered with oak trees, pines, juniper, sassafras, and other aromatic shrubs. Vast flocks of wild-fowl had come in for the winter, such numbers they had never seen before, and in various parts of the bay whales were seen spouting, making the sailors wish they had their harpoons with them, for then they could soon have taken three or four thousand pounds' worth of oil. But the main question was as to the fitness of the land for permanent settlement; and for the purpose of ascertaining this, the same Saturday sixteen well-armed men went on shore to explore, and others to procure firewood. They reported on their return that the land consisted of hills of sand, reminding them of the dunes of Holland, and that the woods were like a grove or park, being free from underwood. The next day being Sunday they quietly rested, and had Sabbath worship, joining in spirit with those they had left behind in what was now a far-off land, and expressing their thankful praise to Him who had brought them safely through so many dangers of the deep.

With the next day came the necessity for decisive action. Jones, the captain of the Mayflower, was impatient to take his ship back to England, afraid lest his provisions might run out. Moreover, he refused to allow his vessel to cruise about in search of the best abiding-place. They must find that for themselves, and he would then sail to their chosen settlement and put them ashore. The thing now to do, therefore, at once was to explore the coast in the shallop, a little craft of from twelve to fifteen tons, which they had brought with them between decks, taking it to pieces for convenience of stowage. It was expected that the carpenters would be able to make it seaworthy in a very few days; but all the parts had been so strained on the voyage that it took weeks instead of days to put it to rights. Meantime, several of the men, growing impatient resolved to make the first exploration on land without it. Their readiness was admired, but the danger being great, their expedition was rather permitted than approved. Sixteen men were then told off, equipped with musket, sword, and corslet, and placed under the command of Captain Miles Standish, the one man of the company who had seen military service in the Netherlands, unto whom was adjudged for counsel and advice, William Bradford, Stephen Hopkins and Edward Tilley.

On Wednesday, November 15 [25], they set forth along the shore, and saw six Indians and a dog coming towards them, who at their approach fled into the woods. They followed the trail of these men for ten miles, hoping to open communication with them, but night coming on, they built a barricade of logs, kindled a fire, and fixed their sentries. Next day they continued their exploration, forcing their way up hill and down through dense thickets which tore their very armour apart. About the middle of the forenoon they came upon deer, deer-paths, and abundant and excellent springs of water. Then, turning to the inner shore, they reached a point on the great circle of the harbour only four miles across the water from the anchorage of the Mayflower. Here, according to previous agreement, they kindled a fire, to assure those on board of their safety. Subsequently they came upon a clearing of land where the Indians had formerly sown corn, found some Indian graves, and, further on, stubble of this year's corn, the remains of a house and a great iron kettle, which some ship's crew had left behind them. What was more to the purpose, under some heaps of sand they came upon 'divers fair Indian baskets filled with corn, and some in ears fair and good, of divers colours, which seemed to them a very goodly sight.' With some of this, burying the rest again, they made their way back to the ship, 'and so, like the men from Eshcol, carried with them of the fruits of the land and showed their brethren; of which and their return they were marvellously glad and their hearts encouraged.'

The shallop being ready at length, a body of twenty-four men set out in this and the long boat, accompanied by Jones and some of the crew, on the second exploration. This was on Monday, November 27 (O.S.), December 7 (N.S.). As this was an expedition by water Jones was made leader instead of Standish. They encountered heavy seas with head winds, and wading ashore were met with blinding snow-storms. So extreme was the cold and so severe their sufferings that of some of those who died later, Bradford says they 'took the original of their death here.' On the following Thursday they were back in the Mayflower. They had found some interesting relics of a French fishing-ship wrecked on Cape Cod four years ago, some Indian wigwams and divers articles of more or less value, but no place of settlement. The Pamet region they had explored had a good harbour for boats, and corn-land, fish and whales also abounded along the shore, but there was no harbour for ships and no supply of fresh water. If they settled here, they would soon have to change again. This was not to be their home. While they had been away Peregrine White, the first English child born in New England, saw the light on board the Mayflower.

On Wednesday, December 6 [16] ten of their principal men selected from volunteers set forth in the shallop on the third and last exploration, taking with them three of the seamen, together with the mate and pilot, Clarke and Coppin, their object being a thorough survey of the bay. Some stayed on board the shallop, while the others explored the land, as far as possible keeping sight of their comrades in the boat. After coasting along the inner side of the cape for about twenty miles they sailed up Wellfleet Bay, but finding it unsuitable for their purpose turned about to the south. On the third morning the land party were attacked by Indians, a shower of arrows being poured in upon them as they breakfasted by their bivouac. Happily no one was seriously injured, and a few musket shots were sufficient to scatter their assailants. After a prayer of thanksgiving for their deliverance they named the spot 'the First Encounter.' Then standing away before an easterly and southerly wind they intended to reconnoitre the shore farther round the bay. After some hours they were driven by snow-storms and rough seas till at nightfall they were fain to find themselves in a sheltered position between what is now known as Clark's Island and Saquish Head, then also an island. Afraid to land in the darkness for fear of the Indians, yet wet through with the storm, some of the more venturesome at length went on to Clark's Island, so called ever after because Clark, the mate, was the first man to step ashore, and there they kindled a fire in the rain ; the rest of the party about midnight being driven by the freezing temperature to join them. Such was the first cheerless entry of the Pilgrims to this part of Plymouth Harbour. The next day was Saturday, which they spent in repairing the shallop, which had been roughly used by the storm, and then this being, as their historian says, 'the last day of the week, they prepared there to keep the Sabbath.' Morton's journal quietly says, 'On the Sabbath day we rested ;' spending much of it in worship, no doubt, as their Sabbaths were wont to be spent.

Monday, December 11 [N.S. 21], 'they sounded the harbour, and found it fit for shipping ; and marched into the land and found divers corn-fields and little running brooks,—a place (as they supposed) fit for situation ; at least it was the best they could find.' This then was the technical landing of the Pilgrims, and here setting foot upon Plymouth Rock they had at length reached their long-sought resting-place.

Meantime the people in the Mayflower, lying at anchor

five-and-twenty miles away, looked out anxiously for the return of the men in the shallop. For one of these thus returning the welcome back was dashed with tears. William Bradford learnt to his sorrow that while he had been away his wife—the Dorothy May, of Wisbech, he had married at Amsterdam seven years before—had fallen overboard and was drowned. So chequered with chance and change at every step was the Pilgrims' course. So had the strong man to bow himself, and still go forward. Within a day or two more the Mayflower herself was in the harbour of Plymouth Bay, battered and beaten by storm and tempest, but her work gallantly accomplished, and her people safe in the possession of freedom in their New England home.

VIII.

PLYMOUTH PLANTATION.

THESE wanderers from the Old World to the New had found settlement at last, but under such stern conditions as to prove that William Brewster was right when he said, 'It is not with us as with men whom small things can discourage, or small discontentments cause to wish themselves at home again.' When they left Leyden, they hoped to reach their destination in time to be able to erect needful dwellings before winter set in. But the delays occasioned by the condition and return of the Speedwell, and by Atlantic storms, had had the effect of throwing them homeless on the bleak New England coast in the very depth of winter. Their houses had yet to be built at the very time that shelter was needed most.

It is not the manner of brave men, however, to waste time in vain regrets. The first thing to be determined was the best position for the settlement, a point which they felt should be decided by the whole body of emigrants. On Monday, December 28 (N.S.), therefore, the men of the company proceeded by way of the woods to reconnoitre the region round Plymouth previously approved by the exploring party. For further satisfaction they also next day journeyed some miles to the north, in the direction of what is now known as Kingston, after which it was agreed to seek Divine guidance and decide the matter by vote. 'The conclusion by most voices was to set on the mainland on the first place,' that is, at Plymouth, as first recommended by the pioneers.

This important point being settled, some twenty of the party began that same afternoon to build barricades, resolving to spend the night on shore. The others were to return to the vessel, coming back next morning with food for their companions, and to join them in their building operations. But that night one of the wildest of tempests burst in fury over sea and land. It needed all the three anchors of the Mayflower to enable her to stand the strain of the storm; and the unfortunate shore party, without a roof to shelter them, had to spend that long and weary night in torrents of rain, drenched to the skin. Moreover, the storm still continuing, it was far on in the next day before the shallop was able to bring them food from the ship.

But the storm abating at length, the work of building began in earnest, all who were able going ashore to fell and carry timber, returning at night to the vessel to sleep, and leaving a guard of about twenty men on shore. These remained over the Sunday, in the course of which they were alarmed by an outcry of unseen Indians, against whom, therefore, it behoved them to be on their guard. According to Old Style, Monday was Christmas Day, but, as their journal reports, 'no man rested all that day.' Working with a will, they proceeded to erect a common house some twenty feet square, intended for general use till all had houses of their own, and to serve as a place of meeting afterwards. In four days the timber work was up and the roof half thatched, when the scare of the Sunday led them to erect a platform on the hill, on which to plant cannon from the ship, in case of a further surprise from the Indians. They then divided the whole company into nineteen families, assigning the single men to the different households, so as to require for the present as few houses as possible. It was arranged that each family should build its own house, having a plot of land three rods long and half a rod broad for each of its members, the homesteads to be staked out after the choice of position had been determined by lot. These houses were to be built so as to form a single street parallel with the stream, now known as the Townbrook, and with land for each family on each side. This street, since 1823 called Leyden Street, still leads up from Plymouth Rock and from the beach to the hill beyond.

It was well that the building went on apace, for before many days were past there was sore need of houses in which to shelter the sick and the dying. The stern severity and exposure of that winter time, joined to hard toil and poor fare, after close and unhealthy crowding on ship-board, began seriously to tell on the condition of the community. In January and February they died sometimes at the rate of two or three a day. It seemed as if the whole colony would be swept away, for at one time there were only six or seven at all able to attend upon the sick and discharge the necessary offices of life. Bradford, who was one of those laid prostrate, speaks especially with grateful affection of William Brewster and Miles Standish, as those who, in the general calamity, never succumbed, and who were unceasing in their loving care for the stricken in their sick and low condition. 'What,' says he, 'I have said of these, I may say of many others who died in the general visitation, and others yet living, that, whilst they had health, yea, or any strength continuing, they were not wanting to any that had need of them.' The first house finished had to be used as a hospital for the sick, and by the end of February thirty-one of these had died, the mortality still continuing. The eminence above the beach, now known as Coles Hill, was set apart for the burial-place of the dead, the graves being levelled and grassed over, lest the Indians should discover how few and weak the settlers were becoming. Of the hundred who, less than three months before, had reached the shores of New England, only about fifty survived. It seemed, indeed, as if this heroic enterprise of theirs would turn out, after all, to be only one failure more; but happily, about the middle of March, the turning-point was reached, and the mortality began to abate. There is something pathetic in the entry in their journal which tells us that at this time the sun began to be warm about noon, and that the birds sang in the woods most pleasantly. It is but a gleam, but it shows that with the return of spring there was a return of life and hope to weary hearts, now that their long winter was over and gone.

Strangers in a strange land, the diminished settlers were naturally haunted by vague anxieties as to the sort of neighbours they might have. Wolves had been heard howling in the woods at night and had been seen prowling by day; but wolves were not so much to be dreaded as Indians intent on surprise and massacre. The shower of arrows from their bows at the place named First Encounter was not reassuring, and there were not wanting signs of them here at Plymouth. In a hunting excursion the captain found a dead deer, from which they had cut off the horns; a week later one of the colonists saw twelve Indians pass by his hiding-place, as if making for the plantation; tools left in the wood by Standish and Cooke had been carried off, and two Indians had been seen on the hill on the other side of the Townbrook, who suddenly disappeared when Standish and Hopkins tried to come to parley with them. It was clear the utmost precaution must be exercised; it was agreed therefore that in addition to the civil government a military organisation should be established, to be under the command of Miles Standish, and that the five cannon brought ashore from the Mayflower should be so placed on the Fort Hill platform as to command the approaches to the village on every side.

After-events, however, soon showed that their fears were

groundless. One morning towards the end of March a solitary Indian walked down the main street and came towards them. Save for the fringed leathern girdle about his loins, he was naked, had straight black hair, short in front and long behind, with no beard, and his only weapons were a bow and two arrows, one of which was headless. Of a good presence, he advanced boldly, and to their surprise, addressing them in English, bade them welcome. He made as if he would enter the common house, but fearing he might be a spy, they kept him outside till they had learnt more about him. In broken English he then told them that his name was Samoset, that he did not belong to that neighbourhood, but was the sachem or chief of Monhegan, an island on the coast between the Kennebec and Penobscot rivers, where from the men on the fishing vessels he had learnt what English he knew. A year ago he had come to Cape Cod with Captain Dermer, and had simply remained eight months on a visit. He further informed them that the Indian name of the place where they were was Patuxet, or the 'little bay,' that nearly four years ago the original inhabitants had all been swept away by a plague, so that there was no one left to dispute the possession of the place with the new-comers. Their nearest neighbours to the west, he said, were Massasoit's people, a tribe numbering some sixty warriors, while those to the east were the Nansets, the people who had made the attack upon them when they were exploring the bay. After volunteering this interesting information, their unexpected visitor stayed the night, and next day left for the Wampanoags, saying that he would soon return with some of them, bringing beaver skins, a fur till then unknown to the English.

Samoset was as good as his word. Next day he returned, bringing with him five tall, powerfully-built Indians. Their faces were painted, some with a black band five fingers broad from forehead to chin, others striped and coloured in various styles. Each had a deerskin hung on his shoulder, and long hose of dressed deerskin extending upwards and meeting at a leathern girdle; and each had the hair short in front, but behind reaching down to the shoulders. As a sign of peace, they left their bows and arrows a quarter of a mile from the town and brought back the tools taken in the woods a month before. Being hospitably entertained, they offered to repay their Puritan hosts with an exhibition of Indian song and dance, which, as it was the Sabbath day, would have been a curious contrast to their Sabbath service. They offered also beaver skins for sale; but as the Pilgrims declined all trade as well as Indian war-song and dance on Sundays, they left what stock they had with them and promised to bring more some other day. Their main object, however, was to prepare the way for a visit from the great sachem Massasoit himself.

The following Thursday Samoset reappeared, bringing with him another Indian, who proved to be an invaluable friend to the settlers. This was Tisquantum, or Squanto, as he came to be called, the only man left of the Patuxet tribe once living at Plymouth. Fact would indeed seem stranger than fiction, when the colonists found that this last of the Patuxets had lived more than three years in London, and knew London streets better than most of themselves. The fact was he was one of four-and-twenty Indians whom Thomas Hunt had kidnapped on board ship in 1614 to sell as slaves in Spain. Contriving to escape, and making his way to England, he entered the service of Sir Ferdinando Gorges, and afterwards that of a London merchant who was treasurer of the Newfoundland Company. Then, some six months before the landing of the Pilgrims, Captain Dermer had brought him back to Plymouth, where he found himself, as we have seen, the sole survivor of the tribe to which he belonged. He now, along with Samoset, came on in advance, to announce that Massasoit, the grand sachem of the confederate tribes of Pokanoket, was at hand with his warriors.

The colonists felt at once that much might depend on the approaching interview. If friendly relations could be established with this great chief, peace might be secured with all the tribes from Narragansett Bay to the end of Cape Cod; even the fierce Nansets, with whom they had already been in conflict, might become their allies. Expectation was on tiptoe; within the space of an hour Massasoit with his sixty braves appeared on the hill south of the Townbrook, and Tisquantum came on, with a request that a messenger might be sent over to confer with the chief. It was perhaps a perilous venture, but Edward Winslow at once volunteered the service. Wearing armour and bearing side-arms, he descended to the ford of the stream, and ascending the slope of what is now known as Watson's Hill, he disappeared from the sight of his friends into the midst of the crowd of Indians who formed the body-guard of the chief.

Presenting certain gifts, meant to propitiate, Winslow found himself the central object of interest, Massasoit examining his sword and armour with lively curiosity, and offering to buy them. Winslow, on his part, assured him that their sovereign, King James, saluted him with peace and good-will, desiring him for his ally; and also that their own governor, whom he had just left, desired to see him, that he might confirm a peace with him, and open a trade for their mutual benefit. Massasoit expressed himself gratified with the interview; therefore leaving Winslow behind as a hostage, and taking with him a body-guard of some twenty armed warriors, he started for the village. To receive him with due honour, Standish and Allerton, with six musketeers, went down to the stream, and as the Indian chief crossed the ford gave him a military salute, escorting him afterwards to the town house, where he was received with such modest state of carpets and cushions as they could muster from their scanty stores. Governor Carver, attended with body-guard of musketeers, met their distinguished guest with courtly salutations, after which they ate and drank together. The chief, a man in the prime of life, of grave manner and few words, presented much the same appearance as his attendants, save that he was distinguished by a great necklace of white bone beads, and that he carried in his bosom a long knife suspended by a cord. His face was painted a dull red, while those of his attendants were painted some black, some red, and others yellow or white, laid on in crosses or curious figures. Some were clad in the skins of wild animals, others were naked; all were tall and powerfully built.

Courtesies being ended, business began; a treaty offensive and defensive being entered into by which each side bound itself to refrain from injuring the other, in the event of war to render aid, and in case of conference to come unarmed to the interview. Thus, in a spirit of independence, and in the exercise of sovereign power, the colony made its first foreign treaty and entered into its first alliance. It was a good beginning, for the treaty thus made stood firm, and was honourably observed for more than half a century. Massasoit outlived all the leaders who took part in that day's proceedings, yet he had been years in his grave before the alliance entered into was seriously shaken, and the disastrous war with his son Philip came to its direful issue.

The treaty being thus concluded, Samoset returned to his own tribe in the north, in what is now the State of Maine, while Tisquantum remained with the colonists as their valued friend. To the colonists themselves this had been an eventful and memorable week. They had learnt much of their surroundings and possibilities; had made friends where they had expected to meet with foes; fears had been dissipated, the sense of dread had given way to a feeling of security; and it may well have been that when the next Sabbath came its round, and the little community gathered for worship in their simple conventicle, they were ready to say to each other: 'The Lord hath done great things for us, whereof we are glad.'

As the spring advanced, the time came on for the Mayflower to return. From December to April she had remained at anchor in the bay, a link of connection with the far-off world from which they had come. Various circumstances had delayed her departure—a succession of storms, the necessity of housing the Pilgrims till the buildings on shore were ready, the sickness of the colonists, and most of all, the sickness on board, from which the boatswain died, the gunner, the cook, and three of the quartermasters, besides several of the ordinary seamen. It was not till the 5th of April, therefore, that the remainder of the crew hoisted sail and prepared to depart. It was a testing-time for the Pilgrims on shore. When the Mayflower was gone, their nearest civilised neighbours would be the French of Nova Scotia, five hundred miles to the north, and the English settlement in Virginia, five hundred miles to the south. Still weakened and reduced in numbers as they were, like brave Englishmen they held resolutely to their purpose. They might have had opportunity to have returned to the dear old land they had left behind, but did not. We can well believe that, with tearful eyes and fast-beating hearts, men, women and children stood on the hillside wistfully watching the vessel as she passed out of the bay and towards the distant horizon, and till she vanished out of sight.

But the best cure for sorrow is work, and the daily demands of daily life left but scant room for sentiment. For there was land to be dressed and corn to be sown, and all hands must needs be busy in preparing for the necessities of the coming time. Here their new Indian acquaintance proved of eminent service. As strangers to the soil, they knew little as to what would thrive best, and under what conditions. Tisquantum therefore gave them the benefit of his knowledge and experience, telling them that Indian corn, which was to be their main dependence, should be sown when the young leaves on the oak tree were as big as the ears of a mouse. He showed them, also, how to put the fish known as ale-wives round the roots of the maize, so as to secure good result when the harvest came, and also when these ale-wives were most plentifully to be caught. So all went briskly to work, sometimes planting and sowing, sometimes felling timber and building, and sometimes, from the necessity for food, hunting and fishing. Though after the sickness had done its work there were only twenty-one men and six growing lads left to do the work of the colony, yet that season twenty-one acres of corn-land were tilled, six acres more were sown with wheat, rye, and barley; in addition to which the gardens round their houses were also brought into cultivation.

In the midst of these industrial activities a great sorrow fell upon the little community, in the sudden death of John Carver, their governor. Coming one day in April from the cornfield, complaining of a pain in the head, he lay down to rest, became insensible, and, though lingering for two or three days, never spoke again. As their governor, and esteemed for his Christian worth, his funeral was conducted with as much of state as they could command, the musketeers firing mournful volleys over his grave. There is a further touch of pathos in the fact that his good wife, Katharine, of frail and delicate build, and worn out with hardship, was also laid by his side in the same quiet resting-place overlooking the sea.

The funeral over, there was a successor to be chosen. There was only one man who could be thought of for the vacant place. William Brewster, as elder and practically sole pastor and preacher, was sufficiently occupied; his friend William Bradford therefore was at once chosen by the suffrages of the brethren as their governor, Isaac Allerton to be his assistant in the duties of his office. Regarding the history of this early New England commonwealth as a prelude to that of the great Federal Republic, it has been pointed out that there is a peculiar interest attaching to this election of Bradford as that of the first American citizen of the English race who bore rule by the free choice of his brethren, as standing at the head of the bead-roll of those governors of the West who, without having any early training in political life, and lacking much that the Old World has deemed needful in her rulers, have yet by inborn strength of mind and lofty public spirit shown themselves in all things worthy of the high office to which they were called.[1]

The government being now settled in the hands of Bradford and his assistant, and the earlier work of planting and sowing being all over, it was deemed advisable that same summer to send out one or two expeditions. And first, by way of consolidating the friendly alliance already established, Edward Winslow and Stephen Hopkins, with Tisquantum as guide and interpreter, were commissioned as an embassy to Massasoit, and charged to make careful observation of the country on their way. Travelling for some fifteen miles, they came to Namasket, a village at the rapids, where they were kindly treated by the Indians, and by sunset had reached another camp of the same tribe, four or five miles farther up the river. The next afternoon they entered the territory of the Wampanoags, the home-tribe of Massasoit; his principal seat was at Sowams, now known as Warren on Narragansett Bay, which the travellers

---

[1] Doyle's *English in America*, vol. i., p. 71.

reached at nightfall, and where they were received with cordial welcome. Seated by the side of the chief, and surrounded by a crowd of Indian spectators, by the aid of their interpreter they delivered their message. Presenting him, on behalf of their governor, with a gay trooper's coat trimmed with lace, and also with an ornamental copper chain, having a medal attached, they informed him that the chain was intended to be lent as a token to any friend of his whom he desired to be hospitably received by them, and would ensure their kindness. Among other matters, they referred to the corn they had found buried, when they landed at Cape Cod the previous winter, asking that the owner might be known, that they might pay him for what they had taken. Assenting to their requests, the chief then arrayed himself in the gay coat they had brought him, and placing the chain round his neck, sat in state to his own eminent satisfaction, and to the admiration of his braves. After making a lengthy harangue, which his people received with assent and applause, the chief spent the rest of the evening in smoking with his guests, and in making inquiries about England and King James. When it was time for bed the situation became embarrassing, for Winslow and Hopkins found they were to sleep in the chief's own bed, he and his wife at one end, and they at the other. Moreover, as two of the chief men also crowded upon the royal couch, too strait for so many, and as the bed consisted of rude planks merely covered with a mat, Winslow declared that he was more wearied with his bed than with his journey.

After tarrying two nights and a day, Massasoit urged them to prolong their stay; but while his welcome was cordial, Indian fare was somewhat hard, and they were disposed to turn homewards. Returning by a different route, they passed for miles through a country which must once have been thickly populated, but over which the plague had swept, leaving the bleaching bones of unburied thousands, a gruesome sight to see. On and on they travelled in solitude through once cultivated fields lying along the streams, and through park-like woods of oak, walnut and beech and exceeding great chestnut trees. After being absent for five days, they reached home once more, 'wet, weary and surbated;' but to their own relief and the joy of their brethren.

About the same time another expedition was sent out, in search of a son of one of the settlers who had lost himself in the woods, and subsisting on berries, had wandered on for five days, till he found himself at the head of Buzzard's Bay, twenty miles from home. Hearing from Massasoit that the lad was in the hands of the Nanset Indians, ten men, well armed, started in the shallop to recover the wanderer. Reaching, after varied adventure, the abiding-place of Aspinet, the sachem of the Nansets, whom they found surrounded by a hundred of his attendants, the lost one, profusely decorated with beads, was handed back to his countrymen. In the month of August a more significant expedition started for Middleborough. Rumours had reached Plymouth that Corbitant, the chief of the Pocassets, had captured Massasoit, and was denouncing the friendly relations established between the colonists and the sachems of the Cape. Tisquantum and another Indian named Hobomok, going to Namasket to ascertain the truth, were captured by Corbitant, who threatened to take their lives. While he was holding a knife to the breast of Tisquantum, saying that with the death of their interpreter the English would lose their tongue, Hobomok contrived to escape and make his way through the woods to Plymouth. A council of war was held at once. It was felt that a timid policy would be dangerous, and that to neglect their ally Massasoit would be to prevent other Indians making alliance with them. It was decided at once therefore that Standish, with ten armed men, should start next day for Namasket, and that if Tisquantum were really killed, Corbitant should be beheaded. The house pointed out by Hobomok was surrounded at midnight, Corbitant called for, and notice given that no one should leave the building till search had been made. It turned out that Corbitant had gone away, leaving Tisquantum in the village unharmed, he coming out to welcome his friends. Returning with him, they left a message for Corbitant to the effect that if he continued his hostile course, forming conspiracies against them, rebelling against Massasoit, their friend, or offering violence to their friends or his, no place should secure him. The effect of this promptitude was felt at once both far and near. The story of this faithful defence of an ally secured other allies. The sachem of Capawack (now Martha's Vineyard), of whom the colonists knew nothing, sent to make peace and acknowledge the English king, as also did Aspinet and Canacum of Manomet. Five other chiefs followed, even Corbitant sought the good offices of Massasoit to make his peace with foes so formidable as the men of Plymouth. That same autumn, and as a sequel to this expedition, five chiefs set their marks to a document acknowledging themselves the loyal subjects of King James.

Encouraged by the result of their expeditions thus far, the settlers resolved to send some of their number to Massachusetts Bay, to establish, if possible, peace and commercial relations with the Indians to the north, who, they were given to understand, were hostile to them. They succeeded in making friendship with the tribe of the Shawmuts; but the expedition was of interest chiefly as making the English acquainted with what was to be known hereafter as Boston Harbour, which they greatly admired as a place for shipping. As in their shallop they glided in and out among its forty-seven beautiful islands, they began to regret that they had not made this their place of settlement. But, pleased with their reception, and bringing with them store of beaver skins to lighten their indebtedness to the Merchant Adventurers at home, they sailed back by the light of the harvest moon, reaching Plymouth the following day.

As the autumn of their first year in the colony was veering towards winter, they were now able to look back with some measure of satisfaction. Heavy sorrows had befallen them, friends and comrades had fallen by their side, still, the experiment of founding a new home began to justify itself. Seven dwelling-houses and four public buildings on the main street were the outcome of their patient toil. Of the latter, one served for worship and for town meetings, the others as storehouses for provisions, clothing, trading stock and general supplies. Though some of the smaller crops had failed, the corn had repaid them for their labour; furs were stored and prepared timber made ready for the next ship to England. Finally they were at peace with the Indians round about, with some of them, indeed, on terms of intimate friendship. They resolved therefore with public rejoicings to keep what may be called their Feast of Tabernacles. In this way and at the end of their first year in the colony, commenced the New England festival of Thanksgiving Day. It was observed as a time of recreation, and also as an opportunity of extending their hospitality to their Indian ally Massasoit, who came on their invitation, bringing ninety of his people with him. These guests of theirs remained for three days, during which they captured five deer, to add to the colony's stock of provisions; they also contributed their share towards the amusements of the time, while the colonists on their part entertained their guests with some small show of military display. This time of rest after toil was observed also as a time of praise for mercies received. They placed it upon record that they had 'found the Lord to be with them in all their ways, and to bless their outgoings and incomings, for which,' said they, 'let His holy name have the praise for ever to all posterity!'

In the month of November the Nanset Indians passed on to Plymouth the intelligence that a ship was seen making her way into the Cape harbour. What could it be? No vessel had been seen since the Mayflower left, nor were they expecting any till the spring came round. England and France were then at war; could it be that these were Frenchmen, with hostile intent? A cannon was at once fired from the battery, to call in all who were out in the fields, and soon every man who could shoulder a musket fell into his place, and stood on the outlook. The alarm turned out to be needless. The stranger drawing nearer proved to be a friend, for the English flag was seen floating at her masthead. It was the ship Fortune, bringing thirty-five new colonists, among them being William Brewster's eldest son, John Winslow a brother of Edward, and Robert Cushman. 'The plantation,' says Bradford, 'was glad of this addition to its strength, but could have wished that many of them had been of better condition, and all of them better furnished with provisions; but that could not be helped.'

In addition to her passengers, the Fortune brought the colonists a patent of their land from the Council of New England, drawn up in the name of John Pierce and his associates, in the same manner as the New York grant formerly received from the Virginia Company. This document, bearing date June 1, 1621, is still preserved in the Pilgrim Hall at Plymouth, and bears the signatures and seals of the Duke of Lenox, the Marquis of Hamilton, the Earl of Warwick, and Sir Ferdinando Gorges. It defined no boundaries, but, under certain conditions, gave to Pierce and each of his associates a hundred acres of land. It remained in force, however, only for a year, being superseded by one by means of which Pierce hoped, but in vain, to get the Plymouth people into his own power.

The Fortune, besides this patent, brought a letter from Weston, complaining that when the Mayflower returned she brought back no profitable cargo from the colonists. That they had sent back no lading in the ship, he said, was wonderful, and worthily distasted. He had heard of their weakness and its cause, but for his part he thought it was weakness of judgment rather than weakness of hands, and that a quarter of the time they had spent in discoursing, arguing and consulting, spent in other ways, might have produced better results. Taunts like these uttered to men who had had to watch day after day by the sick and the dying, and many of whom had narrowly escaped death themselves, were felt to be ungenerous and uncalled-for.

Bradford repelled these unworthy imputations in language at once pathetic and dignified. Weston's letter had been addressed to Carver as governor. 'Touching him,' says Bradford, 'he is departed this life, and now is at rest in the Lord from all those troubles and encumbrances with which we are yet to strive. He needs not my apology, he who for the common good oppressed himself and shortened his days. If the company had lost their profits, these were not to be set over against the loss of the lives of honest and industrious men, which could not be valued at any price. It had pleased God to visit them with death daily, and with so general a disease that the living were scarce able to bury the dead, and the well not in any measure to tend the sick. And now to be greatly blamed for not freighting the ship at such a time doth indeed go near us and much discourage us.' He concluded by telling Weston that the colonists had conceded the points at issue, had signed the controverted articles, and were sending back the ship well-laden. He hoped, therefore, that friendship would be re-established, and that the promises made by the Merchant Adventurers on their side would not be forgotten.

When the Fortune returned, she took back for the company a cargo of beaver fur, prepared timber, and profitable sassafras to the value of about £500. This hardly-earned consignment, however, never reached its destination. When off the English coast the vessel was captured, and her cargo seized by the French, and carried to Isle Dieu. The cargo was retained, but at the end of fourteen days the ship and ship's company were released, and Cushman, who was on board, secured all the papers, among which was Bradford's and Winslow's Journal, known as Mourt's Relation. There was also a letter from Edward Winslow to his 'loving and old friend,' George Morton, who was about to come out in the next vessel, advising him as to what he and his companions were to bring with them—good store of clothes and bedding, and each man a musket or fowling-piece, the piece to be long in the barrel, and as the shooting was from stands, they need not fear the weight of it; juice of lemons they would find of use to take fasting, and for hot waters, aniseed was the best, but should be used sparingly. As glass was then much too great a luxury for a New England home, he recommends they should bring paper and linseed oil for their windows, and much store of powder and shot. Besides this letter of Winslow's, there was another from William Hilton, one of the emigrants who had come to Plymouth in the Fortune, and who was sending back home his first impressions of the colony, which were considerably *couleur de rose*. He tells his friends in this letter that he found the country pleasant and temperate, yielding naturally of itself great store of fruits, with vines of divers sorts in great abundance. Timber of varied kind abounds, and there are great flocks of wild birds—turkeys, quails, pigeons and partridges; while lake and sea were well stored with fish.

Better grain than Indian corn, he thinks, no man need desire, and best of all, says he, 'we are all freeholders; the rent-day doth not trouble us; and all those good blessings we have, of which, and what we list in their seasons for taking. Our company are, for most part, very religious, honest people; the word of God sincerely taught us every Sabbath; so that I know not anything a contented mind can here want.'[1]

Early in 1662 there were disquieting rumours as to possible hostilities on the part of the Narragansett Indians. About the beginning of April, a messenger from that tribe left a sheaf of arrows tied round with a rattlesnake skin, which Tisquantum interpreted as a declaration of war. To show fear would be to invite destruction. Governor Bradford at once, therefore, sent back the snake-skin stuffed with bullets and powder and accompanied with a defiant message. The chief, Canonicus, alarmed at the look of the missive, refused to receive it; back, therefore, it was sent from place to place, till it found its way to Plymouth again. A feeling of insecurity was occasioned by this event, and was intensified by the news which reached them about the same time from Virginia. For the English settlers there, apprehensive of no danger, had scattered their dwellings far apart from each other; and taking advantage of this fact, the Indians had treacherously risen on the 22nd of March and massacred men, women, and children to the number of 347.[2] Not one would have been left alive to tell the tale, but for the fact that a settler named Pace was warned by an Indian convert who lived in his house. Unfortunately, the scattered state of the colony made it impossible for the English to combine in any plan of resistance, or even to send warning to the most

[1] This letter was first printed in 1622 in Smith's *New England's Trials*.
[2] *Colonial Papers*, vol. ii., July 13.

distant plantations. The news of this massacre reaching Plymouth at the very time the Narragansetts were showing signs of hostility created a feeling of alarm, and led these colonists in the north to take such precautions as had been neglected by the settlers in the south. In five weeks they had constructed a strong line of palisade on the north side, beginning at the shore line, and extending along the upper part of the hill as far as the Townbrook. In this line of palisade there were four flanking-bastions, from which musketry could command the outside, and in three of these bastions were gates, which were kept locked at night and guarded by sentinels. Standish further placed all able to bear arms under a general muster or training, forming with the new-comers a battalion some fifty strong.

In the midst of these precautions and alarms there arrived a shallop from a fishing-vessel in the harbour, partly owned by Weston, and bringing letters from him. In these he informed the Plymouth people that he was about to form a settlement of his own near to them, and asking them to maintain the seven men in the shallop till the main body should arrive. The quartering of these men upon them that summer was an unwelcome additional strain on their scanty resources. For though their crops were sown, they were not grown, and June found their storehouses almost empty of provision; moreover, wild-fowl were out of season, and though of fish there were bass in the outer harbour and cod in the bay, they had neither nets nor deep-water tackle to take them. All through the summer, having neither bread, meat, nor vegetables, they were reduced to subsist on what shell-fish they could find. To complicate the situation still further, two of Weston's emigrant ships arrived, landing sixty more men, who, while drawing their food from the vessels, trusted for lodgment to the people on shore. Some of the new-comers were of doubtful sort, and finding that green corn roasted in the ear was an agreeable food, they robbed the cornfields remorselessly, seriously reducing the moderate crop of maize on which the colony had to depend for next year's sustenance. After six weeks the vessels fortunately returned and took off these men to the new colony to be started at Wessagusset, since known as Weymouth ; they went, leaving their sick behind, and but scanty thanks for the hospitality received. As the result of frequent depredations, the crop harvested that autumn proved altogether too light and insufficient to feed their people, even through the winter; and all the food they could purchase from the Indians north and south of them would go but a little way towards their subsistence till harvest-time came round.

In the autumn of 1622 their faithful friend Tisquantum died of fever, leaving his little property to his English friends, and asking Bradford, who had nursed him like a woman, to pray for him that his soul might go to the Englishman's God in heaven. The following March also news reached Plymouth that their friend and ally Massasoit lay dangerously ill at Sowams. The Indian custom of visits of ceremony to their chiefs in time of sickness rendered it desirable to send an embassy. Taking Hobomok as interpreter, Winslow therefore set forth, reaching the dwelling-place of the chief late at night. He found him still alive, his wigwam crowded with people, and the powahs in the midst of charms and incantations, making, as Winslow says, 'such hellish noise as distempered us that were well, and therefore unlike to ease him that was sick.' The patient had not slept for two days, and had gone quite blind. He was able to understand, however, that Winslow had come to see him, and desired to have him near. Winslow expressed on behalf of the governor at Plymouth the sorrow he felt at hearing of Massasoit's condition, and saying that he had sent such things as were likely to relieve him. Winslow then took the case in hand, dismissing powahs and all the officious crowd who were hindering rather than helping the patient's recovery. It was very simple medical treatment he resorted to, but under it the complaint, after a time, began to yield; long sleep came over the wearied man, and gradually he rose once more from what was thought would prove the bed of death. On his recovery he gratefully declared, 'Now I see the English are my friends and love me, and while I live I will never forget this kindness they have shown me.'

The opportunity of showing his gratitude was even now within his reach, and he used it. As the messengers were on the point of returning, the chief called Hobomok aside, and told him of a plot which was being set on foot by the Massachusett Indians, which he was to reveal to Winslow on their way home. To understand the meaning of the secret thus confided to Hobomok, we must go back a step or two in the narrative. The colonists whom Weston had planted, as we have seen, at Wessagusset on Boston Bay, proved to be not well-disciplined or self-controlled. By the middle of March they had exhausted their stores and even devoured their seed-corn. Reduced to extremities, some of them hired themselves out to the Indians for a cap-full of corn to fetch wood and water; others less honestly disposed took to robbing the Indians, for which their own governor had them put into the stocks and whipped. Eventually food was refused to them on any terms. Upon this, the question of making a raid on the Indian stores was discussed. Before this extreme step was taken, however, some thought that advice should first be sought from Governor Bradford at Plymouth. This was done by letter, their leader stating that they had used all means both to buy and borrow of the Indians, who had stores, as he knew, but who, maliciously as he thought, withheld them. On receipt of this, Bradford summoned a town's meeting to advise thereon. After due deliberation, a letter was drawn up in reply, and signed by many of the townsmen, to the effect that they altogether disliked this purpose of theirs, as being contrary alike to the law of God and the law of nature. If they carried out that purpose, it would be fatal both to the peaceable enlargement of the king's dominion and to the propagation of the law and knowledge of God and the glad tidings of salvation, and would breed a distaste in the savages against their persons and professions.

In speaking thus, they were not unmindful of the hardships their neighbours were going through, for they themselves were in the same case, having but little corn left, and being compelled to subsist on ground-nuts and shell-fish. They might do the same, and should remember that even if they did rob the stores of the Indians, their ill-gotten gain would last but a little while, and they would then have to seek food among men whom they had made their enemies. It would be better to begin in a course likely to hold out, and on which they might with a good conscience ask and expect the blessing of God.

Such was the answer received. Meantime things went from bad to worse at Wessagusset. The settlers having sold nearly all their clothing for food, were half-naked as well as half-starved. Camping out in the woods in search of food, or wandering along the beach, squalid and abject from hunger and disease, they became objects of contempt to the Indians, who began to look on them as enemies who might easily be swept out of life. Such was the situation of affairs when Winslow returned from his visit to Massasoit. The news he brought back to the men of Plymouth was not reassuring. For the secret confided to Hobomok by Massasoit, and which he was to reveal to Winslow, was to the effect that the Neponset Indians had resolved on a general massacre, both of the settlers at Wessagusset and those at Plymouth. They had no cause of complaint against the latter, but they knew that they would never submit to see their fellow-countrymen ruthlessly murdered without rising on their behalf. The safest thing, therefore, would be to put them out of the way too. With this intent, they entered into a league with the seven tribes south and west of Plymouth, and also, even in his sickness, tried to induce Massasoit to join them. In this way he came to be aware of their plot, and, out of gratitude to Winslow, revealed it. His advice was that the Plymouth settlers should strike the first blow, seizing and executing the main conspirators among the Neponsets. If, as was their custom, they waited for the other side to become the aggressors, they would find that that meant a massacre of sixty of their countrymen at Wessagusset, whom no subsequent energy could bring back to life again; and immediately after that, a host of Indians let loose upon themselves, excited and infuriated with bloodshed.

The situation was serious, and as it was now the time for holding the court or annual town meeting for the election of officers, Bradford laid the matter before the whole body of the people in their chief assembly. It was an anxious debate. They were unwilling to shed the blood of those whose good they sought, and whose conversion they had hoped for. But the massacre of the previous year in Virginia and the very decided words of Massasoit seemed to leave them no alternative. It was agreed therefore that Standish, taking with him a sufficient force, should start, as if on a trading expedition, warn their countrymen at Wessagusset, and then strike home at the chief conspirators. On arriving, he found to his dismay that their vessel, the Swan, was in the harbour, without a soul on board, that the settlers were scattered in different directions, and the whole plantation in fancied security, letting the Indians come in and out among their dwellings as they pleased. By Standish's advice all the men were called home, and on pain of death ordered to stay there.

The first day being stormy, nothing could be done; but an Indian spy coming in under pretence of selling furs, saw the course affairs were taking, and went back with his report. From this the conspirators saw their secret was out, and at once assumed a defiant attitude, surrounding Standish, and sharpening their knives. He kept his self-command, wishing to get the chief conspirators together before commencing action. He so managed matters as to get them at length into one of the dwellings, with an equal number of his own men. He then gave the word of command, on which there was a desperate struggle, and seven Indians fell in the hand-to-hand encounter. Next day the matter came to further issue in the open, Standish securing the strategic advantage of a rising hill, for which both sides were striving. The Indians from behind the trees kept up a shower of arrows, till Hobomok came to the front. Somehow he had obtained the reputation of being a *pinese*, or one who holds communication with the evil spirit; when, therefore, he threw off his coat and ran towards them, they fled like a flock of sheep.

So in comedy ended the tragedy, after which Standish urged the settlers to go on with their plantation, or if they preferred, come to join their neighbours at Plymouth. But they had had enough of colonisation and its attendant experiences, and determined to go back. Putting, therefore, all their movable property on board the Swan, lying out in the bay, they joined the fishing vessels at Monhegan and abandoned the country.

On the return of Standish and his party to Plymouth, it was decided to complete the fort on the hill commenced some ten months before. The work had been delayed through differences of opinion, some deeming it unnecessary, and others regarding it as vainglorious. But recent alarms put an end to these differences, and the fort was completed. It was described as large and square, and by Bradford as 'strong and comely,' and a great work for them. From that time it became the centre both of their civil and religious life. The main room in the building was used as the place of meeting for worship till about 1648, when the first church edifice was erected at the foot of the hill ; here also the town meetings were held henceforth, the common house being used for storage. The fort being thus used as a place of worship, the land on the hill round it became God's Acre, the burial-place of their dead. On the flat roof above the meeting-house artillery was placed behind battlements, and sentinels stationed night and day. The fort itself has, of course, long since disappeared, but a marble tablet still marks the spot where once it stood, and portions of its foundations may still be traced.

Till the spring of 1623, from the necessity of the case, the colony had gone on the communistic system, for being under common obligation to pay back to the Adventurers the money advanced, they were practically trading as one company. But communism had serious drawbacks, as it always must have. It had been tried here at Plymouth under more than ordinarily favourable conditions, for it was tried in a community of sober, industrious and godly men. Yet it was far from successful, for it led to confusion and discontent, discouraged production, and bestowed a premium upon indifference. The strong and able thought it hard that they should have to work for the wives and children of other men, and share no more than those who could not do half their work. On the other hand, grave and aged men felt it to be somewhat of an indignity that they should be reduced to an equality, and made to work in the ranks with the younger and meaner sort. Husbands, too, rebelled at the idea of their wives having to dress the meat and wash the clothes of other men, feeling this to be a kind of slavery hard to brook. That all should be on an equality to have alike and do alike, and should think themselves one as good as another, Bradford says, did ¦much diminish and take off that mutual respect which it is good to preserve in a community. It would have been worse, he thinks, with worse men, and it is to no purpose that the failure lies not with the system, but with the corruption of human nature, for, seeing that all men have this corruption in them, God in His wisdom has seen another course fitter for them.

With this feeling prevalent, before the planting time of 1623, a modified departure from the communistic system was determined upon. Without making provision for inheritance, it was arranged to assign to each family for one year a parcel of land in the proportion of one acre to each person, and as the land varied in quality and value, it should be divided by lot. This arrangement at once infused new life into the community. All now went to work with a will, and planted far more corn than under the old system. Even the women went willingly into the fields, taking their children with them to help.

Still, though the planting season of 1623 was a time of busy industry and willing work, this could not alter the fact that by the time the seed-corn was in the earth their stores of food were spent. Many a night they went to rest without knowing whence the next day's food was to come, and how they were to live till the next harvest came its round, it was impossible to say. They said one to another that now above all people in the world they had need to cast themselves on God's providence, and pray that He would give them daily bread. Yet, as Bradford tells us, they bore their hardships with great patience and alacrity of spirit, though for two or three months together they had neither bread nor any kind of corn; and in spite of scanty fare God in His mercy preserved both health and life. In this hard time, while they trusted in God, they with their usual bravery and good sense vigorously helped them-

IX.

AT THE END OF SEVEN YEARS.

THE thanksgiving celebrated by the Pilgrims at the hill fort had not gone by many days when a vessel was seen making its way into the harbour at Plymouth, which proved to be the ship Anne, bringing additional colonists and stores from the Adventurers in London. Ten days later she was followed by the Little James, a pinnace of forty-four tons, the two vessels together bringing about a hundred new emigrants for the colony. Some of these were so obviously unfit for colonial life that the governor shipped them back at once in the same vessel at his own expense. Many of the others had come out to pursue an independent course of their own; the remainder were old friends and kinsfolk from the Church at Leyden. Among the latter were George Morton and his household, Fear and Patience the two daughters of Elder Brewster, the wife of Samuel Fuller, Mrs. Southworth, who afterwards became the wife of Governor Bradford, and Barbara, subsequently married to Miles Standish. These and the rest of the old friends from Leyden were welcome arrivals indeed, and the greetings on both sides naturally of cordial sort. But the greetings over, the new-comers began to feel disappointed with their new surroundings. For the reality, as they found it, was widely different from the rose-coloured pictures of New England life they had either painted for themselves, or had had suggested to them by such letters as that which William Hilton had sent over. They were startled, on meeting them again, to see the change wrought in those from whom they had parted at Delfshaven little more than two years before. Scanty fare, constant exposure and hard grinding toil had taken the freshness and brightness out of their faces; their clothes were tattered and worn, their log-built huts rude and unattractive to those who had just left the cities of the Old World behind them; and the best dish they could set before their friends when they came to them was a lobster or a piece of fish, without bread or anything else but a cup of fair spring water. It was a process of disillusion, and the disillusion was complete. Some wished themselves back again, while others even fell a-weeping, as they saw in their friends what they themselves might have to come to.

The practical demands of life, however, make short work of regretful sentiment. There was business to be done, and at the very outset stood the necessity of making some amicable adjustment between the claims of the old settlers and the new. For, on the one hand, as the new-comers had only brought sufficient supplies of food for themselves to last till harvest, they were not willing to let these provisions of theirs come into the common stock. On the other hand, the established settlers did not consider it fair that the recent arrivals should have share in the produce of the harvest to which they were looking forward, and for which they alone had toiled. It was agreed, therefore, that the stores in the ship should be the exclusive property of those who had sailed in her, and that the produce of the coming harvest should belong to those who had sown the seed. Then there was a further complication. Besides the sixty emigrants who had come over in the Anne, who were to be merged in the general colony, there were about forty more who wished to form a separate colony within the colony, and who described themselves as 'particulars,' by way of distinction from the body of colonists regarded as 'generals.' After conference held on the matter, it was agreed that these should be received with courtesy, and have competent places assigned them within the town, and that they should be free from the labour expected from the rest, except such public service as might be necessary for the safety of the colony. On the other hand, they were not to be at liberty to carry on trade in furs and other commodities with the Indians; towards the maintenance of the government and all public officers, each male 'particular' above the age of sixteen would be expected to pay into the common store a bushel of Indian corn, or the value of it; and finally they were to be subject to such laws and ordinances as were already or should hereafter be enacted for the public good. The new-comers, ninety-six in all, added to those who came over in the Mayflower, with the thirty-five brought by the Fortune, two hundred and thirty-three in all, make up the company of those known in America as the Pilgrims, or First Comers or Forefathers. Out of the two hundred and thirty-three there were about a hundred and eighty survivors at the end of 1623.

Up to this time the government of the colony had necessarily been of the simplest and most rudimentary kind. As Professor Freeman has pointed out, the smallness of the scale of the settlement led them to reproduce in not a few points the England of an earlier age than their own; that, in fact, a New England town-meeting was essentially the same thing as the Homeric agoré, the Athenian ekklesia, the Roman comitia, the Swiss Landesgemeinde, and the English folk-moot. The circumstances of the case called again into being the primitive assembly which had not long died out in the Frisian sea-lands, which still lived on in the Swabian mountain-lands, but which, in the older England, was well-nigh forgotten.[1]

The town-meeting being thus the central source of

---

[1] *Introduction to American Institutional History*, by E. A. Freeman; John Hopkins' University Studies, Series I., p. 15. 1882.

authority, all arrangements at first were simplicity itself. Fresh laws were added as fresh laws were needed, but no statute-book was deemed necessary, an entry in the governor's note-book being all that was thought requisite. But towards the end of 1623, the Colony Record-book was started, and the first entry, under date December 17, marks an important development in criminal procedure. Hitherto, the few trials there were had been conducted by the whole body of the townsmen, the governor presiding and carrying out their decision. This arrangement, natural enough at first, became cumbrous at length, as the townsmen increased, leading to waste of time. The first entry in the new records marks a great step onward in the establishment of trial by jury, it being enacted and provided that 'all criminal facts, and also all matters of trespass and debt between man and man, shall be tried by the verdict of twelve honest men, to be empanelled by authority in the form of a jury upon their oath.' The following New Year's day also (March 25), a further development in the government ensued when the colony, for the third time, elected William Bradford as governor. He demurred to being chosen again, urging that the very purpose and intent of an annual election was the constant change from one to another of all posts of honour or labour. If honour there were, others should share it ; if burden, others should help to bear it. He urged also his opinion that the governor, whoever he was, ought to have associated with him a council for his assistance. Notwithstanding this protest, the townsmen re-elected him, but deferred so far to his wishes as to create a council of five, giving him a double vote at the board.

About the time of this election there arrived at Plymouth the ship Charity, bringing the last communications they were ever to receive from John Robinson, their former pastor, for whose coming to them they still continued to hope. One letter, dated Leyden, December 19, was for his 'loving and much beloved friend,' Governor Bradford, in which he expresses his regret at hearing of the killing of the Indians at Wessagusset by Standish: 'How happy a thing it had been,' says he, 'if you had converted some before you had killed any!' He exhorts them to have a care of the military spirit of Standish. He loves him right well, and is persuaded that God has given him to them in mercy and for much good, if he is used aright; but he fears there may be wanting in him 'that tenderness of the life of man (made after God's image) which is meet.'

Robinson's other letter to his 'loving and dear friend and brother,' William Brewster, deals mainly with the difficulties continually raised by some of the Merchant Adventurers in the way of the coming over of himself and the rest of the Leyden brethren. Not by all of them, for there were five or six on the board who were their warm friends; about as many more were opposed to the establishment of free worship in the colony; the remainder, the main body, he thinks are honestly minded towards them, but at the same time they 'have others (namely, the forward preachers) nearer unto them than us, and whose course, so far as there is any difference, they would rather advance than ours.' He is persuaded they are unwilling that he, above all others, should be sent over, they having ecclesiastical purposes of another sort for the colony. And as one restive jade can hinder by hanging back more than two or three can draw forward, so in this case. He knows that even while the messenger from Plymouth was present, the hostile section 'constrained the company to promise that none of the money now gathered should be expended or employed to the help of any of us toward you.' He can only say: 'Your God and ours, and the God of all His, bring us together if it be His will, and keep us in the meanwhile, and always to His glory, and make us serviceable to His Majesty, and faithful to the end.'

Robinson's surmise as to the purpose of the Adventurers to establish the Episcopal form of Church government in the colony was not without foundation. In 1623, Robert Gorges, commissioned by the Council for New England as governor-general of the whole country, took out another company of settlers to the deserted village of Weymouth, formerly known as Wessagusset. He brought with him an Episcopalian clergyman of the name of William Morrell, to whom the council had given general powers of regulation and control over the religious affairs of the country. Bradford says : ' He had I know not what power and authority of superintendency over other churches granted him, and sundry instructions for that end.' A man of good sense and tolerant temper, he soon found it was easier to confer large powers in the old country than to exercise them in the new. He spent a year at Plymouth, studying anthropology among the Indians, and accumulating observations in natural history, but remaining silent on the matter of his ecclesiastical commission till he was on the point of leaving. Only after he had gone away was it fully realised that all the time he had lived so amiably and innocently among them he was possessed of full powers authorising him to compel the Pilgrim Fathers to conform to that Church of England from which at so great a cost they had severed themselves. But though this first endeavour to set up conformity came to nothing, those of the Adventurers who were opposed to religious freedom did not abandom their intention. The emigrants who had come over in the Anne, and who kept themselves separate from the rest of the colonists as ' particulars,' formed the centre from which this new movement was to emanate. They began by sending complaints privately to London to the effect that there was much religious controversy in the colony, that family exercises on Sunday were neglected, that both sacraments were disused, and that children were not catechised, or even taught to read. So that when, in 1624, the ship Charity arrived from England, bringing cattle and other supplies, she brought also a series of inquiries on these points from the board in London, and at the same time brought John Lyford, an Episcopal clergyman of Puritan sympathies, whom the Adventurers opposed to Free Church principles had selected for the accomplishment of their purpose.

Both Edward Winslow and Robert Cushman were at the meeting of the company where he was appointed, and opposed his being sent out, but yielded at length for peace sake, thinking, as they said, that he was 'a honest and plain man, though none of the most eminent or rare.' They gained their point so far, however, that it was agreed that Lyford should have no official position in the colony until the Church at Plymouth should see fit to choose him as their pastor. He was civilly received on his arrival, housed and provided with a servant till his obsequious manner began to excite misgiving. 'When this man first came,' says Bradford, 'he saluted them with that reverence and humility as is seldom to be seen, and indeed made them ashamed, he so bowed and cringed unto them; yea, he wept and shed many tears, blessing God who had brought him to see their faces, and admiring the things they had done.' After a time he sought Church-membership with them, made a large confession of his faith, and as acknowledgment of his formerly disorderly walking, blessing God for the liberty he now possessed of enjoying the ordinances of God in purity among His people. They felt he was altogether too effusive. These shrewd Englishmen would have liked him better had he protested less. Their misgivings were confirmed as they found him often engaged in secret conference with Oldham and others of the 'particulars.' They came to know, too, that he was writing letters home to the Adventurers of defamatory sort, letters he was seen showing to his confederates, and at which they chuckled and laughed. Feeling how seriously these letters might affect the interests of the colony in England, the governor intercepted them on board the vessel in which they were to be sent out. He found, as he expected, that they contained slanders and false accusations against the original settlers; and in one of them Lyford informed the Adventurers that he and Oldham intended a reformation in church and commonwealth, and that as soon as the ship bearing his letters had sailed they would set up Episcopal worship. Without knowing that the governor was in possession of these letters, these men began to seek occasions of quarrel with the Plymouth leaders. Oldham stormed at Standish when in his capacity as captain he called upon him to take his place in order as sentinel at the fort, called him evil names, and even drew his knife. The governor, hearing the tumult, came out to quiet it, at which he stamped and raved, calling them traitors and rebels; 'but after he was clapt up awhile he came to himself,' and was let go. Eventually the party associated with Lyford and Oldham, without communicating with the rest, withdrew themselves and set up public worship apart.

The governor now felt the time had come to confront Lyford with the letters which had been intercepted, and for this purpose summoned a court of the townsmen at the fort on the hill. In the presence of all he charged Lyford and Oldham with secretly plotting to destroy the government. They indignantly denied the charge, demanding proof, upon which Lyford's letters were produced and some of them read, on which he was struck dumb. The governor explained that in his capacity as magistrate he had opened the letters, it being his first duty to prevent mischief and ruin to the colony by conspiracies and plots.

These letters contained a series of charges as to the civil management of the colony: unfair distribution and partiality; also waste of tools and vessels. But points of more serious moment related to the advice Lyford sent home to the Adventurers as to the mode of proceeding in future. He advised first of all that John Robinson and the rest of the Church at Leyden should be kept out of the colony, or all would be spoilt. Care should be exercised not only that they should not be shipped from Leyden, but also that they should not be landed privately on any part of the English coast. To prevent this, it would be well to change the captain, who was friendly to the colony. He further urged that a number of new colonists should be sent over sufficient to outnumber the present settlers; that those known as 'particulars,' though by their own arrangement having separate interests, should yet have a voice in all courts and elections, and be free to hold any office in the town; and that every 'particular,' though only a servant, should rank as an Adventurer. If by these means they cannot be strengthened to carry and overbear things, it would be best for them, he thinks, to go elsewhere, and start a plantation for themselves; he therefore asks for authority from the board to do this, if it should be found necessary. Finally he concludes by saying: 'I pray you conceal me in the discovery of these things.'[1]

In the presence of the whole body of townsmen Lyford was asked what explanation he had to give of these letters, taking the charges point by point. He had little to say except that he had heard complaints from this man and that, but possibly he had been misled.

They reminded him that when he sought admission to the Church, he declared that he no longer regarded himself as a minister, though episcopally ordained, till he received

---

[1] Bradford's *History of Plymouth Plantation*, pp. 177-181.

a call from them; yet now he contested against them, and drew a company apart, without even speaking a word to them, either as magistrates or brethren. Thus confronted, the man broke down, confessed that he feared he was a reprobate, and that his sins were so great that he doubted whether God would ever pardon them; he admitted that he had so wronged them that he could never make amends, and that he was unsavoury salt. 'All this he did with as much fullness as words and tears could express.'

The court decided that the leaders of this movement should depart the colony, Oldham to go at once, leaving his family behind, till he could make provision for them; Lyford might remain six months longer. They gave him further space, hoping he might change his course. He admitted he was leniently dealt with, and afterwards publicly confessed his sin to the Church, 'with tears more largely than before.' Upon this they began again to conceive good thoughts of him, and admitted him once more to teach among them.

In the course of a month or two, however, he was again writing secretly to the Adventurers, justifying his former letters, and complaining that there was no ordained minister in the colony, Elder Brewster being still their preacher. This also coming to the knowledge of the townsmen, they made reply to the various points urged against them, as to their having no ordained minister among them—

'We answer, the more is our wrong, that our pastor is kept from us by these men's means, and then reproach us for it when they have done. Yet have we not been wholly destitute of the means of salvation, as this man would make the world believe; for our reverend elder hath laboured diligently in dispensing the Word of God unto us, before he came, and since hath taken equal pains with himself in preaching the same. And be it spoken without ostentation, he is not inferior to Mr. Lyford (and some of his betters) either in gifts or learning, though he would never be persuaded to take higher office upon him.'

This letter of Lyford's was written towards the end of August, 1624, after which he remained at Plymouth through the following winter, living as before from the public stores, ultimately joining Oldham at Nantasket, where there were a few straggling settlers. Next year Oldham sailed into Plymouth Harbour once more; but as he came only to assail the colonists 'beyond the limits of all reason and modesty, calling them a hundred rebels and traitors, and I know not what,' there was nothing for it but to commit him till he grew more reasonable, after which, led out between two lines of musketeers, he was ignominiously expelled the colony; and so for all the purposes of this narrative he goes on his way, and we see him no more.

It will probably be said that the ejectment of Episcopalians from Plymouth colony was an inconsistent piece of intolerance on the part of men who had fled from intolerance at home. But it may fairly be replied that judgment must be forbearing towards men who feared, rightly or wrongly, that the object of the new-comers was not so much religious equality as ecclesiastical absorption. Bradford, speaking on behalf of the colonists, says that—'all the world knew they came hither to enjoy the liberty of their conscience and the free use of God's ordinances, and for that end had ventured their lives, and passed through grievous hardships.' Their past experience might well make them fearful of the introduction of the national system, at a time when Laud was beginning to be in the ascendant, and with iron will and heavy hand driving men into conformity. Was there any reason to suppose they would long retain that freedom for which they had sacrificed so much, if the Episcopal system, with the royal power to enforce it, were once introduced among them?

Using quaint illustration, William Bradford contended that it would turn out to be a modern instance of an ancient fable—the fable of the coney, who out of pity received a hedgehog into his burrow one stormy day. Once fairly lodged, the hedgehog, not content with merely sharing quarters with the original owner, by vigorous use of his prickly spines compelled the coney to vacate her burrow and leave the whole of it to him.

The breach with Lyford at Plymouth led to a breach with the Board of Merchant Adventurers at home. Returning from England in the early part of 1625, Edward Winslow brought a communication from them to the effect that only on certain conditions would they consent to continue their connection with the plantation. One of the main reasons for their change of attitude was that the Church at Plymouth had received Lyford to their fellowship, who, on his confession before them, had renounced national and diocesan churches. It was clear, they said, from this, that though they had renounced the name, practically they were Brownists still, and it would be sin against God, therefore, on their part, were they to support them. They will, however, still co-operate on these conditions, namely: that as they, the Adventurers, were partners in trade, they should also be partners in the government of the plantation; that the French or Presbyterian discipline should be adopted both in substance and detail, so that both the name of Brownist and differences resulting therefrom would be done away with; and finally, that their former pastor, John Robinson, and the remaining portion of the Church at Leyden, should not be allowed to come over and join their brethren at Plymouth, unless they should first reconcile themselves to the system which the Adventurers speak of as 'our Church,' that is, the Church of England, by written recantation signed under their own hands.

To these demands the colonists made reply that in effect they did hold and practise the discipline of the French and other Reformed Churches, as set forth in the *Harmony of the Confessions* of 1586, but that to tie themselves down to that discipline in every particular would be to give away the liberty they had in Christ Jesus. Even Paul himself would have no man follow him except as he followed Christ; and that it was too great arrogancy for any man or any Church to think that he or they have so sounded the Word of God to all its depths as to be able to set down precisely the Church's discipline without error in substance or circumstance; it would not be difficult, indeed, to show that the Reformed Churches themselves differ in many things among themselves. What they had to say as to Robinson and his friends at Leyden signing a recantation, Bradford in his History omits 'for brevity's sake,' and possibly for other reasons.

While that portion of the Adventurers to whom this reply was addressed disappear now from the history, the section still favourable to the plantation sent by Winslow a reply of their own. In this they state that the joint account has been closed, that £1400 remained due, and that the goods to meet this should be shipped as trade permitted. They go on to say they are persuaded that the reason of the withdrawal of the other Adventurers is really want of money (for need whereof men use to make many excuses), though other reasons are pretended, as that they were Brownists and the like. Still, though it might be too late to stay these things, it was not too late to exercise patience, wisdom, and conscience in bearing them. The right thing for them to do was to keep a fair and honest course, and see what time would bring forth, and how God in His providence would work for them. We are persuaded, they say, that you are the people that must make a plantation where all others fail and return. Go on, good friends, pluck up your spirits and quit yourselves like men in your difficulties, so that, in spite of all the displeasures and threats of men, the work to which you have put your hand may still go forward, a work which is so much for the glory of God and the welfare of our countrymen that it were better for a man to spend his days for that than to live the life of Methuselah in wasting the plenty of tilled land or eating the fruit of a grown tree.

In the summer of 1625 Miles Standish took a voyage to England in the interests of the colony, having with him letters in reply to those they had received. This mission was undertaken at an unfortunate time. The king had died at the end of March, his son Charles I. was giving all the weight of his influence to Laud, who was vigorously enforcing uniformity ; and London was being ravaged by the plague, the tale of death rising week by week, and trade being almost at a standstill. All that Standish could accomplish during the five months of his stay was to obtain the loan of £150 at fifty per cent. interest, wherewith to purchase goods for the colony. Returning in a fishing vessel bound for the coast of Maine, his arrival there was notified by some Indian messenger, and the shallop was sent up the coast to bring him and his goods on to Plymouth.

He had serious tidings to relate. He brought them the first news of the death of the king they had received, though by that time he had been dead more than a year ; Prince Maurice also was gone, he who had been Stadtholder of Holland during the time they were at Leyden ; their friend Robert Cushman, too, whom they looked upon as their right hand with the Adventurers, had died at the early age of forty-five ; Fletcher, another friend of theirs, had been ruined by Turkish pirates ; and many who were knit to them in bonds of Christian brotherhood both in England and Holland had died of the plague. It was indeed a changing world. But, most sorrowful of all, Standish had to tell them that all hope of their ever seeing John Robinson once more among them must now be abandoned. He had letters with him, one from Roger White, Robinson's brother-in-law, one from Thomas Blossom, a leading member of the Leyden brotherhood, and also a joint letter from the Church at Leyden, addressed to Bradford and Brewster, telling them that their former pastor had been seized with illness on Saturday, February 22, and that though he had rallied sufficiently to be able to preach twice the following day, before another Sabbath came its round he had entered into rest, departing this life on March 1, 1625. Roger White wrote pathetically that: 'If either prayers, tears, or means would have saved his life, he had not gone hence.' In like strain of sorrow Thomas Blossom's letter mourned the departure of their loved and honoured pastor, 'whom the Lord (as it were) took away even as fruit falleth before it was ripe; when neither length of days nor infirmity of body did seem to call for his end. The loss of his ministry,' he adds, 'was very great indeed unto me, for I ever counted myself happy in the enjoyment of it, notwithstanding all the crosses and losses otherwise I sustained . . . We may take up that doleful complaint in the Psalm, that there is no prophet left among us, nor any that knoweth how long. Alas! you would fain have had him with you, and he would as fain have come to you.'

The letter from the Church was signed by four of the brethren in the name of the rest. In it they say that, though 'it hath pleased the Lord to take to Himself, out of this miserable world, our dearly beloved pastor, yet for ourselves we are minded, as formerly, to come unto you when and as the Lord affordeth means. And now, brethren, what shall we say further unto you? Our desire and prayer to God is (if such were His good-will and pleasure) we might be re-united for the edifying and mutual comfort of both, which when He sees fit He will accomplish. In the meantime we commit you unto Him and to the word of His grace.'

Sorrow over Robinson's death was felt, and respect for his memory manifested beyond the bounds of their own community. Winslow tells us that—

'When God took him away from them and us by death, the University and ministers of the city accompanied him to his grave with all their accustomed solemnities; bewailing the great loss that not only that particular Church had whereof he was pastor, but some of the chief of them sadly affirmed that all the Churches of Christ sustained a loss by the death of that worthy instrument of the Gospel.'[1]

John Robinson was buried under the pavement of St. Peter's, the church near to his own house. The official record of the fact has been discovered in recent years, and is as follows, making, as usual, Dutch mistakes in recording English names. '1624, 4 March. John Roelends, Preacher of the English Community by the belfry—buried in the Peter's Church.'

Another officer, giving the receipt for his burial, enters it thus:

1625   } Open and hire for John Robens
10 March }   English Preacher—9 florins.

He died in the house already described on the Klok-steeg. In a census of the city taken October, 1622, he is registered as Jan Robberson, his wife's name being Bridget; their children were Isaac, Mercy, Fear, and James; and they have Maria Hardy as their domestic. Isaac joined the Pilgrims in New England, but Robinson's widow and the rest of his household appear to have remained at Leyden. The Church of which he was pastor continued to exist and apparently to flourish for many years after his

---

[1] *The Ground of First Planting of New England*, p. 95; London, 1646.

death. In 1644, when the Reformed Churches contributed 17,567 florins to aid their brethren in Ireland, this community sent 558 florins, a sum equal to about £200 of present value. As time went on, however, those who originally came over from England died off gradually, so that the Dutch-speaking element came eventually to be the only one left; and in 1658, as Hoornbeek tells us, the Church united itself with the Reformed Church of Holland. After a period of more than two centuries, the interest in Robinson's memory was revived by the discovery of Scrooby as the starting-point of the Pilgrim Church; and on July 24, 1891, a bronze memorial tablet, fixed in a recess of the exterior of St Peter's Church at Leyden, was unveiled under the auspices of the National Council of Congregational Churches of the United States. The ceremony took place in the presence of delegates from England and America, the burgomaster, and the representatives of the Ecclesiastical Commissioners of the city and of the University of Leyden.

About the time that Brewster received at Plymouth the tidings of the death of his former friend and pastor, his own wife was called away from his side, at the age of fifty-six. Troubles, therefore, still gathered round him, the clouds returning after the rain. Yet it is often at such times that God is nearest to His own, and Bradford, in his brave, godly way, tells us that 'the Lord, whose work they had in hand, so helped them that now when they were at the lowest they began to rise again; and being stripped in a manner of all human helps and hopes, He brought things about otherwise in His divine providence as that they were not only helped and sustained, but their proceedings were both honoured and imitated by others, as by the sequel will more appear.'

As these words imply, from this time onward the outlook of life grew wider for the colonists. Their agriculture prospered, for the produce of their Indian corn growing beyond their own requirements, they found they could get ready sale for the surplus at six shillings the bushel; they therefore used great diligence in planting the same. They felt also that, in order to meet their liabilities in England, it was necessary to establish in addition a more general trade with their neighbours. It having been agreed that no one colonist should trade on his own behalf separately, this matter was left in the hands of the governor and some others, to be managed for the general good of the colony. The difficulty felt at the outset was as to where goods could be procured for the purpose of this more general trade. Fortunately, the opportunity presented itself when it was most needed. A trading post established at Monhegan by merchants from the English Plymouth was about to be broken up, and the remainder of the stock offered for sale. Hearing of this, Governor Bradford and Edward Winslow went over, and acquired half the property, to the value of £400. About that time, also, a French ship, having a cargo of Biscay rugs and other commodities on board, was wrecked at Sagadahoc; these goods also, through some Bristol merchants, they acquired, paying for the most part in beaver fur and other barter obtained during the previous season; for the rest, their note of hand was accepted, to fall due the following year.

Having in this way become better furnished for trade, and with their corn after harvest, they were now able to meet their various engagements against time, get clothing for their people, and have some commodities beforehand. One serious difficulty in the way of their carrying on anything like an extensive trade lay in the fact that they possessed only one small open boat, which was dangerous for long voyages, especially in the winter season. The ship-carpenter was dead, but fortunately the house-carpenter was a man of resource, and at their request resolved to try what he could do. Taking one of the largest shallops, he lengthened her five or six feet, strengthened her with timbers, built her up, and laid a deck upon her, and so fitted her with sails and anchors that she did them good service for seven long years, and so enabled them to build up a trade on the Kennebec.

Still, while their trade was growing, they felt hampered by their engagements with the Merchant Adventurers and by the restrictions placed upon them in the matter of their friends and brethren at Leyden, who were anxious to come to them, and whose company they desired to have. The governor and some of their chief friends, therefore, had serious consideration, and 'resolved to run a high course, and of great adventure.' The plan they proposed was to hire the trade of the company for a certain term of years, and during that time to pay off the £1800 due from the plantation to the London Adventurers, and also their trading debts, amounting to some £600 more. For purposes of negotiation on this and other matters, Isaac Allerton was sent over to England in 1626, and returned the following year 'at the usual season of the coming of ships.' He had been able to obtain a loan of £200 for the colony at thirty per cent. interest, with which he purchased trading goods, 'which goods they got safely home and well conditioned, much to the comfort and content of the plantation.'

With regard to the main matters of his commission, he had, 'with much ado and no small trouble,' and by 'the help of sundry of their faithful friends there, who also took much pains thereabout,' come to an arrangement by which the company in London surrendered all claim to stock, shares, land, merchandise and chattels, in consideration of the sum of £1800 of lawful money of England, to be paid 'at the place appointed for the receipt of money on the west side of the Royal Exchange in London,' £200 to be paid yearly, and every year, on the Feast of St. Michael, the first payment to be made in the year 1628. This agreement made by Allerton on their behalf was very well liked and approved of by the plantation, and consented to. As the colony was not a chartered corporation, the responsibility must, of course, be personal, and was jointly borne by Bradford, Brewster, Standish, Allerton, Winslow, Howland, Alden, and Prince, and a deed duly drawn up, signed and sealed to that effect, was taken over to England by Allerton the following season. These brethren, who, as the bondsmen of the colony, engaged with the Adventurers on the one side to pay off the public debt, engaged also with the colonists themselves on the other side to do so within six years, and further would import every year £50 worth of hose and shoes, to be sold to the colonists in exchange for corn at six shillings per bushel, on the understanding that the entire trade of the colony with the outside world should be carried on by themselves alone; that each purchaser among the colonists should pay to them, year by year for the six years, three bushels of corn or six pounds of tobacco, as might be preferred; and that they, having undertaken these responsibilities, should have and freely enjoy the boats with their equipment, and also the whole stock of furs, fells, beads, corn, hatchets, and knives now in the stores. At the end of the said term of six years the whole of the trade was to return to the use and benefit of the colony as before. The men who undertook these responsibilities were afterwards known as the 'Undertakers.' In this way the property in the colony passed from the Adventurers to the colonists, and for a period of six years from the colonists to the Undertakers.

This fundamental change in the direction of independence brought about other changes of wide-reaching economical effect. First of all, the responsibility incurred by the eight securities was divided over the whole community, by the payments in corn and tobacco to be made year by year, and also by the arrangement that if the trade profits were not sufficient to meet the yearly payments in London, the deficiency should be made up in equal proportions by all the settlers who were described as purchasers and were to be enrolled as such. In return for this liability, the land being divided into shares of twenty acres each, every purchaser should have one share, in addition to the land he already possessed, the heads of households to have as many shares, and therefore as many liabilities, as they had persons in their families. By this arrangement the more recent comers, such of the 'particulars' as still remained, and others in the colony not so described, who yet had arrived later than those who came in the Mayflower, would be on equal footing with the rest. In pursuance of this arrangement, strips of land along the river-side, five acres by four, were marked out for tillage and assigned by lot. The meadow land, however, was not to be divided in perpetuity, but held in common, except that every season, for the purpose of hay for his cattle, each purchaser had assigned to him a certain portion which he was at liberty to mow.

This was the carrying out of a plan to which Bradford and Brewster had probably been accustomed in the old Austerfield and Scrooby days. Those who have scientifically investigated the rural economy of Britain seem to have established the fact that, throughout the whole period from pre-Roman to modern times, two parallel systems have obtained undisturbed by all invasions—Roman, English and Norman—that of the *village* community, on the eastern side of Britain, and that of the *tribal* community, in the western districts of the island, neither of which seems to have been introduced later, at any rate, than two thousand years ago.[1] Each system was marked by the two notes of

[1] *The English Village Community.* By Frederick Seebohm, p. 437. 1883.

community and equality; but the tribal system, belonging to an earlier stage, was pastoral rather than agricultural, whereas in the case of the village community only a small proportion of the land of the township was in meadow or pasture, each occupier having certain defined rights of common thereon. These commons were divided as Green Commons and Lammas Meadows; to the former the cows of the township were daily driven, the latter were subject to temporary occupancy by individuals on a regular system for the one purpose of haymaking.[1] This ancient system, going back in Britain farther than the historic period, seems to have been the plan carried out by the Plymouth colonists as soon as they were free to act. Side by side with this arrangement as to the land, there was a quaint method of distributing the few cattle which, as yet, were all they possessed. These were too few and too precious to be the sole property of individuals, and were therefore assigned to small partnerships. For it was not till 1624 that they had any horned cattle, and the following year the four they had were only increased to nine. In 1627 there appear to have been twelve cows, which were divided at a town meeting. There being one hundred and fifty-six persons at this time in the colony, namely, fifty-seven men, thirty-four boys, twenty-nine matrons and thirty-six girls—servants and indentured persons not being reckoned—there were therefore thirteen persons to each cow, these to have the use of her for ten years, after which she was to be restored to the common stock, with half her increase, if increase there were. In case of abuse or neglect, all the thirteen were to be held responsible. The cattle, like the land, were assigned by lot, and to each of the divisions, except the fourth, was granted in addition a pair of she-goats. Equality of possession, however, could not long be maintained here

[1] *The English Village Community.* By Frederick Seebohm, pp. 11. 13. 1883.

any more than elsewhere, for the next year we find that Miles Standish, probably with the view of removing to Duxbury, had bought out the other partners in his division, and therefore for the remainder of the ten years had the cow to himself.

The whole of this arrangement is most methodically laid down in the records, and the names of all the one hundred and fifty-six shareholders, men, women and children, carefully given, so that we are able pretty definitely to see how the colony actually stood at the end of the seven years dating from the landing of the Mayflower in 1620. Taking all those who had at various times come to the colony, and adding to their number those who had been born there, they came altogether to two hundred and sixty-seven. Of these fifty-eight had died, and fifty-three had removed elsewhere, leaving, as we have seen, one hundred and fifty-six still remaining. It is ominously significant of the fearful hardships of the first year when we find that, while only six died during the remaining six years, no fewer than fifty-two died that year.

It so happens that in 1627 we have not only the means of measuring the growth of the colony from within, but have also testimony from without as to its general appearance at the end of the first seven years of its history. It will be remembered that in 1620 negotiations were being carried on between the Dutch merchants and the Pilgrims then in Leyden with a view to settlement together on the Hudson River. Three years later a permanent Dutch colony was established at Manhattan, the modern New York, but no further communication took place between this plantation and that at Plymouth for several years. In March, 1627, however, Bradford, in his capacity as governor, received a friendly letter from Isaac de Rassières, the secretary of the colony at Manhattan, addressed to the 'noble, worshipful, wise and prudent lords, the Governor

AT THE END OF SEVEN YEARS.

and Councillors of Nieu Pliemŭen, wishing their welfare in Christ Jesus our Lord.' 'It is their manner,' says Bradford, 'to be full of complementall titles.' In this letter, they had often wished, they say, to congratulate their friends at Plymouth on their prosperous undertakings as colonists ; the more so that they themselves also had made good beginning to pitch the foundation of a colony where they were ; and seeing also that, their native countries lying not far apart from each other, their ancestors centuries ago had held friendship and alliance both for war and traffic, as might be read in old chronicles by all the world. And now they on their part are willing to renew this intercourse, and to carry on trade with them as neighbours which may be of mutual service. If they, too, are agreeable to this, some one shall be deputed to deal with them at such time and place as they may appoint.

This letter was acknowledged on the part of the Plymouth people with friendly civility, except that they modestly demurred to 'the over-high titles more than belongs to us or is meet for us to receive' with which the letter was addressed ; they reciprocate the good feeling expressed by these neighbours of theirs, and cannot forget, they say, the hospitable reception given to them at Leyden in days gone by ; having lived there many years with freedom and good content, as many of their friends did still ; for which they and their children will ever be grateful to the Dutch nation. They further express their readiness to trade with them in commodities or merchandise as desired, and they trust that this offer of theirs may work out to good and fruitful result in days to come. This reply of the Plymouth people being written in Dutch, they pray to be excused for their rude and imperfect writing in that language, seeing that, for want of use, they cannot so well express themselves as they would desire. This correspondence in the spring of 1627 was followed in the autumn by a visit from the Dutch secretary, who came in state, making solemn entry heralded by trumpeters, and attended by some of the pageantry dear to the hearts of his countrymen. He remained several days, spent a Sunday with them, attending their religious services, and finally departed, having established trading communication between New Plymouth and New Amsterdam which continued for several years.

Some time after, De Rassières returned to Holland, where he wrote to Herr Blommaert, a director of his company, an account of his visit to the Plymouth plantation. This letter, as lately as 1847, found its way to the Royal Library in Holland, and has since been printed,[1] giving an interesting description of the colony as seen by a contemporary at the end of the first seven years of its history.

After describing the bay as lying to the north of Cape Cod, the point of which can be easily seen in clear weather; the sandbank of Plymouth Beach, twenty paces broad, over which the sea breaks violently with an easterly and northeasterly wind; the small island of Saguish, and the river of fresh water, rapid but shallow, on the south side of the town, flowing down to the sea from inland lakes above, he then describes the town itself.

'New Plymouth,' he tells us, 'lies on the slope of a hill, stretching east toward the sea-coast, with a broad street about a cannon-shot of eight hundred feet long leading down the hill, with a crossing in the middle, northward to the rivulet and southward to the land.' One may stop by the way here to point out that the street is nearly twelve hundred feet long, and that De Rassières has unwittingly reversed the bearings of rivulet and land. He goes on to say that 'the houses are constructed of hewn planks, with gardens also enclosed behind and at the sides with hewn

[1] New York *Historical Collections*, New Series, vol. ii.; also in the Appendix to *New England's Memorial*, p. 495.

planks, so that their houses and courtyards are arranged in very good order, with a stockade against a sudden attack; and at the ends of the streets there are three wooden gates. In the centre, on the cross street, stands the governor's house, before which is a square enclosure upon which four small cannon are mounted, so as to flank along the streets.'

He next proceeds to describe the fort on the Burial Hill, which played so important a part both in their civil and ecclesiastical life.

• 'Upon the hill they have a large square house with a flat roof, made of thick sawn planks stayed with oak beams, upon the top of which they have six cannon, which shoot iron balls of four and five pounds and command the surrounding country. The lower part they use for their church, where they preach on Sundays and the usual holidays. They assemble by beat of drum, each with his musket or firelock, in front of the captain's door; they have their cloaks on, and place themselves in order, three abreast, and are led by a sergeant without beat of drum. Behind comes the governor in a long robe; beside him, on the right hand, comes the preacher with his cloak on, and on the left hand the captain with his side-arms and cloak on, and with a small cane in his hand; and so they march in good order, and each sets his arms down near him. Thus they are constantly on their guard, night and day.'

Possibly, in honour of the visit of the Dutch secretary, there may have been on that particular Sunday more formality and state than usual as the Pilgrims went up for the worship of God to their Mount Zion on Burial Hill. Be that as it may, that worship of theirs was in spirit and truth, and was associated, as all worship ought to be, with righteousness and integrity in daily life. De Rassières, speaking of the Indians, is candid enough to say—and to the honour of the Pilgrim Fathers let it be said—'The tribes in their neighbourhood have all the same customs as ours, only they are better conducted than ours, because the English give them the example of better ordinances and a better life ; and who also, to a certain degree, give them laws by means of the respect they from the first have established among them.'

X.

ARRIVAL OF NEW NEIGHBOURS.

IN that same year of grace, 1627, in which De Rassières paid his visit to the Plymouth plantation, 'some friends being together in Lincolnshire fell into discourse about New England and the planting of the Gospel there.' So wrote Thomas Dudley in 1631 to the Lady Bridget, Countess of Lincoln, giving the story of the beginnings of that second Puritan exodus to New England, out of which came the settlements round Massachusetts Bay. Thus Lincolnshire has the honour of being connected with the beginning of both movements, the one which, starting at Gainsborough, resulted in the formation of Plymouth Colony, and that which, taking its rise in the friendly discourse referred to, issued in the creation of the settlements in Massachusetts.

So far as permanent results are concerned this second movement was even more important than the first. In romance of circumstance and the charm of personal heroism the story of the Pilgrim Fathers is pre-eminent. They were the pioneers who made it easy for the rest of the host to follow. But it was not so much what they achieved as what they suggested that gives them the place of honour in the history of their country. If the second Puritan exodus, which lasted over the twelve years between 1628 and 1640, had not followed, that of 1620, at its slow rate of increase, would not have been sufficient to create a power strong enough to overcome the combined influence of Indians, Dutchmen, and Frenchmen, and make the English language and the English tradition paramount on North American soil. The second movement, out of which came the settlements round Massachusetts Bay and along the valley of the Connecticut river, has been justly described as the greatest effort at colonisation which Englishmen had yet made since the projects of Raleigh and Gilbert entered the national mind. For the men who made it were not a mere band of traders bent simply on money-making, but a worthily representative body of citizens animated with the desire of reproducing in the New World what was best in the life of the Old. Some of them came from stately homes and were possessed of wealth and social position, while others had occupied influential positions as ministers of the Church. Before the movement had spent itself, something like ninety university men, three-fourths of them from Cambridge, had emigrated to New England. It is impossible to exaggerate the importance of this fact in its bearing on the future of American life.[1]

It has frequently been noted that the eastern side of England was ever foremost in the matter of Protestant Reformation. As it was in the sixteenth century under the Tudors, so was it in the seventeenth century under the Stuarts. While all the forty counties of England were more or less represented among the emigrants to Massachusetts, the shires on the eastern side contributed far more than all the rest. It is estimated that two-thirds of the American people came from these, one-sixth from Devon, Dorset, and Somerset, and the remaining one-sixth from all other parts of England. It is, therefore, not by accident that Boston in Lincolnshire gave its name to the chief city of New England, and that the earliest counties of Massachusetts were called Norfolk, Suffolk, and Essex. An

---

[1] Doyle's *English in America*, i. 135. *The Influence of the English Universities in the Development of New England*. By Franklin B. Dexter. 1880.

American writer has noted the fact that the native of Connecticut and Massachusetts who wanders in the rural England of to-day finds no part of it so homelike as the homesteads, villages, and quaint market towns he passes as he fares forward in not too straight a line, sayıfrom Ipswich to the Humber or the Trent. The farmhouses with their long sloping roofs and gable end towards the road, their spacious chimneys and narrow casements, also the names over the shop-doors or on the tombstones in the neighbouring churchyards, all remind him of what he has left behind in his home across the sea.[1]

But while Suffolk in the southern portion of eastern England made an important contribution to the Puritanism of America when it sent John Winthrop from Groton Manor-house, Lincolnshire made the most important contribution of all when it sent the men of mark who met in those days for conference in Boston town, or Sempringham Manor-house, or Tattershall Castle—the last two places being the seats of Theophilus Clinton, the fourth Earl of Lincoln. Cotton Mather speaks of 'the religious family of the Earl of Lincoln—the best family of any nobleman then in England.' A staunch Protestant, Lord Lincoln when only twenty-four received permission from the king to raise a troop of horse to join Count Mansfeld in the service of the Elector of Bohemia, and was himself colonel in one of the six regiments engaged. He was not less strenuous as an advocate of constitutional right. In 1627 he was sent to the Tower for refusing to subscribe to the general forced loan resorted to by Charles I. and for actively dissuading his neighbours from subscribing; and later on we find him trying to gain access to Sir John Eliot when he too was sent to the Tower for the constitutional part he took in the struggle of the time. Joined with the earl in his refusal to subscribe to the king's loan were Atherton

[1] *The Beginnings of New England.* By John Fiske. 1889.

Hough, Thomas Dudley, and Thomas Leverett—three men prominent among those who afterwards went to New England.

Tattershall Castle, a stately mansion built by the Lord Treasurer Cromwell in the time of Henry VIII., and the other family seat of Lord Lincoln at Sempringham, became identified with the Puritan movement with which we are now concerned. Roger Williams speaks of riding with John Cotton 'and one other of precious memory, Master Hooper, to and from Sempringham,' Williams saying, as he rode along, why he could not use the Book of Common Prayer as Cotton did, and Cotton defending himself by saying that he 'selected the good and best prayers in his use of that book, as Sarpi did in his using of the Masse-book.' To Tattershall Castle, too, John Cotton used to retire as to a second home when broken down in health under the heavy strain of his ministerial life at Boston Church. And though the earl himself did not go over to New England, two of his sisters did, Susan, who was married to John Humphrey, and Arbella, the wife of Isaac Johnson. Thomas Dudley also, Lord Lincoln's steward and confidential adviser, and Simon Bradstreet, who succeeded him in that office, were associated with the movement, as were also Richard Bellingham, the Recorder of Boston, Thomas Leverett, an alderman of the borough, and Atherton Hough, the mayor of the town in 1628, all of whom, as we have seen, followed his lordship's lead in resistance to the forced loan.

In the matter of religion Lincolnshire had long been strenuous in its resistance to the ceremonies imposed upon the Puritan clergy. In the reports of proceedings in the Ecclesiastical Courts, preserved in the old Alnwick Tower at Lincoln, we find the father of Simon Bradstreet, the Puritan minister of Horbling, again and again before the court for nonconformity, and flatly telling them at last that

conformed he had not, and conform he would not. And
so left Lincolnshire for Middleburgh and the Puritan community there. Dr. John Burgess also, the rector of another
church in the county, was deprived in 1604 for preaching
against ceremonies, 'which were not worth a man's life or
livelihood ;' and at the end of that same year the Lincolnshire ministers presented King James with a long and
elaborate defence of their godly brethren, who were being
suspended and deprived for refusing subscription and
conformity to the rites and ceremonies enjoined by law.
They did not hesitate to tell the king that 'the greatest
number of resident preachers and fruitful ministers do dislike them and have seldom used them for many years past.'
Many years after this again Sir John Lambe, Dean of
Arches, spoke of 'the Puritan town of Boston,' and in
1621 the Government thought it worth while to send down
a commission to make serious inquiry as to who had cut
off the crosses at the top of the maces 'carried before
the mayor to the church on Sundays and Thursdays and
solemn times.' It was thought to be a piece of Puritan
hostility to what some regarded as a mere Popish symbol,
but the town-clerk said that John Cotton, the vicar, in his
hearing, 'did condemn the doing of the said fact.' One
also, who was afterwards among the New England men,
'Atherton Houghe, gentleman, one of the churchwardens
of the town of Boston, being examined, saith that he
neither did cut off the top of the crosses from the maces
nor doth know who did it . . . . But he confesseth he
did before . . . . that year break off the hand and arm
of the picture of a pope (as it seemeth) standing over a
pillar of the outside of the steeple very high, which hand
had the form of a church in it; which he did as he
thought by warrant of the injunctions made primo of
Queen Elizabeth, willing all images to be taken out of
the walls of churches: and for that he heard that some

of the town had taken note of such pictures as were in the outside of the church.'[1]

Following these records we thus come into the circle of those friends who, in the year 1627, 'being together in Lincolnshire fell into discourse about New England and the planting of the Gospel there.' The times were growingly serious. The storm of civil war had not yet burst over the nation, but ominous signs of its coming were beginning to darken the face of the sky. Within a few months Parliament placed foremost among the nation's grievances Laud's oppressive treatment of the Puritan party in the Church. In an address to the king they speak of the general fear existing among the people of some secret working and combination to bring about 'a change of our holy religion more precious unto us than our lives and whatever this world can afford.' It is well known, they say, that to side with Laud is the surest way to preferment in the Church; that the books and opinions of that party are suffered to be printed and published while those in defence of the orthodox religion are hindered and prohibited under colour of the king's proclamation. Their fears are increased by the fact that means have been sought out to depress and discountenance pious, painful and orthodox preachers, *how conformable soever*, and peaceable in their disposition and carriage they may be. These, instead of being encouraged, are molested with vexatious courses and pursuits, and are hardly permitted to lecture, even in those places where there are no constant preaching ministers.

This address of the Commons to the king throws light on the distinctive character of the men who composed the Puritan exodus which began in 1628, the year of the Petition of Right, and ended for the most part in 1640 when the Long Parliament came into power. These were not Separatists by conviction as were the Pilgrim Fathers who

[1] *State Papers*, Dom.

went over in 1620; but, while Puritans in doctrine, were conformable Churchmen and loyal in their attachment to the Church of England. They themselves were anxious to emphasise this fact. The 'Planter's Plea,' published in 1630 by one actively concerned in the movement, disavows in the strongest terms the suspicion which had gone abroad that 'under colour of planting a colony they intended to raise and erect a seminary of faction and separation.' The writer urges all men 'to forbear that base and unchristian course of traducing innocent persons under these odious names of Separatists and enemies to the Church and State.' There can be no manner of doubt that the spirit of this 'Plea' was that which from the first animated those settlers who went out under the auspices of the Massachusetts Bay Company. Francis Higginson went out in 1629, and, when the vessel in which he sailed was off the Land's End, he called his family, with some of the other passengers round him, to take the last farewell look of the land they were leaving and which they loved so well. Standing there, and looking eastward till the coast-line faded out of sight, he said: 'We will not say, as the Separatists were wont to say at their leaving of England, " Farewell Babylon, farewell Rome;" but we will say, " Farewell dear England, farewell the Church of God in England, and all the Christian friends there!" *We do not go to New England as Separatists* from the Church of England, though we cannot but separate from the corruptions in it; but we go to practise the positive part of Church reformation, and propagate the Gospel in America.' John Winthrop also, and the company who sailed with him in 1630, when on board the Arbella, sent from Yarmouth a 'Humble request to the rest of their brethren in and of the Church of England for the obtaining of their prayers,' and desiring to be thought of by them 'as those who esteem it our honour to call the Church of England from whence we rise, our dear Mother; and cannot part from our native country where she especially resideth, without much sadness of heart and many tears in our eyes, ever acknowledging that such hope and part as we have obtained in the common salvation we have received in her bosom, and sucked it from her breasts. We leave it not, therefore, as loathing that milk wherewith we were nourished there; but, blessing God for the parentage and education as members of the same body, shall always rejoice in her good and unfeignedly grieve for any sorrow that shall ever betide her.'

The Lincolnshire men who, in 1627, 'fell into discourse about New England,' did not let the matter end in discourse, but proceeded to decisive action. As a preliminary step they entered into correspondence with men whom they knew to be of like mind with themselves both in London and the West. Those in the West were chiefly in the neighbourhood of Dorchester, from which town a private company of merchants had from 1623 onwards sent out fishing vessels year by year to the coast near Kennebec, and had landed fourteen men at Cape Ann to establish a permanent station for the benefit of their vessels. After a three years' trial this settlement was abandoned and the partnership dissolved. John White, the Puritan rector of Dorchester, saw in the failure of the one enterprise the opportunity of starting another of a more important kind. The first project of a Commonwealth of Massachusetts is said to have been started by him, and it is possible that some letters of his led to that conversation in Lincolnshire to which reference has been made. The Dorchester Company being dissolved and their settlement at Cape Ann broken up, some of the settlers removed fifteen miles to the south-west to the Indian village of Naumkeag, now better known under the name of Salem. Some of the merchants were still of opinion that something might be done with this place if the men who had gone there were reinforced and cattle sent over to them. The matter taking this new shape came to be discussed afresh both in London and the West, and there were some who offered to furnish funds if fitting men could be found to engage their persons in the voyage. In the course of inquiry they made the acquaintance of John Endicott, a man well known to divers persons of good note, who manifested much willingness to accept of the offer as soon as it was tendered,' and who was destined to play an important part in the future history of the enterprise. Little is known of his antecedents except that he was a native of Dorchester, born there in 1588, was a man of strong Puritan convictions, and had attended the preaching of Samuel Skelton, one of the ministers who afterwards went out in 1629. A leader thus being available a patent was obtained from the Council of New England, March 19, 1628, by which the Council 'bargained and sold unto some knights and gentlemen about Dorchester, namely, Sir Henry Roswell, Sir John Young, knights, Thomas Southcoat, John Humphrey, John Endicott and Simon Whetcomb, gentlemen, that part of New England lying between the Merrimac river and the Charles river on the Massachusetts Bay.' The preliminary expedition being ready, on the 20th of June, thirteen days after Charles I. had assented to the famous Petition of Right, Endicott sailed from Weymouth in the Abigail, Henry Gauden master, arriving at Naumkeag on the 6th of September following. He had with him Charles Gott, Richard Brackenbury, Richard Davenport, and some others destined for active service in the future, and was entrusted by the company at home with full powers to act in their name till they themselves, as they intended, should follow.

So far as weather was concerned their voyage was prosperous, but unfortunately their provisions having been preserved in unwholesome salt, sickness began to prevail among the passengers. Reaching land in disabled condition, and being but imperfectly housed on their arrival, these emigrants, like those who went out to Plymouth nine years before, began to die off one after another. Endicott in his distress sent over to Plymouth to Governor Bradford for help, having heard that Samuel Fuller, a deacon of the Church and a physician, had 'cured divers by letting blood and other means.' Fuller was at once sent to the rescue, and his kindly work among the sick brought about a close friendship between the people of Plymouth and the new-comers to Naumkeag—a friendship which resulted in a nearer agreement on the question of the government of the Church. Endicott's conversations with Fuller led to the removal from his mind of certain false impressions as to what separation really meant. Writing to Governor Bradford on May 11, 1629, he says: 'I acknowledge myself much bound to you for your kind love and care in sending Mr. Fuller among us, and rejoice much that I am by him satisfied touching your judgments of the outward form of God's worship. It is, as far as I can gather, no other than is warranted by the evidence of truth, and the same which I have professed and maintained ever since the Lord in mercy revealed Himself unto me; being far from the common report that hath been spread of you touching that particular.' Endicott was bent on closer relations still, seeking Christian alliance which was to have important ecclesiastical results in the future of Massachusetts. In the earlier part of the same letter he says to Bradford: 'It is a thing not usual, that servants to one Master and of the same household should be strangers. I assure you I desire it not, nay, to speak more plainly, I cannot be so to you. God's people are all marked with one and the same mark, and sealed with one and the same seal, and have for the main, one and the same heart, guided by one and the same

Spirit of truth; and where this is there can be no discord, nay, here must needs be sweet harmony. And the same request (with you) I make unto the Lord that we may, as Christian brethren, be united by a heavenly and unfeigned love; bending all our hearts and forces in furthering a work beyond our strength, with reverence and fear, fastening our eyes always on Him that only is able to direct and prosper all our ways.'

While feelings of brotherhood were thus springing up between Endicott's advance party at Salem and the Plymouth Plantation, the movement in favour of further Puritan emigration to New England was daily growing stronger at home. Endicott sent back a good account of his voyage and of his first impressions of the country to which he had come, and as a consequence more adventurers were disposed to join in the undertaking. Men of competent estate, feeling that they had no special employment at home and might be serviceable in planting a colony abroad, came forward to help on the movement. Others of their acquaintance, seeing men such as these of good estate joining in the enterprise, were induced to join also. Among the men of social standing thus attracted to this undertaking were John Winthrop, of Groton, in Suffolk; Isaac Johnson, of Clipsham, in the county of Rutland, who had married Lady Arbella, the sister of the Earl of Lincoln; John Humphrey, of the county of Kent, who had married another sister; Matthew Cradock, a wealthy London merchant, who became one of the largest contributors, and in after years a member of the Long Parliament; Thomas Goffe, also of London; and Sir Richard Saltonstall, of Halifax, nephew of another Sir Richard, who was Lord Mayor of London in 1597.

These men bought of the first comers all their right and interest on Massachusetts Bay acquired under the deed of March 19, 1628, and being desirous to be something more than a mere private trading company, sought for their venture the authority of the Crown, so as to make good their title, patents having from time to time been granted in the most careless and contradictory fashion. An important step forward was taken when, on March 4, 1629, a royal charter was obtained constituting the company a legal corporation under the title of the 'Governor and Company of the Massachusetts Bay in New England.' The corporation thus formed were to elect annually a governor, deputy-governor, and eighteen assistants, who were to hold monthly meetings, and in addition general meetings four times a year. Matthew Cradock was elected as governor, and one of the first things done after his election was to create a second government to be resident in the colony itself, consisting of a governor, deputy-governor, and twelve councillors, three of these to be chosen by the planters whom Endicott found in the colony when he arrived. The government thus constituted was to be free from control on the part of the Company at home, both in the matter of legislation and the appointment of officers, as though its founders had already in view the coming change when the Company should no longer exist as a separate corporation, but should be merged in the legislature of the colony itself. The ordinance by which it was created provided that 'they shall have full power and authority, and are hereby authorised by power derived from His Majesty's Letters Patent to make, order, and establish all manner of wholesome and reasonable orders, laws, statutes, ordinances, directions, and instructions not contrary to the laws of the realm of England ; a copy of which orders from time to time shall be sent to the Company in England.' Land was to be allotted, so that each shareholder should have two hundred acres for every £50 he invested. If he himself went over and settled in the colony, in addition to investing his money, he was to have fifty acres more for himself and fifty for each member of his family. Emigrants who were not shareholders were to have an allotment of fifty acres, and fifty additional for each servant exported; the governor and council to have power to grant more to such emigrants 'according to their charge and quality.'

Holding the question of the religious life to be of primary importance, the Company did not overlook provision for the spiritual needs of the new settlement in their arrangements. In a letter to Endicott, April 17, 1629, acknowledging one from him sent over the previous September, they say: 'For that the propagation of the Gospel is a thing we do profess above all to be our aim in settling this plantation, we have been careful to make plentiful provision of godly ministers, by whose faithful preaching, godly conversation, and exemplary life we trust not only those of our own nation will be built up in the knowledge of God, but also the Indians may in God's appointed time be reduced to the obedience of the Gospel of Christ.' The three ministers first sent out were Samuel Skelton, a Lincolnshire minister, who was chosen because the Company had learnt that John Endicott had formerly received much good from his ministry; Francis Higginson, of Leicester; and Francis Bright, of Rayleigh, in Essex. The Company, in sending out these men, gave charge to Endicott to accommodate them with necessaries, to build houses for them as soon as convenient, 'and because their doctrine will hardly be well esteemed whose persons are not reverenced, we desire that both by your own example and by commanding all others to do the like, our ministers may receive due honour.'

All that is known of Skelton, beyond his former connection with Endicott, is that he was of Clare Hall, Cambridge, where he graduated in 1611. Of Francis Higginson we first hear at a meeting of the Company, held March 23, 1629, when letters were read from Isaac

Johnson describing him as an able man, as one 'approved for a reverend grave minister, fit for our present occasions,' and as willing to go to the plantation. On this John Humphrey was requested to ride down to Leicester at once, and if he found that Higginson could be ready to go in the vessels about to start, and if his removal should be consented to by the best affected of the people there, and with the approbation of Mr. Hildersham, of Ashby-de-la-Zouch, he was then and there to make arrangements with him.

These conditions being met, Higginson prepared to sail from Gravesend on the 25th of April. He was the son of the vicar of Claybrook, in Leicestershire, where he was born in 1587, and where after graduating at Jesus College, Cambridge, in 1610, he was associated with his father as curate. Eventually, however, he left Claybrook to become the vicar of one of the five parish churches of Leicester. Here, about the year 1627, he made a decided stand for purity of fellowship by refusing to allow immoral persons to come to the Lord's Table. His Puritan proclivities soon made him a marked man with the Laudian party, and being removed from his living for not conforming to the ecclesiastical requirements imposed, the people of the town maintained him by one of those lectureships in the Church which were the special creation of the Puritan feeling of the time. It was while he was thus engaged that John Humphrey rode down to Leicester and had that conference with him which ended in his consent to go to New England at the request of the Company. His removal was felt to be a grievous loss by the godly people of the town. In after years his son John mentioned in a sermon that before leaving England his father gave 'some account of his grounds in a great assembly of many thousands at Leicester;' and that when he and his family set out for London, the streets were filled with people who with prayers and tears bade them farewell. The reasons for his going he gave to the great assembly referred to were that he approved of the patent of the Company, which granted to the people the right to choose their own rulers, and to admit into freedom such as they should think meet, and further, because religion was the principal end aimed at in the establishment of the plantation. A pamphlet of the time, entitled *General Considerations for the Plantation of New England*,[1] is said to be from his pen. If so, it is evident he thought the prospects of religious freedom at home to be but dark and gloomy, and that it was the part of a wise man to seek for shelter before the storm should burst. The Protestants of Bohemia, he thought, might serve as a warning, who sat still at home till the Palgrave was defeated, the fires of persecution kindled, and the Catholic religion thrust by force into the Palatinate. They ought not to forget either that only last October the Huguenots in Rochelle were reduced by famine and siege, and their local privileges cancelled. Experiences like these might well teach men to avoid the plague while it was foreseen, and not wait till it was making havoc among them. Even if the attempt to escape had miscarried, it would not have been so disastrous as that backsliding and abjuring the truth into which the Protestants of Bohemia and their posterity were plunged. With these views Francis Higginson decided to leave his fatherland and sail for the West.

Five vessels were to take out him and the party sailing with him—the Talbot, a good and strong ship of 300 tons, carrying above a hundred planters and provisions for a twelvemonth; the George, another strong ship of 300 tons, also carrying fifty-two planters and provisions; the Lion's Whelp, a 'neat and nimble ship of 120 tons,' carrying many mariners and above forty planters specially from the town

[1] Reprinted in *Young's Chronicles* (Massachusetts), pp. 271-278.

of Dorchester and the neighbourhood; the Four Sisters, of 300 tons, carrying more passengers with cattle and provisions; and, finally, the world-renowned Mayflower, which had thus the honour of being concerned in the foundation of the settlement of Massachusetts Bay as well as of that of the Plymouth plantation. The Governor and Company, in sending out this expedition, were much more generous in its equipment than were the Merchant Adventurers with the settlers at Plymouth. Large supplies of clothing were sent out, including 200 suits, doublets, and hose of leather; 100 suits of northern 'dussens' or Hampshire kerseys lined, the hose with skins, the doublets with linen of Guildford or 'Gedlyman' serges; 300 plain falling bands such as had taken the place of the great ruffs of Elizabeth's time; 100 waistcoats of green cotton bound about with red tape; 100 Monmouth capes and 100 leather girdles, besides hooks and eyes for 'mandilions,' these being garments large and full of folds, with which ''gainst cold in night did soldiers use to wrap.' Besides these quaint and picturesque 17th century garments, there were provisions on board sufficient for the voyage, and seeds and cereals for use when they reached the other side, not forgetting rundlets of Spanish wine, and casks of Malaga and Canary. Then besides horses and cattle, fishing-nets and fowling-pieces, there were equipments of military sort in case of need—drums, ensigns, partisans and halberds, swords and belts, corselets, pikes and half-pikes, bastard muskets with snaphances without rests, and full muskets with matchcocks and rests; they also provided land ordnance for the five forts, including culverins, demi-culverins, sakers and iron drakes, with stores of powder and shot.

As men were even of more importance than material, those who were skilled in the making of pitch and salt, and in planting vines, were enlisted in the service, William Sherman having been allowed fourteen days to fetch his

ARRIVAL OF NEW NEIGHBOURS. 281

vines from Northampton; men also skilled in working iron, and a surgeon and barber-surgeon were sent out along with Thomas Graves of Gravesend, who appears to have been a kind of universal genius, professing himself skilled and experienced in the discovery and finding out of mines of all sorts, iron, lead, copper, and mineral salt; in making fortifications; in surveying buildings, measuring lands and describing a country by map. No wonder the Company specially charged Endicott to take advice of this man, who had travelled in divers foreign parts, as to where it would be best to settle down, fortify and build a town.

With these artificers and skilled men of various grades the Company send over, they say, many religious, discreet, and well-ordered persons to be set over the rest, dividing them into families, placing some with the ministers, and others under such honest men as shall see them well educated in their general callings as Christians, and according to their several trades. They prudently remark that where so many are being sent out, there may be, in spite of all their care, some libertines among them; if there are, let them be corrected, and should they prove incorrigible, let them be shipped back again in the Lion's Whelp when she returns, for it is better to do that than to keep them in the colony as a source of infection and an occasion of scandal. 'Above all,' they add, 'we pray you be careful that there be none in our precincts permitted to do any injury in the least kind to the heathen people; and if any offend in that way let them receive due correction.' Should any of the Indians claim right of inheritance in any part of the lands granted in the patents, 'we pray you endeavour to purchase their title, that we may avoid the least scruple of intrusion.' Further, 'to the end the Sabbath may be celebrated in a religious manner, we appoint that all that inhabit the plantation both for the general and particular employments may surcease their labour every Saturday throughout the year at three of the clock in the afternoon ; and that they spend the rest of that day in catechism and preparations for the Sabbath as the ministers shall direct.' Finally, they inform Endicott that they have agreed with Lambert Wilson, the chirurgeon, that he is to remain in the service of the plantation for three years, during which time he is not only to be at the service of the planters themselves, but also of the Indians, as from time to time he shall be directed by the governor. He is also to educate and instruct in his art one or more youths fit to learn his profession and succeed him—one of these to be the son of Francis Higginson the minister, if his father approve thereof, the rather because having been educated at the Leicester Grammar School he hath been trained in literature.

This general letter of April 17, 1629, was sent over along with the Company's patent under the broad seal, and also the Company's own seal in silver, which had engraved upon it the figure of an Indian with the legend inscribed : 'Come over and help us.' This letter was further supplemented by one written at Gravesend four days later, while the vessels waited there, in which the Company charge the settlers that special care be taken that family prayer be observed morning and evening, and a watchful eye be held over all in each family, and so disorders may be prevented and ill weeds nipped before they take too great a head. It is well to begin well and let punishment follow infractions of law, otherwise government will be looked upon as no better than a scarecrow. Their desire is for lenity all that may be ; but if necessity arise then the other thing is not to be neglected, knowing that correction is ordained for a fool's back. Finally, 'we heartily pray you that all be kept to labour as the only means to reduce them to civil, yea, a godly life, and to keep youth from falling into many enormities which by nature we are all too much inclined to.

God, who alone is able and powerful, enable you to this great work, and grant that our chiefest aim may be His honour and glory. Thus wishing you all happy and prosperous success we end and rest.'

Thus equipped and thus instructed those who went out in 1629 set forth, the George about the middle of April, the Talbot and Lion's Whelp hoisting sail at Gravesend on the morning of the 25th; and the Four Sisters and the Mayflower following three weeks later. Francis Higginson, who sailed in the Talbot, kept a journal, in which he describes the usual experiences, sights and scenes of an Atlantic voyage. They had, he says, a pious and Christianlike passage, having a company of religious, honest, and kind seamen. The shipmaster and his men used every night to set their eight and twelve o'clock watches with singing a psalm and 'prayer that was not read out of a book.' They constantly served God, too, morning and evening, by reading and expounding a chapter, singing and prayer. The Sabbath also was solemnly kept by preaching twice and catechising; and in times of great need 'two solemn fasts were observed with gracious effect.' Instruction as well as delight they received in beholding the wonders of the Lord in the deep waters, sometimes seeing the sea round them appearing with a terrible countenance, as it were full of high hills and deep valleys, and sometimes as a most plain and even meadow. Gazing on all the ocean sights and scenes new to a landsman, he exclaims: 'Those that love their own chimney corner, and dare not go beyond their own town's end, shall never have the honour to see these wonderful works of Almighty God!'

Writing back in September to old friends in Leicester who were purposing to come out and join the settlement, he advises them as to what they ought to bring for the voyage and for use in the colony. It will be wise for them to look ahead, 'for when you are once parted with England you shall meet neither with taverns nor alehouse, nor butchers', nor grocers', nor apothecaries' shops to help what things you need in the midst of the great ocean, nor when you are come to land; here are yet neither markets nor fairs to buy what you want.'

On arriving at Salem, the name now given to Naumkeag, the three ministers entered at once into conference with Endicott and the rest of the godly people as to the ecclesiastical future of the colony, explaining that for themselves they desired to see a Reformed Congregation. They then learnt what had already taken place as the result of Samuel Fuller's visit and influence, and how the people had seen their way to the adoption of those church principles in operation in the Plymouth plantation. Both Higginson and Skelton seem to have agreed with the course already taken, while Francis Bright dissented, and, being unwilling to work with them, removed to Charlestown. Three weeks after they had landed, a solemn day of fasting and prayer was set apart for the choice of a pastor and teacher. Some time having been spent in prayer, certain questions were then propounded to Higginson and Skelton as to their views of a minister's calling. They replied that they held that calling to be twofold—first the inward, or God's calling, by which the man was endowed with the necessary gifts and his heart moved to desire the work; next the outward call which comes from God's people, when a company of believers are joined together in covenant to walk together in the ways of God, and when the men thus gathered have a free voice in the choice of their officers. These views being regarded as satisfactory, the brethren proceeded to election in the freest possible manner, except that the voting was confined to the men. Each duly qualified member wrote on a slip of paper the name of the man whom the Lord moved him to think to be fit for a pastor, and in like manner whom he would have for

ARRIVAL OF NEW NEIGHBOURS. 285

teacher. The votes being counted, it was found that Skelton was chosen as pastor and Higginson as teacher, the difference between the two being explained when John Eliot tells us that 'Mr. Skelton being farther advanced in years was constituted as pastor of Salem Church, Mr. Higginson the teacher.' The difference in office was thus mainly a question of seniority. Among the abuses charged against the Puritans during Bishop Neile's primary visitation of the diocese of Lincoln in 1614 was that precedence was given to ministers in preaching and at table according to age rather than university degree—'after the German fashion the elder minister is held more worthy.' The two ministers having signified their acceptance of the choice thus made of them, they were then commended to God in prayer in the following manner : 'first, Mr. Higginson, with three or four of the gravest members of the church, laid their hands on Mr. Skelton, using prayer therewith. This being done, there was imposition of hands on Mr. Higginson also.' Charles Gott, who came over to Salem with Endicott in 1628, wrote to Governor Bradford an account of these proceedings, which took place on the 20th of July, concluding his letter by saying : 'And now, good sir, I hope that you and the rest of God's people (who are acquainted with the ways of God) with you, will say that here was a right foundation laid, and that these blessed servants of the Lord came in at the door and not at the window.'

The service thus described seems like a re-ordination of men already ordained ; but the probability is that it was not so regarded by the men themselves. The following year a similar service was held in the case of Mr. Wilson, who was chosen as the minister of Charlestown, and concerning which Winthrop writes : 'We used imposition of hands, but with this protestation by all, that it was only as a sign of election and confirmation, not of any intent that Mr. Wilson should renounce his ministry he received in

England.'[1] Morton, in his *Memorial*, speaks as if the ordination of Higginson and Skelton took place on the 6th of August, not on the 20th of July, and that Governor Bradford and some others from Plymouth who intended to be present, 'coming by sea were hindered by cross winds that they could not be there at the beginning of the day; but they came into the assembly afterward, and gave them the right hand of fellowship, wishing all prosperity and all blessedness to such good beginnings.' It is probable, however, that Gott's account is the more accurate of the two, and that, as he tells us, the 6th of August was appointed for another day of humiliation for the choice of *elders and deacons* and ordaining of them; and when the two ministers gave their assent publicly to the Confession and Covenant which they themselves had drawn up beforehand.

This 6th of August being observed as a day of fasting and prayer, there were sermons and prayers by both ministers, and towards the end of the day the Confession and Covenant were solemnly read and assented to. It was clearly stated at the time, however, that these were only acknowledged as a direction pointing unto that faith and covenant contained in the Scriptures, and therefore no man was held to be bound by the mere form of words, but only to the substance, end, and scope of the matter contained therein. Mather, in his *Magnalia* (I., 18), gives us this covenant made at Salem, in which they covenant with the Lord and one another to walk together in all His ways so far as He reveals Himself to them in His Word, and this through the power and grace of our Lord Jesus Christ, avouching the Lord to be our God, and ourselves to be His people in the truth and simplicity of our spirits; to give themselves to the Lord Jesus Christ to be governed by Him, resolving to cleave unto Him alone for life and

---

[1] Winthrop's *History of New England*, 1630-1649. Edited by James Savage, 2 vols. Boston, 1853.

glory, and to reject all contrary ways, canons, and constitutions of men in His worship; to walk with their brethren in all brotherliness, avoiding jealousy, suspicion, and censure ; to avoid all occasions of dishonouring Christ in the church ; to study the advancement of the Gospel in all truth and peace, not slighting sister churches, but taking counsel of them as need shall be ; to carry themselves in all lawful obedience to those that are over them in church and commonwealth; to approve themselves to the Lord in their worldly callings, shunning idleness as the bane of any State, and not to deal hardly or oppressively with any ; and, finally, promising to the best of their ability to teach their children and servants the knowledge of God and of His will that they may serve Him also. This covenant thus accepted that day, and afterwards renewed on special occasions from time to time, became the basis of church fellowship, some being admitted into the church by expressing their assent thereto, others by answering questions publicly propounded, or by presenting the substance thereof in writing, or by giving their religious experience and conviction in their own way.

The step thus taken was however not taken unanimously, as after events showed. Francis Bright, one of the three ministers sent out, withdrew, and went to Charlestown ; and two members of the Council, John and Samuel Browne, 'men of estates and men of parts and port in the place,' openly expressed their dissatisfaction that the ministers did not use the Book of Common Prayer, did not administer the ordinances of Baptism and the Lord's Supper with the ceremonies usually observed in England, and had expressed their intention of denying admission to the Lord's Table of scandalous persons. Proceeding from protest to action, they gathered a company for worship separate from the public assembly, conducting the service according to the order of the Book of Common Prayer. Endicott, as

Governor, seeing that disturbance was growing out of this, summoned the two brothers before him. In the course of their examination they charged the two ministers with departing from the orders of the Church of England, and with being Separatists, who would soon become Anabaptists. Skelton and Higginson made answer that they were neither Separatists nor Anabaptists, that they were not separating from the Church of England, or from the ordinances of God therein, but only from the corruptions and disorders which had sprung up in that Church in recent years. They had come away from their native land, they said, after suffering much on behalf of their convictions, that they might get away from the Prayer Book and the ceremonies, and being now in a place where they could have their liberty, they neither could nor would use them, judging as they did that the imposition of these things was a sinful corruption of the worship of God. Having duly weighed this answer, the governor and council and the generality of the people did well approve thereof, and finding John and Samuel Browne very resolute in a course tending, as they believed, to mutiny and faction, they plainly told them that New England was no place for them; and, acting upon this conviction, shipped them back to England the same year, the two brothers breathing out threatenings as they went.

The course thus pursued by Endicott and the council in this case, and the similar proceedings taken at Plymouth in reference to Lyford and Oldham, as well as by Governor Winthrop in later years, have again and again been condemned as intolerant, and as grossly inconsistent on the part of men who had themselves fled from intolerance at home. But as so impartial an historian as Professor Gardiner has pointed out,[1] their own religious liberty would have been in danger if a population had grown up around

[1] *History of England*, vol. vii. 156.

them ready to offer a helping hand to any repressive measures adopted against them by the Government at home. As he truly says, the objection to toleration on the part of the men of New England was not merely intellectual. The question as it presented itself to them at that particular time was not whether they were to tolerate others, but whether they were to give to others the opportunity of being intolerant to themselves. The cases, therefore, are not parallel between a strong government harrying out of the land a little community of conscientious men, far too weak to be dangerous, and that little community fighting as for dear life to guard the liberty which has cost them so much, and which might easily be taken from them again.

On the surface of the narrative it seems strangely inconsistent that the men who went out to New England with Endicott in 1628, with Skelton and Higginson in 1629, and, if we may anticipate for a moment, with Winthrop in 1630, while expressing themselves with such ardent affection towards the Church of England, and such dislike of Separatism as they did when they left the old country, should so soon have made the fundamental changes in church life we find they did. The explanation is not to be found altogether from their having come into the near neighbourhood and under the influence of the Separatists of Plymouth Plantation. John Cotton, who went out in 1634, speaking of the church at Salem as organised under Endicott, Skelton, and Higginson, writes thus: 'How far they of Salem take up any practice from Plymouth I do not know. Sure I am that Mr. Skelton was studious of that way before he left Lincolnshire.' He adds that those who really knew the spirit of these men 'would easily discern that they were not such as would be leavened by vicinity of neighbours, but by the divinity of the truth of God shining forth from the Word.' The real explanation lies deeper. First, it must be noticed that the men themselves never admitted or supposed that, in making the changes they did, they ceased to be Church of England men. In a brotherly explanation they gave to friends at home, they granted that on going into exile they began to search and try their ways, and came to see that some things which in the beginning of their ministry they had regarded as matters of indifference, or had practised without serious thought, when weighed in the balances of the sanctuary had not sufficient warrant in the Word of God to justify them in establishing them under new conditions in a new country. It must also be remembered that the whole question of episcopal government had not at that time taken the definite position in the Church of England which it has since assumed. The most prominent bishops and divines of the early part of Elizabeth's reign were in close sympathy and friendly intercourse with the Swiss Reformers, and it is well known that under the influence of Cartwright great numbers of the clergy were in favour of a Presbyterian form of church government, and even proceeded to set up that system openly in the parish churches of Northamptonshire and Warwickshire. Even while practising Presbyterianism, they none the less claimed to belong to the National Church. Till the time of Laud himself the doctrine of the divine right of episcopacy was a comparative novelty, received by a minority only even among Churchmen themselves. It was first broached by Bancroft, in his sermon at Paul's Cross in 1588, was even by him suggested rather than asserted, and that rather as an anti-Puritan polemic to the claim to divine right which was being made for Presbyterianism than as expressing the matured and solid conviction of the main body of Churchmen. When Lord Burleigh referred Bancroft's statement to Dr. Hammond, then chancellor of the diocese of London, for his opinion, in a letter still in existence, he replied that the authority of bishops was derived solely from the statute passed in the twenty-fifth year of the reign of Henry VIII., and recited in the first year of Elizabeth's reign ; that it was not reasonable on their part to make any other claim ; and that 'if it had pleased Her Majesty with the wisdom of the realm to have used no bishops at all, we could not have complained justly of any defect in our Church.'[1] Long years after this when Laud himself, in his exercise for the degree of B.D. at Oxford, took up the position that 'there could be no true Church without diocesan bishops,' Heylin tells us that he was 'shrewdly rattled' by Dr. Holland, the Regius Professor of Divinity, 'as one that did cast a bone of discord betwixt the Church of England and the Reformed Churches beyond the seas ;' and his thesis was denounced as 'a novel Popish position.' Dr. Washburn, an American episcopal clergyman of our own day, who would naturally regret the setting aside of episcopacy in the early New England churches, yet candidly admits that 'there was not one leading divine from Hooper to Hooker who ever claimed more than historic and primitive usage as the ground of episcopal authority, or pretended that it was of the essence of a Church. . . . Not only so, no notion of an exclusive episcopacy, even to later times, when Bancroft and Laud had naturalised it, gained footing as a Church principle.'[2]

As with the question of episcopal government so with the use of the Prayer Book, the wearing of the surplice and the practice of various ceremonies ; they contended that these were still open questions and that the views they held on these points were more in accordance with the principles of the Reformation than were those of their opponents ; that in fact they were the true representatives

[1] *Hatfield MSS.*, Nov. 4, 1588, No. 754.
[2] *Epochs in Church History.* By Dr. E. A. Washburn, p. 120.

of the National Church of England. It must be noted further that they had adopted two principles in relation to church life which carried them further in the direction of Separatism than they themselves were aware of. In reply to their brethren in England they contended that Christian character was indispensable to church life. Francis Higginson, as we have seen, even in Leicester days had made a stand for purity of fellowship, and refused to allow immoral persons to come to the Lord's Table; and in New England they acknowledged that their practice differed from that of the Reformed Churches in that 'we receive to our churches only visible saints and believers; in common with many good men we desire all separation of the precious from the vile. This day hath discovered what kind of people are to be found everywhere in the parishes of England. Can light and darkness, Christ and Belial agree together? Popish and Episcopal enemies cleave together in our church of Christ with the saints of God.'

The second principle which carried them further in the direction of Separatism than they realised grew out of the first; it was that of 'giving discipline as well as other ordinances to particular churches, not subjecting them to any government out of themselves, but only to take the brotherly counsel and help of one another.' 'If,' said they, 'the Church be pure and have such officers as the New Testament requires, we need not fear to betrust the Church with that power which we conceive Christ hath given to the same, other churches watching over them and counselling them in the Lord. The reforming the material of a church and the recalling of the power of government to the church tends much to further the work of reformation, and in no way hinders the same.'

Thus while they protested they were not Separatists, but heart and soul true Church of England men, they had adopted the two main foundation principles on which

Separatism was based, viz. that to be true members of a Christian Church men must be Christians, and if they are Christians they are illuminated by the Spirit of God, and therefore capable of self-government. The difference between the men of Salem and the men of Plymouth lay in this, that the former retained the State-church principle in spirit, the latter did not. When Francis Higginson was desired to draw up a Confession of Faith, seeing that the wilderness in which they were might be looked upon as a place of liberty and they might in time be troubled with erroneous spirits, 'therefore they did put in one article into the Confession of Faith on purpose about the duty and power of the magistrate in matters of religion.' This principle once adopted was in after years extended. John Cotton contended for a scriptural theocracy. To secure the best legislation they deemed it right to limit the political franchise to men of consistent religious character, united in church fellowship. Church-membership was made the essential pre-requisite to citizenship, and the formation of churches came under the direct supervision of the civic authority. Discipline was no doubt for the most part observed in the Christian society without external interference, but when the censures of the Church were disregarded, the State stepped in and imposed the penalty of political disfranchisement, fine or imprisonment. In this way came about the troubles and intolerance of a later time.

But during the period between 1629 and 1634 this was not foreseen, and the men who acted with Endicott, Skelton and Higginson contended that the course they took was the only course possible to them. It had become impossible for them to remain at home. 'Was it not a time when human worship and human inventions were grown to such an intolerable height that the consciences of God's saints, enlightened by the truth, could no longer bear them? Was not the power of the tyrannical prelates so great that, like a strong current, it carried all down stream before it? Did not the hearts of men generally fail them? Might we not say, "This is not our resting place?". We might, no doubt, have remained at home and found a way to have filled the prisons, but whether we were called to that when there was an open door of liberty placed before us we leave to be considered. The Lord Himself knew the motives which animated us in going abroad. He that seeth in secret and rewardeth openly knew what prayers and tears had been poured out to God, by many alone, and in days of fasting and prayer, by God's servants together for His counsel, direction and blessing in this work. Many longings and pantings of heart had there been in many after the Lord Jesus to see His goings in the sanctuary; and this liberty of New England we have looked upon and thankfully received from God as the fruit of these prayers and desires.'

XI.

MASSACHUSETTS BAY AND CONNECTICUT VALLEY.

ALREADY two bands of settlers had gone out to Massachusetts in 1628 and 1629; a still larger expedition was to follow in 1630. But there was an important preliminary question to be settled. Those who composed the Massachusetts Bay Company were not content that it should be a mere trading adventure, having its headquarters in London, and liable at any time to be interfered with by the Crown. The vision of a Free State across the sea invested with the prerogatives of self-government rose before them as a possibility to be realised. But how to realise it without arousing the ever-watchful jealousy of Laud and the king was the difficulty which at once presented itself. This difficulty was met by the adoption of a resolution which, on the face of it, appeared innocent enough, but which meant more than appeared. At a general court of the Company, held July 28, 1629, the governor, Matthew Cradock, suggested that for the purpose of inducing persons of worth and quality to transplant themselves and their families to the new settlement, and for other weighty reasons not mentioned but perfectly well understood, it was expedient to 'transfer the government of the plantation to those that shall inhabit, and not to continue the same in subordination to the Company here as now it is.' This important matter was, after due debate, left till the next meeting to each man's private consideration, the strictest secrecy to be observed meanwhile. Before that next meeting, however, Sir Richard Saltonstall, John Winthrop,

Thomas Dudley, Isaac Johnson, and eight other governors met privately at Cambridge and bound themselves by written agreement, 'on the word of a Christian and in the presence of God, who is the searcher of all hearts,' that they would be ready by the 1st of March to embark themselves and their families for the plantation, provided that by the end of September the whole government of the plantation's patent be by order of the court legally transferred and established to remain with those who shall inhabit the plantation. This was on the 26th of August, and three days later, at a formal court of governors, the provision thus laid down was agreed to by general consent and an order to that effect drawn up. The practical result of this order was to place the entire control of affairs in the hands of the ten members of the Company, who were themselves going out to the colony, and therefore interested in its future.

As Cradock was not going out, it was necessary under this arrangement to choose as governor some one who was. Therefore, at a court held on the 20th of October, 'having received extraordinary great commendations of Mr. John Winthrop both for his integrity and sufficiency,' he was, 'with a general vote and full consent of this court, by erection of hands, chosen to be governor for the ensuing year, to begin on the present day.' The election thus made speedily justified the expectations formed of it, and was repeated no fewer than eleven times in the after-history of the colony. Governor Winthrop is one of the great names in American history, taking its place in their temple of fame side by side with that of Washington himself. Descended of an ancient and honourable family in Suffolk, he was born at Groton Manor-house, near Sudbury, in 1588. Trained to the law, a member of the Inner Temple, and subsequently one of the attorneys of the Court of Wards and Liveries, he was at the same time a typical example of the grave and earnest country gentleman of Puritan times. Sorrowful experience of life had in his case chastened to a deeper seriousness a nature early inclined to serious thought, for when only twenty-eight he was for the second time left a widower with six motherless children. His third marriage with Margaret Tyndal, in 1618, brought into his home the brightness and charm of sweet Puritan womanhood at a time when his spirit had become too sombre for so young a man. Early in life, when only ten years old, he had, he says, some notions of God, prayed to Him in danger, and 'found manifest answer;' at twelve 'began to have some more savour of religion, and thought he had more understanding in divinity than many of his years;' and at eighteen, under the ministry of Ezekiel Culverwell, the Word came home to him with power, he having found only light before. Now came he 'to some peace and comfort in God and in His ways; loved a Christian and the very ground he trod upon; honoured a faithful minister in his heart and could have kissed his feet; had an insatiable thirst after the Word of God, and could not miss a good sermon though many miles off, especially of such as did search deep into the conscience.' As his character matured his cheerfulness increased : 'Now could my soul close with Christ and rest there with sweet content, so ravished with His love as that I desired nothing nor feared anything, but was filled with joy unspeakable and glorious, and with a spirit of adoption could now cry "My Father" with more confidence.' When riding along the country roads to London 'it pleased God that I now made great use of my time both in praying, singing, and meditating with good intention and much comfort; my meditation being often as to how the Spirit of God reveals the love of God to us and causeth us to love Him again ; how He unites all the faithful in deed and in affection ; how He opens our understanding in the mysteries of the Gospel and makes us believe and obey. I found great sweetness therein, it shortened my way and lightened all such troubles and difficulties as I was wont to meet with.'

As the times grew more and more ominous and men were sent to the Tower or the Fleet for resisting an unconstitutional loan, or were harassed in the High Commission Court for refusing conformity to what they deemed superstitious worship, Winthrop began to fear for his country and to think of leaving it. In a letter to his wife in the spring of 1629 he says: 'The Lord hath admonished, threatened, corrected and astonished us, yet we grow worse and worse. He hath smitten all the other churches before our eyes, and hath made them to drink of the bitter cup of tribulation even unto death. We saw this and humbled not ourselves to turn from our evil ways . . . . I am verily persuaded God will bring some heavy affliction upon this land and that speedily. Yet He will not forsake us; though He correct us with the rods of men, yet if He take not His mercy and loving-kindness from us we shall be safe. He only is all-sufficient; if we have Him we have all things.' Further, for economic reasons, he was of opinion that emigration had become a necessity. Even in those days men were talking of surplus population in England. Winthrop writes: 'This land grows weary of her inhabitants, so as man who is most precious of all creatures is here more vile and base than the earth we tread upon, and of less price among us than a horse or a sheep . . . . We use the authority of law to hinder the increase of the people as by urging a statute against cottages and inmates; and thus it is come to pass that children, servants, and neighbours, especially if they be poor, are counted the greatest burdens, which, if things were right, would be the chiefest earthly blessings. The whole earth is the Lord's garden and He hath given it to the sons of men . . . . why then should we stand striving here for places of habitation and in the meantime suffer a whole continent, as fruitful and convenient for the use of man, to lie waste without any improvement?'

It may easily be supposed there were not wanting zealous friends anxious to retain men like John Winthrop at home. His neighbour, Robert Ryece, the Suffolk antiquary, pleaded that 'the Church and Commonwealth here at home hath more need of your best ability in these dangerous times than any remote plantation.' He suggested that nothing was easier than to be misled by fancy-drawn pictures of foreign lands. 'The pipe goeth sweet till the bird be in the net,' and his neighbour who is in the forties should remember that 'plantations are for young men that can endure all pains and hunger.'[1] These pleadings, written August 12, 1629, came too late, for, under date July 28, John Winthrop has the following entry: 'My brother Downing and myself, riding into Lincolnshire by Ely, my horse fell under me in a bog in the fens, so as I was almost to the waist in water; but the Lord preserved me from further danger—blessed be His name.' This ride into Lincolnshire meant that he had been to Sempringham or Tattershall Castle in earnest conference with Isaac Johnson, John Humphrey, Thomas Dudley and others of the Boston men, about the New England scheme. On the 26th August he was one of the twelve who signed the solemn agreement entered into at Cambridge; and, on the 20th October, he was, as we have seen, chosen as the first governor to be resident in the colony.

On March 23, 1630, Winthrop and his associates sailed from Southampton in four vessels; the Arbella, the Jewel, the Ambrose and the Talbot; two others preceded them in February and March, while ten others, including the Mayflower among them, followed in May and June.

[1] *Life and Letters of John Winthrop.* By Robert C. Winthrop. Boston, 1864.

Touching at Yarmouth, in the Isle of Wight, on the 7th of April they issued a document entitled 'The humble request of his majesty's loyal subjects' to the rest of their Brethren in and of the Church of England 'for the obtaining of their prayers,' promising in return, 'so far as God shall enable us, to give Him no rest on your behalfs, wishing our heads and hearts may be fountains of tears for your everlasting welfare when we shall be in our poor cottages in the wilderness.' Leaving Yarmouth on the 8th of April, and passing the Scilly Isles on the 11th, they reached land on the American side on the 12th of June. The following winter Thomas Dudley wrote to the Countess of Lincoln an account of their voyage and of what they saw when they landed. He can only do it rudely, he says, 'having yet no table, nor other room to write in, than by the fireside, upon my knee, in this sharp winter.' Writing in this colonial fashion he tells her that seventeen vessels had arrived safe in New England, and that the four in which Winthrop and his companions had sailed had made a long, troublesome and costly voyage, being all wind-bound at starting and hindered by contrary winds after they set sail, being scattered with mists and tempests so that few of them arrived together. They had scarcely lost sight of the English coast when they descried from the mast-head eight sail astern of them. They had been warned before leaving Yarmouth that ten French vessels were waiting for them, these surely were they! Preparations were at once made for action; Lady Arbella and the other women and children were removed to the lower deck to be out of danger, gun-room and gun-deck were cleared, hammocks taken down, ordnance loaded, powder-chests and fireworks made ready, every man was armed and written down for his quarter; 'and for an experiment our captain shot a ball of wildfire fastened to an arrow out of a crossbow, which burnt in the water a good time. All things being thus fitted we went to prayer upon the upper deck. It was much to see how cheerful and comfortable all the company appeared; not a woman or child that showed fear, though all did apprehend the danger to have been great. Our trust was in the Lord of Hosts and the courage of our captain who tacked about and stood to meet them.' It was a false alarm; the suspected enemies turned out to be friends: 'so when we drew near, every ship (as they met) saluted each other; and so (God be praised) our fear and danger was turned into mirth and friendly entertainment.'[1] The rest of their adventures were for the most part such as are usually met with on an Atlantic voyage; on the seventieth day out land was seen, on the seventy-second day 'there came a smell of the shore, like the smell of a garden,' and on the seventy-sixth day, by Saturday the 12th of June, the Arbella came to anchor a little within the islands. The Pilgrim Fathers landed in the depth of winter, these their successors in the height of summer, and 'most of our people went on shore upon the land of Cape Ann which lay very near us and gathered store of fine strawberries.'

Winthrop, on landing at Salem, at once assumed office as governor of the colony. It was a position of grave responsibility, for something like a thousand persons were added to its population about the time of his arrival, and a second thousand came shortly afterwards, so that before long there were from two to three thousand people with a governor and legislature of their own, engaged in erecting towns and villages and preparing the way for the great republic that was to be. Moreover it was a time of sore discouragement when the new governor entered upon his office. 'We found the colony,' says Dudley, 'in a sad and unexpected condition, above eighty of them being dead the winter before, and many of those alive being weak and

[1] Winthrop's *History of New England*, i. 6, 7.

sick, all the corn and bread amongst them all hardly sufficient to feed them a fortnight.' The new comers therefore had from the first to feed the settlers out of their stores as well as themselves. Winthrop came to be looked upon as the Joseph unto whom the whole of the people repaired when their corn failed them; and the story was told in after years how that, six months after his arrival, as he was in the act of giving out to a poor man the last handful of meal in the barrel, a ship with stores arrived at the harbour's mouth. A hundred and eighty bond-servants also, who had been brought out by Endicott at a cost of from £16 to £20 each, had to be set at liberty for the simple reason that food could not be found for them.

Like other colonists since their time, Winthrop and his companions found, on their arrival, that the reports which had reached them at home had been too highly coloured. Dudley speaks of the 'too large commendations of the country and the commodities thereof.' He says also: 'Salem, when we landed, pleased us not;' since this was the case, further explorations were made about the bay, with the result that the people planted themselves dispersedly, some at Charlestown on the north side of the Charles river, others at Boston on the south side; others again at Medford, Watertown, Roxbury and Dorchester. Winthrop himself settled first of all at Charlestown, but presently his new timber-house was transferred across the river to Boston, which, in a kind of informal way, became from that time the capital. Within a year of their arrival there were no fewer than eight separate settlements dotted along the shores of the bay from Salem to Dorchester, Watertown, five miles up the river from Charlestown, being the farthest settlement.

During that year heavy sorrows befell the little community. Winthrop's own son, Henry, was accidentally drowned at Salem, and under date September 30th the governor has this sorrowful entry: 'About two in the morning Mr. Isaac Johnson died; his wife, the Lady Arbella, of the house of Lincoln, being dead about one month before. He was a holy man and wise and died in sweet peace, leaving some part of his substance to the colony.' Of Lady Arbella, Cotton Mather quaintly says that she left an earthly paradise to encounter the sorrows of a wilderness for the entertainments of a pure worship in the house of God; and then left that wilderness for paradise, taking New England on her way to heaven. Earlier also in the same month Francis Higginson, to their great grief, was taken from them, and also William Gager, 'a right godly man, a skilful chirurgeon, and one of the deacons of the congregation.' Dudley estimated that of those who came over no fewer than two hundred passed away between April and December. Some also returned home, but the rest remained brave and undaunted. Winthrop, writing to his wife, piously says: 'The Lord is pleased still to humble us; yet He mixes so many mercies with His corrections, as we are persuaded He will not cast us off, but in His due time will do us good, according to the measure of our afflictions. He stays but till He hath purged our corruptions, healed the hardness and error of our hearts and stripped us of our vain confidence in this arm of flesh, that He may have us rely wholly upon Himself. . . . We may not look at great things here. It is enough that we shall have heaven, though we should pass through hell to it. We here enjoy God and Jesus Christ. Is not this enough? I do not repent my coming; and if I were to come again, I would not have altered my course, though I had foreseen all these afflictions.'

As the plantation grew to be a state, and various towns arose, the problem of government for a scattered community came to be dealt with. The legislature at first was, as we have seen, that of the general court of the Massachusetts

Bay Company transferred to New England. The first movement was in the direction of an oligarchical government. For in October, 1630, the legislative rights were transferred from the court of the freemen to the governor, deputy-governor and assistants, and at the same time the election of the governor was handed over from the freemen to the assistants.[1] This tendency to centralisation was checked, as it has been again and again in our history by the pecuniary needs of government. In the month of August, 1630, the authorities learnt from recent vessels coming from London and Amsterdam, that the French were making preparations of hostile kind against the colony. It was resolved, therefore, to erect frontier fortifications at Newtown, to pay for which a tax of £60 was assessed upon each of the various settlements by order of the governor and his assistants. When the levy came to be made at Watertown, the freemen there objected on the old substantial constitutional ground that Englishmen cannot be rightfully taxed, except with their own consent, and they maintained that the power to tax and to make laws is properly vested in the whole body of freemen. These men of Watertown seem not to have been unreasonably stubborn, for on being summoned to Boston and admonished, they withdrew their opposition. Still their protest was the manifestation of the independent spirit which in the next century brought about the Revolution, and even at the time was not without important results. For the following year the powers of government were more formally defined, and it was enacted by a general court that the whole body of freemen should elect the governor, deputy-governor, and assistants. There was also an extension of self-government in the arrangement that every town should send two representatives to advise the governor and assistants on the question of taxation. These changes following upon the

[1] *Records*, i. 79.

Watertown protest may have been merely a coincidence, but were more probably a consequence.

During 1633, no further change in the government seems to have been made; but in 1634 the freemen in each town elected three representatives, who, twenty-four in number, presented themselves at the general court, demanded to see the patent, and maintained that by that instrument the power of making laws was vested in the whole body of freemen. The governor, on the other hand, pleaded that those who framed the patent had never contemplated so large a body of freemen, and that the colony did not possess the necessary materials for a house of deputies. This conference was not in vain. Before the court broke up the representatives of the freemen had obtained full powers of election and legislation; and henceforth there were to be four courts a year, at one of which the whole body of freemen were to elect the officers of their little commonwealth; and at the other three the representatives of the various towns were to legislate, make grants of land, and transact other necessary public business.

About the same time another question arose, which, in miniature, was not unlike that which arises as to the respective powers of the Lords and Commons in the English Parliament. The relations between the governor and assistants on the one hand, and the deputies from the various towns on the other, and also the distribution of power between them, had remained undefined. At first they all sat in one chamber and deliberated together; but in 1634 the two bodies came into conflict upon a project voted upon, on which it appeared that of the deputies twenty to five were in its favour, while it was negatived by the assistants, of whom only two besides the governor supported it. Then arose, of necessity, the question as to the legislative powers of the two bodies, and as to whether the consent of both was necessary to a valid enactment.

The question was, however, set at rest the following year for a while by the assistants giving way to the views of the deputies.

While freedom was slowly broadening down in one direction it was being seriously narrowed in another. A law was enacted disastrous alike both to religion and politics, the consequences of which were felt for many years to come. With the view of securing Christian government in the state, it was decided no man should be a freeman of the colony unless he were a member of some church. Then after church-membership was thus made a necessary qualification for voting at town meetings, an Act was passed granting to the towns the right of dividing their lands, electing constables and surveyors, and of enforcing their orders by a fine of twenty shillings. So that non-church members were practically disfranchised, and yet absolute control of their secular interests was handed over to men whose one qualification was that they happened to be in church fellowship. Here was the problem of state and church in its acutest form—on the one hand offering unworthy inducements to a religious profession, and on the other creating an element of bitterness and discontent in the colony. Non-members of churches were not excluded from the territory, or relieved of the oath of allegiance or freed from civic duty, but their citizenship was unjustly maimed and incomplete. It is not difficult to forecast the result of such an arrangement.

Still, states as well as men have to learn by their mistakes, and in spite of mistakes the Massachusetts Company steadily prospered. By the year 1634 nearly four thousand Englishmen had come over, and some twenty villages on or near the shores of the bay had been founded. Permanent houses and bridges were erected; roads and fences made; farms were beginning to be remunerative, an increasing trade in timber, furs and salted fish was being carried on with the mother country, and 4000 goats and 1500 head of cattle were grazing in the pastures. In other directions also progress was being made. Political meetings were held, justice was administered by magistrates after English precedents; and religious services were conducted by a score of ministers who were men of education—nearly all of them graduates of Cambridge or Oxford, and most of them having held livings in the Church of England. It is estimated that between 1630 and 1639 the number of university men who went to Massachusetts from the mother country had increased to between sixty and seventy, three-fourths of these remaining within that colony, and that by 1647 their number had mounted up to at least ninety. These men conserved the interests of religion and learning till the colleges of Harvard and Yale commenced their great career, and thus in New England life 'the guiding and directing force was supplied by an element which was itself moulded on the banks of the Cam and the Isis, under the influence and refinements of the best culture which the England of that day could give.'[1]

Not only were the leaders of the colony men of university training but also men of strong individuality of character and native force. We have already seen the sort of men Winthrop and Endicott and Johnson were, it will be instructive and interesting to come into the company of others of the makers of New England. Foremost among these stands the name of John Cotton, a native of Derby, where he was born in 1585, and who at the early age of thirteen entered Trinity College, Cambridge, from which he migrated to Emmanuel, of which he became fellow and tutor. At twenty-three he made a reputation by the funeral sermon in Latin he preached for Dr. Some, Master of Peterhouse. Like John Robinson he was one of those

[1] *The Influence of the English Universities in the Development of New England.* By Franklin B. Dexter.

Cambridge men who came under the powerful spiritual influence of William Perkins, the Puritan preacher at St. Mary's. This influence for a while he tried to resist, smothering his convictions from a fear that if he became a godly man it would spoil him for being a learned man. God's truth was, however, mightier than he, and through great storm and struggle of soul, he came forth at length one of the most spiritual, as well as one of the most intellectually able preachers of his time. In 1612 he entered upon a sphere of service worthy of his powers, for in that year he became vicar of the noblest parish church in England, that of St. Botolph, whose lofty tower is at once the landmark and the pride of Boston town. From the first he impressed men with a sense of power, some evidence of which comes to us from official sources. Among the manuscripts in the possession of the Dean and Chapter of Lincoln Cathedral there has been preserved a description by a contemporary of the primary visitation of the diocese by Bishop Neile in 1614, which is interesting as giving lifelike sketches of the men and the time, and as setting John Cotton before us as he was when he had been two years vicar of Boston.[1] The account was probably drawn up by the bishop's registrar as the bishop went through the different archdeaconries of the diocese, which at that time extended from the Humber to the Thames, the visitation being held at seventeen different centres. At Luton Mr. Rawlinson preached an eloquent and excellent sermon, but was 'too curious in assigning the place of the body of Elijah before the coming of Christ;' at Huntingdon Mr. Hearne preached 'a very acute and witty sermon' on three sorts of sluggards, but after dinner there was 'no table-talk tending to divinity;' at Leicester there was a plain sermon, apparently too plain, urging preachers 'to particularise the faults of

---

[1] There is an abridged copy of this document in the British Museum. *Addl. MSS.* 5853, ff. 249 *sq.*

their parishioners in the pulpit,' and 'the day's conference was to no great purpose;' at Melton Mowbray, as has sometimes been the case elsewhere, 'the text was more proper to the business than the sermon,' and the 'table-talk was not of divinity;' at Kirton there was 'a nimble and censorious sermon,' but no conference at dinner; at Market Rasen 'a good plain sermon' but 'a very mean clergy;' at Louth there were 'many grave and learned ministers,' too grave indeed, for they were 'all silent;' at Horncastle the 'concio prima' was 'a very sweet and eloquent sermon, very handsomely applied to the combinations of the times against the clergy; the second was 'a discreet sermon and well approved,' for the preacher, being led by his text to deal with some neglects of the clergy, 'he very discreetly delivered that point in Latin.'

From Horncastle the bishop proceeded to Boston, where the preacher was John Cotton, whom the registrar describes as 'a young man, but by report a man of great gravity and sanctity of life, a man of rare parts for his learning, eloquent and well-spoken, ready upon a sudden, and very apprehensive to conceive of any point in learning though never so abstruse, insomuch that those his good gifts have won him so much credit and acceptance, not only with his parishioners at Boston, but with all the ministry and men of account in those quarters, that grave and learned men, out of an admiration of those good graces of God in him, have been, and upon every occasion still are, willing to submit their judgments to his in any point of controversy, as though he were some extraordinary Paraclete that could not err.' Our informant seems to have had a very considerable taste of his quality. He says, 'Mr. Chancellor and myself heard three of his sermons in two days, which three were six hours long very near.' The sermons were well conceived, were delivered modestly and soberly, and well worthy of all commendation; but, alas! nothing in this world is perfect: 'there was *mors in olla*'—death in the pot—'every sermon to our judgements was poisoned with some error or other.' In one sermon he maintained that the Pagan world would not be condemned for want of belief in Christ, but only for moral transgressions against the law of nature written in their hearts; in another he contended that the office of apostle was extinct in the Church; that it was a flat error to think any man a lawful minister who was not a preacher; ordination did not make such a man a minister, though God's terrible providence might set him over His people in His anger and heavy displeasure, but not in mercy; he further taught that reading was not preaching; that non-residence was utterly unlawful; that it was not lawful to let the Sabbath pass without two sermons; and that by the order of deacons in the Bible was meant neither more nor less than collectors for the poor.' Clearly registrar and chancellor thought that here was a man who needs watching; he is too modern and is in doubtful company: 'his authors he is most beholding to (I understand) are of the newest stamp, and the place of his dwelling stands better affected to this way than the other.' In conclusion, this official compassionates the people of Boston—as well he may—over their Sunday afternoon service. For they have prayers with psalms after the lessons; after the second lesson a psalm is sung, which is followed by a sermon two hours long; then another psalm, after which the parish clerk calls out the children to be catechised, each one 'answering aloud as they used to do at a sessions with an *Here, Sir.*' After this call there is a long prayer by the minister of the town, and then come the questions 'out of a catechism of his own making,' and, finally, he spends two hours more in explication of questions and answers; so, says our informant, 'if they keep the same tenour all the year, their afternoon worship will be five hours long, where, to my observation, there were as many sleepers as wakers, scarce any man but sometime was forced to wink or nod.'

In the course of time complaints were lodged against Cotton in the Bishop's Court at Lincoln, and he was silenced for a while, but again restored. Altogether he was vicar of Boston for twenty years, and during much of the time seems to have enjoyed more than the usual liberty. For he openly held and taught that, according to the Scripture, bishops were appointed to rule no larger a diocese than a particular congregation, and that the keys of ecclesiastical government are given by the Lord to each separate church. What is more noteworthy still, within the larger parish community a gathered church was set up, some scores of pious people in the town forming themselves into an evangelical church-state by entering into covenant with God and with one another, 'to follow after the Lord in the purity of His worship.' This larger liberty was perhaps due to the fact that from 1621 onwards John Williams was Bishop of Lincoln, a man who had himself considerable leaning to Puritan modes of thought, and, like his successor, Dr. Laney, 'could look through his fingers,' and who, from 1621 to 1626, being Lord Keeper of the Privy Seal, left his diocese very much to take care of itself. But, as jealous eyes were set on the bishop himself, in 1625 he called John Cotton's proceedings in question, and a letter, still in existence, in the minute and beautiful handwriting of the vicar, asks for further time for consideration on the points at issue, 'inasmuch as his forbearance of the ceremonies was not from wilful refusal of conformity but from some doubt in judgement and from some scruple in conscience.' Signing himself, 'Your Lordship's exceedingly much bounden orator, John Cotton,' he adds to the address on the outside, 'This with speed.'[1]

Much exercised in mind, John Cotton took counsel

Addl. MSS. 6394, f. 35.

of various friends as to whether he ought to stand or flee. Among others he put the case before that quaint and witty old Puritan, John Dod of Fawsley, who answered, *suo more*, 'I am old Peter, and therefore must stand still and bear the brunt; but you, being young Peter, may go whither you will.' His enemies, however, growing more resolute, and a long and sore sickness laying him low, on July 8, 1633, he resigned his important charge into the hands of the bishop, seeing, as he says, that neither his bodily health nor the peace of the Church will now stand with his continuance there. As to how he has spent his time and course he must ere long give account at another tribunal, but he takes leave to say to his lordship that the bent of his course has been 'to make and keep a threefold Christian concord among the people—between God and their consciences, between true-hearted Christian loyalty and Christian liberty, and between the fear of God and the love of one another.' He honours the bishops and esteems many hundreds of the divines of the Church, but, while prizing other men's judgment and learning, their wisdom and piety, in things pertaining to God and God's worship, he feels he must live by his own faith, not theirs. Therefore, since he cannot yield obedience of faith, he is willing to yield patience of hope. At an assembly held in the old Guildhall in Boston on the 22nd July, before the mayor, aldermen and common council, two letters were laid before the house—one from John Cotton yielding up his place of being vicar, which the House accepted, and one from John, Lord Bishop of Lincoln, by the hands of Thomas Cony, the town clerk, stating that on the 8th July the said lord bishop did, at his house in the College of Westminster, accept of Mr. John Cotton's resignation of his vicarage. So ended the most memorable ministry Boston has ever known. The resignation was followed by the issue of writs, and if John Cotton meant to leave the country it must be at once. So, travelling in disguise, he made his way to London where John Davenport, the vicar of St. Stephen's, concealed him till he could get away to New England, which he reached on the 4th September, and where, on the 10th October, he was solemnly set apart as the colleague of John Wilson in the pastorate of that other Boston church across the sea.

This John Wilson, with whom John Cotton was thus associated, was a son of a prebendary of St. Paul's, and grand-nephew of Archbishop Grindal, and while at King's College, Cambridge, had shown the serious bent of his mind by visiting with religious intent the prisoners in the county gaol. At the same time he was strongly prejudiced against the Puritans, declining their acquaintance as men of odd notions, whims and crotchets. Happening, however, one day to see in a bookshop the *Seven Treatises* of Richard Rogers, he was so struck with the book as to take a journey to Wethersfield to hear the author preach. From that time he changed his mind about the Puritans, consorted with men of that way of thinking, and held meetings with them in his own rooms for prayer and conference. Acting thus he soon came under the censure of the bishop as visitor of the University, when his father, to avoid trouble, turned him aside to the Inns of Court for his future. Though thus diverted from his course his desires were still towards the Gospel ministry, and eventually he returned to Cambridge, entering Emmanuel College, the very centre and seed-plot of Puritanism. On leaving Emmanuel he became chaplain to Lady Scudamore, but having rebuked her ladyship's guests one Sunday for talking about nothing but hawks and hounds after the morning sermon, he was felt to be undesirable company. We next find him at Sudbury, the successor of a veteran Puritan in the ministry there, but being harassed in the ecclesiastical courts, he made common cause with his neighbour John Winthrop of Groton, and sailed for New England with him in 1630.

While Wilson and Cotton were serving the Church at Boston, across the river at Charlestown might be found Zachary Symmes, who, after being harassed by Sir Nathaniel Brent during his Metropolitical Visitation, had resigned his charge at the Priory Church of Dunstable in Bedfordshire, and came over to New England in company with Peter Bulkely, the founder of Concord and one of Emerson's ancestors. Bulkely also was from Bedfordshire, where he had succeeded his father as rector of Odell, on the banks of the Ouse. The brother-in-law of Oliver St. John, afterwards Cromwell's attorney-general, and of good family, finding himself pressed both at Bedford and Aylesbury by Sir Nathaniel Brent, he joined the Puritan emigration, taking with him some £6000—equal to about £30,000 of present value—and making his way 'through unknown woods' he purchased from the Indians the land on the banks of the Merrimac, and so became the founder and first minister of that town of Concord which has figured so largely in the intellectual life of New England.

Dorchester, a few miles out of Boston, was favoured with the able ministry of Richard Mather, who after many earnest struggles of soul had made his way to the Puritan standpoint. Having for fifteen years served as minister of Toxteth, near Liverpool, he was in 1633 suspended for nonconformity to the ceremonies. The remainder of his life was spent in the ministry of the Church across the sea. His son, Increase Mather, was one of the presidents of Harvard College; and his grandson, Cotton Mather, in his *Magnalia Christi Americana*, has preserved for us the ecclesiastical records of the colony during the first eighty years of its history.

To the north of the new Boston, in the town of Lynn, was another native of the Lincolnshire Boston in the

person of Samuel Whiting, whose father was once mayor of
the town. After leaving Emmanuel College he acted as
chaplain to Sir Nathaniel Bacon, and then became the
colleague of Mr. Price, of Lynn, where his service was
interrupted through complaints made to the Bishop of
Norwich of his nonconformity to certain rites and ceremonies, which, says Cotton Mather, were never of any use
in the Church of God except to become tools by which the
worst men might thrust out the best from serving it.
Cited before the Court of High Commission, proceedings
were suddenly dropped through the death of King James
before the case came on. By the intercession of the Earl
of Lincoln the matter was allowed to rest there, on the
understanding that Whiting would leave the diocese, which
he did, and for the next seven or eight years exercised his
ministry at Skirbeck, near his native town. Proceedings,
however, were renewed against him, and he too in 1636 left
for New England. The spirit of the man may be discerned
from the sermon he preached shortly after his arrival: 'We
in this country,' says he, 'have left our near and our dear
friends, but if we can get nearer to God here, He will be
instead of all and more than all to us. He hath all the
fulness of all the sweetest relations bound up in Himself,
and we may take out of Him that which we forsook in
friends near and dear to us as our own soul.'

Among the early authors of New England and one
whose ministry was among the most spiritually fruitful, was
Thomas Shepard, of Cambridge. A native of Towcester,
in Northamptonshire, he, like so many other of the Puritans,
was of Emmanuel College. After proceeding Master of
Arts, he was invited by the inhabitants of Earls Colne, in
Essex, to be their lecturer, where he produced such an
impression by the 'majesty and energy in his preaching,
and the holiness of his life,' that when he left the country,
many of those whom he had been the means of turning to

a Christian life 'afterwards went a thousand leagues to enjoy his ministry'—in other words, followed him to New England. While in Essex he was within the jurisdiction of Laud, then Bishop of London, who, summoning him into his presence, dealt with him in much the same stormy fashion as Judge Jeffreys, half a century later, dealt with the Nonconformists who appeared before him. Shepard has described the interview, which took place as early as eight o'clock in the morning, and at which Laud was so angry that he 'looked as though blood would have gushed out of his face, and did shake as if he had been haunted with an ague fit.' When Shepard sought to mollify the irate bishop, he called him a prating coxcomb, asked him if he thought that all the learning was in his brain, and finally prohibited him from exercising any ministerial function within his diocese. 'If you do, and I hear of it,' said he, 'I will follow you wherever you go, in any part of the kingdom, and so everlastingly disenable you.' When Shepard besought him not to deal so in regard of a poor town, Laud exclaimed—'A poor town! You have made a company of seditious, factious bedlams. Do not prate to me of a poor town.' Yet once more the Puritan preacher pleaded that if he might neither preach, read, marry nor bury, he might at least be suffered to catechise on Sunday afternoons; but Laud, telling him he might spare his breath, for he would have no such fellows prate in his diocese, bade him begone. 'So away I went,' says Shepard, 'and blessed be God, I may go to Him.'

Journeying from place to place in other dioceses, and enduring many hardships, he at length made his way over to New England, where he became the pastor of a church organised shortly after his arrival at Newtown, afterwards known as Cambridge, the congregation consisting largely of members of his former flock, who had followed him from Essex. Here he remained exercising a memorable spiritual influence till his death in 1649, and Cotton Mather tells us that one of the reasons for establishing Harvard College at Cambridge was that the preachers there to be trained might be brought under the enlightening and powerful influence of Shepard's ministry.

Another name of even still greater eminence in New England Puritan history is that of the saintly pastor of Roxbury, John Eliot, the apostle of the Indians. Little is known of his previous history in the old country beyond the fact that he was a graduate of Cambridge in 1622, and was for a time assistant in a school kept by Thomas Hooker at Little Baddow, near Colchester. Threatened with proceedings in the Ecclesiastical Courts, he also made his way over to New England in 1631, and, after serving the church in Boston, in the absence of John Wilson, he became the honoured and beloved minister of Roxbury, near by, till his death in 1690, at the advanced age of eighty-six. A man of deep prayerfulness of spirit, he seemed, as it was said, to live in heaven while he tarried on earth ; and while he tarried, to ring aloud the curfew bell wherever the fires of animosity were kindled. His ministry to his own countrymen did not prevent him putting forth his energies, as the words of the Massachusetts Bay Company's charter expressed it, 'to win and incite the natives of the country to the knowledge and obedience of the only true God and Saviour of mankind and the Christian faith.' Miserable, degraded, and unpromising as the Indians were, he learnt their language, reduced it to grammatical form, and at the end of his grammar wrote that 'prayers and pains through faith in Christ Jesus will do anything.' Able after a time to preach in their language, he gathered a church of converted Indians in 1651, and gave them the Bible in their own tongue, some copies of which still remain, though no one living now can read them. Increase Mather, writing to Dr. Leusden, of Utrecht, in 1687, stated that there were then no fewer than six churches of baptised Indians and eighteen assemblies of catechumens professing the name of Christ; that among the Indians themselves there were no fewer than four-and-twenty native preachers, in addition to the four English ministers, who could preach in the native tongue. The people, influenced for good by this apostle of Roxbury, came to be distinguished as the 'praying Indians,' and such was the reputation for saintliness of this good man, that there was a New England saying to the effect that the country would never perish while Eliot lived. The story of John Eliot's life-work revived the spirit of Richard Baxter even when his soul was in departing. Raising himself once more, he said: 'I know much of Mr. Eliot from letters I have had from him, and there is no man on earth I honour more. This evangelical work of his is the apostolical succession I plead for; his departing words I make my own: " My understanding faileth, my memory faileth, my tongue faileth, but my charity faileth not."'

The limit of these pages will not permit more than passing reference to many other worthies who did much to mould the new community to which they came—Peter Hobart, born at Hingham, in Norfolk, and who founded that other Hingham, where in its own beautiful grounds, and amid leafy surroundings, still stands the oldest meeting-house in New England; Charles Chauncey, from the Hertfordshire Ware, who had to face fierce fires in the Ecclesiastical Courts of his native land before he left it; Nathaniel and Ezekiel Rogers, the sons of two memorable men of Puritan fame; John Fisk, John Avery, John Norton and Jonathan Burr; and last, but not least, John Harvard, who, dying childless, bequeathed his library and half his estate to endow the great College which bears his name.

When this College was founded by a General Court in 1636, danger seemed to threaten the colony from the

Indians, from the Home Government, and from internal theological dissension. As we find from the Colonial Papers, Laud, with unresting vigilance, was busily drawing up minutes on matters of Colonial administration which boded no good to the cause of freedom. As early as 1635 the colonists were alarmed by a declaration from the king announcing his intention of placing the New England colonies under a governor appointed by himself. Two years later another declaration was issued, and it might have gone ill with the liberties of Massachusetts but for the outbreak of that Scotch rebellion, which not only rejected Laud's Episcopacy and Service-book, but altered the whole aspect of national affairs on both sides of the sea. In 1638, when a strict order came to send back the Massachusetts charter to England, to be replaced by a new one, the increasing troubles arising from the attitude of the Scottish people towards Episcopacy more than anything else made that order of none effect.

As the colonists received allotments of land more and more widely, it began to be necessary for the settlement to look farther afield. The fame of the great Connecticut river valley had reached the people at the Bay, and began to excite expectation among the planters. Agents were sent out to report, and in 1636 there was a considerable migration a hundred miles to westward. Those who came from Cambridge formed a church at Hartford, those from Dorchester at Windsor, those from Watertown at Wethersfield, and those from Roxbury at Springfield. The man who had most influence in directing this westward movement was Thomas Hooker, a native of Leicestershire and Fellow of Emmanuel, who had been settled at Chelmsford as lecturer and assistant. While here it is said 'his lecture was exceedingly frequented and proportionately succeeded, and the light of his ministry shone through the whole county of Essex.' Pressed for his nonconformity to ceremonies in which he did not believe, he laid down his ministry and commenced a school at Little Baddow, where he had John Eliot as his usher. Eliot has told us what the spiritual atmosphere of Thomas Hooker's house was like : 'Here the Lord said unto my dead soul—Live! and through the grace of Christ, I do live, and I shall live for ever. When I came to this blessed family I then saw and never before the power of godliness in its lively vigour and efficacy.' Still further harassed, Hooker went over into Holland, but hearing that some of his Essex friends were taking wing to New England, he joined them at their request, and eventually came to be prominently identified with the migration to the Connecticut valley.

In June, 1636, when the river had become free from ice and the woodland meadows offered pasture, the Cambridge congregation, a hundred or more in number, led by Thomas Hooker, taking with them 160 head of cattle and sending their furniture and supplies round by water, made their way to the new settlement. It was a migration not so much of individuals as of churches, and the first comers being followed by others from Dorchester, Watertown, and Roxbury, by the following May 800 people were living at Windsor, Hartford, and Wethersfield—Springfield being settled later on. In 1636 the municipal independence of the three townships was recognised ; the following year the colony advanced to representative government by a meeting of deputies or committees for the different townships, and in 1638 the three towns together formally declared themselves a commonwealth. The legislature was to consist of a governor, six assistants and deputies, the governor and assistants to be elected annually by the whole body of freemen met in General Court for that purpose. In one important point the constitution of Connecticut was more liberal than that of Massachusetts, inasmuch as the governor was the only person from whom church-membership was required. All freemen who had been admitted by a majority of their township, and had taken the oath of fidelity to the commonwealth, had the right of voting both for deputies and at the General Court of Election.

At the opening session of the General Court of 1638, Thomas Hooker preached a forcible sermon, in which he maintained that the foundation of authority is laid in the free consent of the people, that the choice of public magistrates belongs unto the people by God's own allowance, and that they who have power to appoint officers and magistrates have the right also to set the bounds and limitations of the power and place unto which they call them. This of Connecticut has been described as the first written Constitution known to history that created a government, and as having marked the beginning of that American democracy of which Thomas Hooker more than any other man deserves to be called the father; the government of the United States to-day being in lineal descent more nearly related to that of Connecticut than to that of any of the other thirteen colonies.[1]

The establishment of these settlements in the Connecticut valley had the sorrowful result of bringing the English for the first time into serious conflict with the Indians. For this new plantation was really an outpost projecting into the territory of a powerful and warlike tribe. Three years before Hooker's migration, complications had already arisen through the murder of a crew of traders by the Pequot Indians. Sassacus, their chief sachem, promised the government at Boston to deliver up the murderers, but had evidently no intention of doing so. Then again in the summer of 1636 the Indians on Block Island murdered John Oldham and seized his vessel. By way of teaching these savages that such conduct was not to be endured,

[1] Fiske's *The Beginning of New England*, p. 127.

three vessels were sent out under the command of Endicott, who ravaged Block Island, burnt their wigwams, and sunk their canoes, the men themselves having taken to the woods. Then crossing to the mainland to reckon with the Pequots, they demanded the surrender of the murderers about whom so many promises had been made. Unable to obtain satisfaction, they attacked the Indians, killing several of them, seizing their ripe corn and burning and spoiling what they could not carry away. As war breeds war again, this expedition of Endicott's led to reprisals, which fell heaviest upon the new-comers into the valley, who had taken no part in that expedition.

Next winter the Connecticut towns were kept in a perpetual state of alarm. Men going to their work were killed and horribly mutilated. One Wethersfield man was kidnapped and roasted alive, after which the Pequots attacked Wethersfield itself, massacring ten of its inhabitants and carrying off two English girls to the woods. Goaded to desperation, the settlers sought help from Boston and Plymouth, and ninety men were sent out under the command of John Mason. One brilliant moonlight night in May, 1637, they made for the Pequot stronghold. This was an entrenched fort or walled village containing 700 Pequots, and girdled by an earthen rampart three feet high, and a palisade twelve feet high made of sturdy saplings set firm and deep into the ground. At opposite ends were two openings barely large enough to let a man pass through, and within this enclosure of two or three acres were the crowded wigwams. A little before daybreak both entrances were occupied and the place taken by complete surprise. Seized with panic, the Indians tried to escape through first one outlet and then the other, but were ruthlessly shot down whichever way they turned. Meantime firebrands were thrown over the palisade among the wigwams, and soon the whole place was in flames, the savages perishing in their burning dwellings. Of 700 Pequots only five escaped with their lives, while of the English only two were killed and sixteen wounded. The tribe was all but wiped out of existence. Never had the Indians heard of so terrible a vengeance, and never again till the time of King Philip's war, eight-and-thirty years later, dared the Indian lift his hand against the white man.

The overthrow of the Pequots removed the one obstacle to the consolidation of New England. The Connecticut settlements were no longer isolated, separated from their friends along the coast by the intervention of barbarous tribes, but were brought into direct communication with the rest of the English from the mouth of the Connecticut river to Boston Bay. The rest of the Pequot Indians, to the number of some 200 warriors with their families, submitted to the English in 1638, and at a conference held at Hartford, in September, were divided between the Mohicans and the Narragansetts. So that the conditions were now reversed, and the Indian tribes in their turn detached and hemmed in, and the way prepared for that last wave of migration which brought to an end the great Puritan exodus from England to America.

About a month after the storming of the Pequot stronghold, this last detachment, consisting of a company of wealthy London merchants with their families, arrived in Boston. The two most prominent men among them were Theophilus Eaton, a member of the Massachusetts Bay Company, and John Davenport, the pastor of this migrating community. The two men had known each other before they came together in this enterprise, for Eaton was the son of the minister and Davenport the son of a former mayor of Coventry. After graduating at Oxford, Davenport obtained the living at Coleman Street, London, where his preaching attracted both public attention and official surveillance. When charged to Secretary Conway with being puritanically affected, he denied the charge, saying, 'I have persuaded many to conformity—yea, my own father and uncle, who are aldermen of the city of Coventry, and were otherwise inclined.'[1] In 1628, writing to Lady Mary Vere, he tells her of the troubles gathering round him; the new Bishop of London, Dr. Laud, has a particular aim at him, and he expects ere long to be deprived of his pastoral charge in Coleman Street. 'But I am in God's hands,' says he, 'not in theirs; to whose good pleasure I do contentedly and cheerfully submit myself. If it be His will to have me laid aside as a broken vessel, His will be done.'[2] In later years we find him explaining his position to this same lady: 'The truth is, I have not forsaken my ministry, nor resigned up my place, much less separated from the Church; but am only absent awhile to wait upon God for the settling and quieting of things, for light to discern my way; being willing to lie and die in prison, if the cause may be advantaged by it; but choosing rather to preserve the liberty of my person and ministry for the service of the Church elsewhere. . . . The only cause of my present suffering is the alteration of my judgment in matters of conformity to the ceremonies established; whereby I cannot practise them as formerly I have done; wherein I do not censure those that do conform. I know that I did conform with as much inward peace as now I do forbear; in both my uprightness was the same, but my light different. In this action I walk by that light which shineth unto me.'

From 1634 till 1637 we find him in Holland, but in the latter year one of the informers of the time reports: 'Mr. Davenport hath lately been in these parts, Braintree, and at Hackney, not long since. I am told that he goeth in gray like a country gentleman.'[3] When spies were thus on his

---

[1] *State Papers*, Dom. [2] *Birch MSS.*, 4275.
[3] *State Papers*, Dom.

track clearly he must go ; we learn, therefore, that he arrived in Boston by the ship Hector, June, 1637. In concert with his friend Theophilus Eaton, whom Winthrop describes as a man 'of fair estate and of great esteem for religion and wisdom in outward affairs,' he spent some months in seeking the best site for a new settlement. This they found at length at Quinnipiack, on Long Island Sound, where they made two successive purchases of land extending eight miles north-east and five miles south-west of the river and running ten miles inland. In this way the town of New Haven came to be founded in the spring of 1638. The next year two other parties of emigrants, each forty in number, and each, like New Haven, joined together as an independent church, settled at Guildford and Milford, both settlements placed on lands purchased from the Indians. In 1640 Stamford on the mainland was added to the group, and in 1643 the four towns were made to constitute the republic of New Haven, to which Southold, on the western shore of Long Island, and Branford were afterwards added.

With the advent to power of the Long Parliament in 1640, and the consequent downfall of Archbishop Laud, the reason for the Puritan exodus ceased, and the exodus itself came to an end. Since the arrival of the Mayflower in 1620, the population had grown to 26,000 souls, and after 1640 for more than a century there was no considerable migration to this part of North America. These twenty years and these 26,000 people constitute the formative period and the determining element of New England and American life. Those who believe in a philosophy of history and seek to trace it in the course of events cannot fail to see the special significance of the time. The Dutch had already erected Fort Amsterdam on the island at the mouth of the Hudson, which was afterwards to bear the great commercial city of New York. The French had settled at Port Royal, in Nova Scotia, and had established a trading post with the Indians at Quebec. If, therefore, the power of England and the English spirit of freedom were to become dominant on the great continent of America, the beginnings must be made during the years with which we have been dealing. Not less significant were the men than the time. Those who came over were almost without exception deeply religious men. It has been truly said that it was religious enthusiasm that secured the preponderance of the continent for men of the English race. As England grew in manufacturing skill and in commerce through the coming of the Huguenots whom religious persecution drove on to English soil, so the great republic of the West feels to this day the coming of the moral and religious influence of the men who, in the seventeenth century, valued freedom of conscience as their most sacred possession. The pick and flower of the nation from which they came, their spirit still lives. Had the emigration not started when it did, the solid and godly element there is in American life would not have been what it is. On the other hand, had that emigration continued longer, had England been depleted to exhaustion of her noblest blood, as France was when her Huguenots were banished or slain, her great struggle for constitutional freedom in the seventeenth century might have ended other than it did. That would have been a calamity not for England alone but for the world. It has been well said that the decisive victory of Charles I., the triumph of Stuart despotism, would have been like the Greeks losing Marathon or the Saracens winning Tours.

XII.

THE UNITED COLONIES.'

HAVING followed the rise of the colonies round Massachusetts Bay and in the Connecticut Valley, we may now return to see how the people of the Plymouth Plantation were faring meanwhile. Since the year 1627, when De Rassières paid the visit he himself described, the settlers seem to have been steadily prospering, if we may judge from the fact that in the autumn of 1632 they held a thanksgiving festival, at which they rejoiced 'in an especial manner;' this, too, in spite of 'a plague of mosquitoes and rattlesnakes.' The colony was already beginning to spread beyond its original boundaries; for as their cattle increased the people moved farther and farther in search of pasturage. At first these visits were mere summer sojourns, but eventually they led to the erection of dwellings where the winter could be spent, and to the grief of Governor Bradford issued in the separation of many from the parent settlement. In 1632 permission was given for the organisation of a church nearer home for those who had thus moved some five miles to the north, of which church Elder Brewster was to have the oversight; but the court at Plymouth, which granted this permission, insisted that settlers so far distant from the protection of the fort on Burial Hill should be every man of them armed. As an additional precaution against surprise their houses were palisaded, and a line of defence was built across the entrance of the Nook.

Though not incorporated till 1637, Duxbury thus came to be the first offshoot of the Plymouth stock, and received its name as a reminiscence of Miles Standish's ancestral seat in Lancashire, the Duxbury Hall, not far from Chorley town. To this new settlement, for the sake of more fertile land, several of the leading men of the colony migrated from Plymouth, as there are memorials to remind us. On Captain's Hill, seen for miles both from sea and land, stands the lofty column of Miles Standish's monument. In a field in North Duxbury, not many minutes' walk from the high road, we come upon an inscription which tells us that here stood John Alden's house—that John Alden who wedded Priscilla Mullins the maiden who, as the legend goes, when he first went to plead Miles Standish's suit, witchingly asked: 'Prithee, why don't you speak for yourself, John?' William Brewster, too, was among those who moved their dwellings into Duxbury, and natives of the town say that till recent time there were to be seen traces of the tall clump of whitewood trees that gave the name of the Eagle's Nest to the place where his homestead stood. Others, again, of those who started from London in the Mayflower have left traces of themselves in Duxbury, in such names as Blackfriar's Brook, Billingsgate, and Houndsditch, which they had brought with them from their former home.

Edward Winslow obtained possession of land even beyond Duxbury, at Greenharbour, known afterwards as Marshfield, though as he was governor in 1644 he does not seem to have altogether severed his connection with Plymouth. So that of those who had signed the compact on board the Mayflower, Miles Standish, William Brewster, John Alden, John Howland, George Soule, and Henry Sampson had migrated to Duxbury; as did also, among those who came later, Brewster's son Jonathan, William

Collier, and Thomas Prince. Governor Bradford mourned over these changes and losses, inevitable in a changing world, but at length consent was reluctantly given for the incorporation of the new settlement as the town of Duxbury, the court making a grant which ran, after the manner of the time, 'to be holden of our sovereign lord the king as of his manor and tenure of East Greenwich in the county of Kent.'[1] With the incorporation of the town came the settlement of its first pastor, Ralph Partridge. Marshfield was the next church organised, which was followed by Scituate, Barnstable, Taunton, Yarmouth, and Sandwich, so that Plymouth Colony at the time it entered into the New England Confederacy consisted of eight separate towns.

The relations between the dwellers in this the old colony and those of the Massachusetts Bay, being all Englishmen, were naturally of friendly sort. John Cotton, in his farewell sermon to John Winthrop and his associates at Southampton, urged them to take advice of those already at Plymouth, and do nothing to offend them. We have seen also how Samuel Fuller, the good physician, went over to the help of the people of Salem in time of sickness; and when at a later time John Winthrop's people also were sorely stricken the colonists at Plymouth, at their request, observed the same day as a day of fasting and prayer on their behalf; and as their neighbours grew in numbers and strength Governor Bradford rejoiced with them, pointing out 'how of small beginnings great things have been produced by His hand that made all things of nothing and gives being to all things that are; and as one small candle may light a thousand, so the light here kindled hath shone to many, yea, in some sort to our whole nation. Let the glorious name of Jehovah have all the praise.' During the years between 1630 and 1643

[1] *The Mayflower Town.* By Justin Winsor.

letters of friendship were interchanged and visits paid. In 1629, as we remember, Governor Bradford and his friends went over to the ordination service at Salem; and the week after the arrival of Margaret Winthrop, Bradford paid a visit of congratulation to 'his much-honoured and beloved friend,' her husband, the Governor of Massachusetts. On his part, too, John Winthrop reciprocated the kindness shown, for we find him lending the people of Plymouth twenty-eight pounds of powder 'upon their urgent distress, their own powder proving naught, when they were to send to the rescue of their men at Sowamsett.'[1] In the month of September, 1632, also, as Winthrop himself tells us, he and his pastor, John Wilson, went over to Plymouth, walking the twenty-five miles from Wessagusset; and as towards evening they were nearing the town 'the Governor, Mr. William Bradford (a very discreet and grave man), met them and conducted them to the Governor's house, where they were very kindly entertained and feasted every day at several houses. On the Lord's Day there was a sacrament which they did partake in; and in the afternoon Mr. Roger Williams, according to their custom, propounded a question, to which the pastor, Mr. Smith, spake briefly; then Mr. Williams prophesied [*i.e.* preached]; and after, the Governor of Plymouth spake to the question; after him, Elder Brewster; then some two or three men of the congregation. Then Elder Brewster desired the Governor of Massachusetts and Mr. Wilson to speak to it, which they did. When this was ended the deacon, Mr. Fuller, put the congregation in mind of their duty of contribution; whereupon the Governor and all the rest went down to the deacon's seat, and put into the box, and then returned.' There were thus some memorable men at this old world Sabbath worship—John Winthrop, William Bradford, William Brewster, and Roger

---

[1] Winthrop's *Life and Letters*, ii. 97.

Williams. And the following Wednesday, 'as early as five in the morning, the Governor and his company came out of Plymouth, the Governor of Plymouth, with the pastor, Ralph Smith, and Elder Brewster, etc., accompanying them near half-a-mile out of town in the dark.' Some of the party went with them as far as the great Pembroke Swamp, ten miles from Plymouth. 'When they came to the great river they were carried over by Luddam, their guide (as they had been when they came, the stream being very strong and up to the crotch), so the Governor called that passage Luddam's Ford.'[1]

The friendship thus subsisting between the two colonies was destined to take a closer and more definite form. The time came when there was felt to be urgent need for union between the New England Colonies for the purpose of common jurisdiction, and also for common support against the Indians, the Dutch in New Netherlands, and, to some extent, the French in the north. There was much that might form a common basis of union to start with; for in all the settlements the colonists were of the same English race, were impelled by similar motives, cherished the same hopes, and had been disciplined by the same kind of training. It needed, therefore, but a suggestion to put the idea in motion. By whom the suggestion was first made does not appear, but Winthrop tells us that after the overthrow of the Pequots, as some of the magistrates and ministers of Connecticut were at Boston, an apparently unpremeditated conference was held to discuss a scheme of confederation, notice of which was given to the government of Plymouth, but too late for them to take part in the deliberations. It further appears that in 1638 a scheme of union was proposed by Massachusetts and rejected by Connecticut, the point upon which they differed being as to whether the vote of a majority of Federal commissioners

[1] Winthrop's *Life and Letters*, ii. 105, 106.

should have binding force on the whole Confederation.[1] The matter from this time remained in abeyance for about three years, possibly through some difficulty on the part of Plymouth, inasmuch as on the revival of the scheme in 1642, Winthrop states that now Plymouth was willing to come in. Bradford, however, says nothing of any difficulty arising on their part, merely stating that ever since the Pequot war the Indians were drawn into a general conspiracy against the English in all parts, which led to a more near union and confederation on the part of the plantations under the government of Massachusetts, New Plymouth, Connecticut, and New Haven. Be that as it may, in May, 1643, commissioners from the three latter colonies met at Boston, and after two or three conferences Articles of Confederation were agreed upon and signed by all the commissioners except those from Plymouth, they by the terms of their commission being obliged to refer the matter back to the court of the colony before giving final consent.

Bradford, in his history, has given the Articles of Confederation in full, these being eleven in number. The preamble states that all the four colonies came to America with the same end and aim, that is, to advance the kingdom of our Lord Jesus Christ, and to enjoy the liberties of the Gospel in purity with peace; and living as they do encompassed with people of several nations and strange languages, they conceive it their bounden duty without delay to enter into a present consociation for mutual help and strength. The confederacy thus to be formed was to be called the United Colonies of New England, and to constitute a league of friendship and amity for offence and defence, mutual advice and succour upon all just occasions, both for preserving and propagating the truth and liberties of the Gospel, and for mutual

[1] Winthrop's *History*, i. 237, 284.

THE UNITED COLONIES. 333

safety and welfare. Each colony was to preserve its own jurisdiction; all public charges to be met by contributions levied on the colonies in proportion to the number of their inhabitants; the affairs of the confederation to be managed by commissioners, two from each colony, all being of good standing as church members; and the annual meetings to be held in each of the colonies in rotation, Massachusetts having two turns in succession.

It will be seen that since all power of taxation beyond a common levy was left to the several colonies, and the board of commissioners had but little executive power, and was little more than a consulting body, the confederacy was rather a league than a federal union; still, it is important as being the first American experiment in the direction of Federal government. There were difficulties, of course, to be surmounted. One source of friction, as might be expected, lay in the overwhelming preponderance of Massachusetts; for of the 24,000 people included in the confederacy, no fewer than 15,000 belonged to that colony, the other three colonies having only about 3000 each. Massachusetts, therefore, had the greater responsibility, and naturally sought to exert the greater authority, an authority which was sometimes resented by the rest. There was also one other undesirable result of the union entered into. It has been contended that since Massachusetts was narrower and more intolerant than Plymouth, restricting its franchise as it did to church members, and allowing less latitude of speech and opinion, its tendency was to reduce the more liberally-inclined Plymouth to something like its own level; that while the latter gained in security and industrial progress from association with its more powerful neighbour, it lost something also in the way of freedom and self-reliance, and that from this and other causes, after the important era of 1643, Plymouth ceases to be of continuous interest, except as the heroes of the bygone pilgrimage sink one by one to the rest they had so nobly earned. Still, in spite of all drawbacks, the league of the four colonies was of great value in the development of New England. It worked well as a high court of jurisdiction, and as a means of concentrating the military strength of the colonies for common ends, and by its principle of State freedom and State equality, it prepared the way for that greater Federal union which, in the following century, made of the American people a nation. From 1643 till the memorable 1684, when the British Government interfered and brought it to an untimely end, this league of the four colonies did good service, and prepared the way eventually for greater things.

The commissioners who met at Boston to form this confederacy seem to have been strangely indifferent as to what might be thought of this important step of theirs by the English Government. It has been well said they sought no permission beforehand; they did as they pleased at the time, and defended their conduct afterwards. As Edward Winslow put the case when sent over to London to defend the action of the colonies: 'If we in America should forbear to unite for offence and defence against a common enemy till we have leave from England, our throats might all be cut before the messenger would be half-seas through.' It seemed a daring step to take; in reality it was less daring in 1643 than it would have been some years earlier. For then Laud had been two years in the Tower awaiting that execution which came two years later, and Charles I. was engaged in that life and death struggle with his Parliament which ended so fatally for him. Both king and archbishop therefore had more urgent business on their hands than that of keeping jealous watch on what the New England colonies might do.

It was on May 19, 1643, that the deputies of the four colonies met at Boston, subscribed the Articles of Confederation, and thus created the first Federal Union on the American continent. The greatest man among the founders of Plymouth Plantation did not live to see that day, for a month earlier, on April 10, 'to the great sadness and mourning of them all,' William Brewster passed to 'where beyond these voices there is peace.' With pathos and sorrow his friend and countryman, Governor Bradford, recording the fact, describes him as 'my dear and loving friend; a man that had done and suffered much for the Lord Jesus and the Gospel's sake; and had borne his part in weal and woe with this poor persecuted church above thirty-six years in England, Holland, and in this wilderness, and done the Lord and them faithful service in his place and calling.' In summing up the life-story of his friend, whose course we have followed from Scrooby Manor-house to the quiet homestead near the Eagle's Nest, William Bradford tells us how bravely, through stress and storm, this venerated elder kept on his way; how he was no way unwilling to take his part and bear his burden with the rest. He tells us that more than once he had lived without bread or corn many months together, having many times nothing but fish, and often wanting that also. 'Yet he lived, by the blessing of God, in health until very old age, and would labour with his hands in the fields as long as he was able. And when the Church had no other minister, he taught twice every Sabbath, and that both powerfully and profitably, to the great contentment of the hearers and their comfortable edification. Yea, many were brought to God by his ministry. He did more in their behalf in a year than many that have their hundreds a year do in all their lives.' William Bradford further describes for us the personal characteristics of this friend of his whom he had known ever since his own old Austerfield days: 'He was wise and discreet and well-spoken, having a grave deliberate utterance; of a very cheerful spirit, very sociable and pleasant amongst his friends, of an humble and honest mind; of a peaceable disposition, undervaluing himself and his own abilities and sometimes overvaluing others; inoffensive and innocent in his life and conversation, which gained him the love of those without as well as those within. Yet he would tell them plainly of their faults and evils, both publicly and privately, but in such a manner as usually was well taken from him ... In teaching he was very stirring and moving the affections, also very plain and distinct in what he taught, by which means he became the more profitable to the hearers. He had a singular good gift in prayer, both public and private, in ripping up the heart and conscience before God, in the humble confession of sin and begging the mercies of God in Christ for the pardon thereof. He always thought it were better for ministers to pray oftener, and divide their prayers, than to be long and tedious in the same, except upon solemn and special occasions, as on days of humiliation and the like.'

Like a tired child William Brewster fell asleep when his long day's work was done. 'He was near fourscore years of age (if not all out) when he died. He had this blessing added by the Lord to all the rest, to die in his bed in peace among the midst of his friends, who mourned and wept over him, and ministered what help and comfort they could unto him, and he again re-comforted them whilst he could. His sickness was not long. Until the last day thereof he did not wholly keep his bed. His speech continued until somewhat more than half a day before his death, and then failed him; and about nine or ten of the clock that evening he died, without any pang at all. A few hours before he drew his breath short, and some few minutes before his last he drew his breath long, as a man fallen into a sound sleep without any pangs or gaspings, and so sweetly departed this life into a better.'

Six years after William Brewster went his way, John Winthrop followed him, and the men of Massachusetts bent with sorrow as they laid the body of their governor 'with great solemnity and honour' in the burial-ground of King's Chapel in Boston city. His sepulchre was there, but as they said, his 'epitaph was engraven in the minds of the people, as a worthy gentleman who had done good in Israel, having spent not only his whole estate, but his bodily strength and life in the service of the country, as a burning torch spending his health and wealth for the good of others.' This was in 1649, and in 1652 John Cotton too was called away, while three years later, in three consecutive years, Edward Winslow, Miles Standish and William Bradford went over to the majority. To William Bradford as the simple but graphic historian of Plymouth Plantation we owe a deep debt of gratitude for the records he preserved and the story he told; and we are glad to know that when the parting time came he too was filled with 'ineffable consolations, the good Spirit of God giving him a pledge of the firstfruits of his eternal glory.'

To those remaining it must have seemed as if the heroic age had reached its close. In a new community just setting out on its career it was not easy to make up for the loss of men who had been formed under the best training the Old World could give. Their successors, however, showed their understanding of the needs of the time by doing all they could to foster that spirit of learning which had made the older generation what it had been. An English historian has done them the justice to say that, 'let our sense of the shortcomings of American Puritanism be ever so strong, it should never lead us to forget this its great merit. It carried on the best traditions of the Reformation. It never dealt with learning as the privilege of a class. It might silence its opponents; it never sought to deaden or sophisticate the minds of its disciples.

Bigoted itself, it so dealt with them as to make like bigotry impossible in the future.'[1] The writer in bearing this testimony had especial reference to the fact, that in 1636 the General Court of Massachusetts voted four hundred pounds, a sum equal to the whole taxation of the colony, towards establishing a college or grammar school. This grant was the following year supplemented by the munificence of John Harvard, a graduate of Emmanuel, Cambridge, who bequeathed to the college a sum of seven hundred pounds and his library of two hundred and sixty volumes. In 1642 the college was placed under the control of a board consisting of the governor, deputy-governor, the assistants, the ministers of six neighbouring towns and the president. In 1650 a fuller grant of incorporation was given, and the college further endowed with all the tolls taken at the ferry between Charlestown and Boston. The influence of Harvard College was felt by all the colonies, and in due time Connecticut followed the example of Massachusetts by starting the college at Saybrook which afterwards at New Haven grew to the great University of Yale. These two institutions were the forerunners of many more colleges and universities, to which the American people have recently given noble and generous endowments for the furtherance of education at a time when our own ancient seats of learning at home are suffering from deepening impoverishment and need.

In other ways than by the founding and endowing of Harvard the New England colonies showed their sense of the value of education. In 1647 an order of court established schools of two classes in Massachusetts. Where there were as many as fifty householders there was to be an elementary school at which reading and writing should be taught; and where there were a hundred householders they were to have a grammar school. In Plymouth colony

[1] Doyle, ii. 113.

there appear to have been voluntary schools before the enactment of 1662, under which the court charged each municipality to have 'a schoolmaster set up.' In 1670 the fishing excise from the cape was offered any town which would keep a free school, classical as well as elementary. Plymouth was the town that complied with this condition, and claims to have had the first free school established in New England by law. In 1677, however, it ceased to be free, though in 1704 it became so again.

From 1643, the year of their confederation, for the next one-and-twenty years the New England colonies pursued their course, undisturbed either by king or commonwealth at home. After the Restoration, however, in 1664, a commission was sent out to administer and inspect. The commissioners were charged to secure the king's rights; to enforce the execution of the Navigation Acts, and the free exercise of religion according to the laws of England. They were also to inquire into the administration of justice, the treatment of the natives, and the state of education; and they were entrusted with certain diplomatic powers, which were conveyed in secret orders.[1] This commission seems to have been fruitless, so far as the purpose of the Government was concerned. It did little but leave behind a feeling of irritation in the minds of the people and the abiding dread of an attack on their liberties. The next incident of moment is that ten years later there broke out that disastrous war with the Indians under King Philip, the horrors of which lived long as a terrible memory in New England. While for the Indians it meant utter destruction and the disappearance of the red man from the history of the country, except for occasional raids on the frontier; to the colonists themselves also it brought disastrous consequences in the destruction of life and property. Of ninety towns, twelve were utterly destroyed, while more than forty

[1] *Colonial Papers*, April 23, 1664.

others were the scene of fire and slaughter. One out of every twelve men of military age was killed, together with great numbers of women and children. Nearly every household was in mourning, and the money cost of the war was so great that in 1676 the direct taxation in Massachusetts was sixteen times what was imposed in ordinary years. In Plymouth also it amounted to £3700, a sum which was supposed to exceed the total value of personal property in the colony.

In 1684 came at last the long-expected blow from the Government in England. In the month of June a decree in Chancery annulled the charter of Massachusetts, so that not only were all rights and immunities based upon it swept away, but the title to private property was rendered invalid, and every rood of land claimed for the king. This was followed by the tyrannical administration of Sir Edmund Andros, which made the years from 1685 to 1688 the darkest period in the history of New England. The revolution which brought in William of Orange drove out Andros, but at the same time it put an end to the old Colonial Government. In 1692 Governor Phipps, appointed by the Crown, came over from England with a charter which united Massachusetts Bay, Plymouth Colony, the Vineyard archipelago, Maine, and Acadia, recently won from the French, into the one royal province of Massachusetts, which, with a slight interval, reached all the way from Martha's Vineyard to the Gulf of St. Lawrence. From that eventful year the body politic created by the men of the Mayflower ceased to have separate existence, and that new period in American history was entered upon which, beginning with the erection of a Crown colony under an English governor, ended with the Declaration of Independence of 1776 and the creation of the great nationality of the United States.

The Puritan community whose fortunes we have traced,

created at first on English soil and under English influence, but developed under new conditions, presented, as we might expect, special characteristics of its own. Living in the atmosphere of the seventeenth century, it partook of its narrowness, but inspired by deeply religious forces it developed at the same time those sterling qualities of integrity, patient industry, enterprise and quiet self-control which both in the Old World and the New have ministered both to individual strength and national growth. In what may be designated the heroic period of its history there was a dignified simplicity and an old-world quaintness which gradually grew less as the generations became more and more removed from the original stock. At first wealth increased but slowly, and the habits of the people were averse from anything like luxurious display. Pleasures were few and simple, and men resorted to them only as relaxation from the more serious duties of life, and there was therefore small attraction in New England for such thriftless and pleasure-loving idlers as had made the early attempts at colonisation in Virginia so conspicuous a failure. A man must be possessed of substantial worth and show some sort of capacity if he would make his way in a country so stern in its conditions and requirements as that of New England was then.

Some of the settlements created were little more than mere groups of farmsteads, the people spreading wider as better land became available. Surrounded as they still were by Indians, there was an element of danger in this wider scattering, as the Virginia massacre had only too painfully proved, and therefore, according to the Plymouth Records, it was enacted that no colonist should settle on unoccupied land, unless he had with him 'such a competent company or number of inhabitants as the court shall judge meet to begin a society as may carry on things in a satisfactory way both to civil and religious respects.'

Thus grouped together in what were at first rather brotherhoods than towns, the New England yeoman lived on his own land, and on the produce of his own toil, and the timber house in which he dwelt was usually the work of his own hands. Landlords and rent such as were found in the old country were almost unknown, and none of the colonial codes so much as contain such words as 'lease' or 'tenant.' But time brought its changes, and wealth, and the comforts and refinements which wealth creates, naturally increased. Early in colonial history Edward Johnson describes the 'city like town' of Boston with its 'comely streets,' and its 'buildings beautiful and large, some fairly set forth with brick, tile and stone,' and tells us how New Haven stood forth with its 'complete streets, and its 'stately and costly houses.' At the same time there continued to be that wholesome blending of town and country life which in these later days has become less possible, as the rural populations crowd more and more into the congested districts of our large cities and towns.

For the first century at least the centre of interest in a New England town or village of the olden times was the meeting house of the place, as the church was called. It was usually among the earlier buildings erected; but to make sure of this, in 1675 it was enacted that a meeting-house should be erected in every town in the colony; if the people failed in this, the magistrates were empowered to build it and charge the cost of its erection on the town. At first these buildings were simple enough, but eventually gave place to those of the second period, which were square wooden buildings surmounted by a belfry, or a turret containing a bell. The meeting house erected at Hingham in 1681, now the oldest in New England, is a fine specimen of the meeting houses of this period. These were followed by those with tower and spire, like that of the Old South at Boston, a style which was repeated far and near.

and in 1664 it was ordered that if the wolf-slayer wished to obtain his reward he must bring the wolf's head, 'nail it to the meeting-house, and give notice thereof.'

In the simpler times of colonial history, the people were called to their Sabbath worship by sound of horn or beat of drum, or by the blowing of a large conch-shell. In some places three guns were fired as the signal for 'church-time.' Like the call to prayer from the minaret towers at Cairo, the summons to worship was made more distinct by coming from the temple-roof. At Windsor, in 1638, a platform was erected on the top of the meeting-house, 'from the lanthorn to the ridge, to walk conveniently to sound a trumpet or a drum to give warning to meeting;' and in 1647 it was the duty of Robert Basset, at New Haven, to 'drum twice upon the Lord's days and Lecture days, upon the meeting-house, that so those that live far off may hear the more distinctly.' In some cases the hour for worship was notified by the hoisting of a flag in addition to beat of drum or sound of horn. In process of time the ringing of a bell succeeded to these more primitive modes of call, the bell being hung, at first, on some tree, and afterwards in the bell-turret on the meeting-house roof.

The house of prayer being reached, the worshippers seated themselves in the deep old-fashioned pews with their not too comfortable benches. While an almost rude political equality prevailed in the town meeting, very marked deference was paid in the meeting-house to social and family distinctions, as well as to age and official standing. In the earliest times of all, the congregation sat on mere benches, the men on one side and the women on the other. Then came the division of the floor-space into pews, and a formal assignment of seats according to social rank. In 1694, the town of Braintree authorised the select men to 'seat the meeting-house,' but as they showed themselves not over forward in settling the delicate matter of personal precedence, a special committee was appointed to see to the business, which they did, but, as may well be supposed, 'not to general satisfaction.' This New England custom of 'seating the meeting' in conformity with the social position of the congregation was one which the early Fathers of the colony may have brought with them from the old country churches in England which they had known in their youth, and where it used not infrequently to breed ill-blood. In John Bunyan's native parish of Elstow, in Bedfordshire, for example, two of the parishioners were presented to the archdeacon's court, one of them charged with 'refusing to sit in a seat of the church where the churchwardens placed him,' the other, who was Bunyan's grandfather, for taking his neighbour's part, and telling the churchwardens they were 'forsworne men.' In like manner, in New England, it required pressure of fine and authority to put down discontent in this matter of settling the due order of precedence according to rank and importance. Whittier tells us how—

> 'In the goodly house of worship, where in order due and fit,
> As by public vote directed, classed and ranked the people sit;
> Mistress first and good wife after, clerkly squire before the clown,
> From the brave coat, lace embroidered, to the gray frock shading down.'

Besides 'seating the meeting,' the officials had also to 'dignify the meeting,' that is, so to arrange as that certain seats, though in different localities, should still be reckoned as equal in dignity. For example, the seating committee at Sutton used their 'best discretion' in deciding that 'the third seat below be equal in dignity with the foreseat in the front gallery, and the fourth seat below be equal in dignity with the foreseat in the side gallery.' In some towns rules amusing for their punctilious minuteness were found to prevail. Each year of the person's age counted one degree, military service eight degrees, and the magistrate's office ten degrees; further, every forty shillings paid in on the church-rate counted one degree.

Little attention was, in earlier times, paid to the personal comfort of the congregation when gathered for worship. There was no attempt to warm the buildings, however stern the winter. If the weather were unusually bitter, the women brought footstoves filled with hot coals from the fire at home, or thrust their feet into fur bags made of wolfskins, but the men held on their way with Spartan severity, looking upon all warming arrangements beyond jack-boots, frieze stockings, and many-caped great-coats, as mere effeminacy. When the select men in a certain town on Buzzard's Bay proposed 'to purchase a stove and pipes, and furnish wood and attendance,' the majority at a town meeting decided by vote 'not to purchase a stove and pipes; not to furnish wood and attendance.' And Judge Sewall, a typical character of the time, the Pepys Diarist of New England life, records of a certain Sunday thus: 'Extraordinary cold storm of wind and snow; blows much more as coming home at noon, and holds on. Bread was frozen at Lord's Table.... Yet was very comfortable at meeting.' On another occasion, again, he tells us the day was so bitterly cold that 'the Communion bread was frozen pretty hard, and rattled sadly into the plates.' Still the worthy judge and his stout-hearted contemporaries held on their way, and it was not till 1773 that the first church in Boston took the lead in setting up a stove to warm the shivering limbs of the worshippers.

The weather might be cold, but the service was not necessarily shortened on that account. It is stated that at the planting of the first church in Woburn, Massachusetts, good Zachary Symmes showed his godliness and endurance by preaching between four and five hours. How his hearers showed theirs, the historian has not told us. The occasion was special, possibly the patience of the

THE UNITED COLONIES. 317

audience was special also. Even the laymen when they turned preachers, as they sometimes did, were not much more merciful than the ministers. Judge Sewall, after expounding at a service at Plymouth Meeting, writes somewhat remorsefully, 'being afraid to look at the glass,' that is, the hour-glass which measured the time, 'ignorantly and unwittingly I stood two hours and a half.' We can see from this how needful it might be for the select men of Salem in 1676 to order 'that the three constables do attend at the three great doors of the meeting-house every Lord's Day, at the end of the sermon both forenoon and afternoon, and to keep the doors fast and suffer none to go out before the whole exercise be ended.' Under such lengthy prelections, it is not wonderful that some of the carnal were seen making stealthily for the door when that was possible, and that even devout listeners felt a sense of drowsiness which could only be resisted by standing up, or by taking off their heavy coats, or by going out to quiet their horses; the tithing man, too, must have found his office no sinecure, as he moved from place to place in the meeting-house recalling the sleepers in this pew and that to consciousness with his wand.

A New England service in those days was probably not very exhilarating from a poetical or musical point of view. Few services in the seventeenth century were, either on one side of the Atlantic or the other. Even in the Church of England, as Thomas Fuller reminds us, the piety of the hymns was better than the poetry, and nearly a century later John Wesley went so far as to call it scandalous doggrel. As for the music, even a Churchman describes it as that 'shameful mode of psalmody almost confined to the wretched solo of a parish clerk, or to a few persons huddled together in one corner of the church, who sang to the praise and glory of themselves for the entertainment and often to the wearisomeness of the congregation.' This being the state of things in the national church at home, even on into the eighteenth century, it is scarcely wonderful if the congregations of New England were not altogether models as to the best form of practising psalmody in public worship.

The Pilgrim Fathers themselves, while in Holland, like the English Church at home, used Sternhold and Hopkins' Version of the Psalms until, in 1612, Henry Ainsworth, the teacher of the Separatist Church in Amsterdam, brought out another version under the title, ' *The Book of Psalms*. Englished both in Prose and Metre.' It commenced with a ' Preface declaring the use and reason of the Book,' also, ' for the use and edification of saints,' what were thought to be appropriate tunes were printed above each psalm in the lozenge-shaped notes of Queen Elizabeth's time ' The singing notes,' says the author, ' I have most taken from our Englished psalms when they will fit the measure of the verse,' for the other long verses 'the gravest and easiest tunes of the French and Dutch Psalms.' This book of Ainsworth's the Pilgrims brought over with them to New England, and it was used in the church at Plymouth as late as 1692, although a later version had been compiled and printed in Boston as early as 1640. In some churches both the two versions were used side by side for several years, till at length the style of the more modern proved too much even for the sacred associations of the more ancient.

This later version, which little by little superseded that made by Ainsworth, and was known as *The Bay Psalm Book*, was compiled by several divines, revised by President Dunster, of Harvard College, and printed in his house in 1643. If we except a small almanac which preceded it, this was the first book printed in New England. By 1709, after various revisions, it had gone through sixteen editions, some of these being printed abroad, in England and Scot-

THE UNITED COLONIES. 349

land. Altogether, about seventy editions were issued, but by the end of the eighteenth century the Bay Psalm Book had fallen into disuse, and has now become a literary curiosity. A copy of the first edition, which once belonged to Bishop Tanner, is preserved in the Bodleian, another was, in 1855, purchased for the Lenox Library in New York for eighty pounds, and a third was sold in Boston, in 1876, for over a thousand dollars.

The musical rendering of this Bay Psalm Book in the worship of the churches was of the simplest sort, for previous to 1700 there seem only to have been about ten tunes in use, such as Oxford, Litchfield, York, Windsor, Cambridge, St. David's and Martyrs. The preface to the edition of the Psalm Book printed in 1698, gave 'some few directions' on the concluding pages, so as to secure that the tune might be sung within the compass of the people's voices 'without squeaking above or grumbling below.' In the earlier time there seems to have been no separate choir or official precentor, and, therefore, the 'tuning the Psalm,' as it was called, was left to some member of the congregation who volunteered the performance. No less a person than Judge Sewall himself undertook this function at Boston, and it is both pathetic and amusing to find from his diary how often he was baffled in the execution of the simple service he had undertaken. Sometimes he is self-complacent, and flatters himself he 'set the psalm well,' at other times he is just as crestfallen. Says he, on one occasion: 'I intended Windsor, and fell into high Dutch, and then essaying to set another tune, went into a key much too high. So I prayed to Mr. White to set it, which he did well. Litchfield Tune. The Lord humble me and instruct me that I should be the occasion of any interruption in the worship of God.' Sometimes, when he had the right tune, the congregation were too strong for him, and carried another tune against him. Thus runs his diary on a certain day: 'In the morning I set York tune, and in the second going over the gallery carried it irresistibly to St. David's, which discouraged me very much.' Nor was this the only time; later on he writes: 'I set York tune, and the congregation went out of it into St. David's in the very second going over. They did the same three weeks before. This is the second sign. It seems to me an intimation for me to resign the precentor's place for a better voice. I have through the Divine long-suffering and favour done it for twenty-four years, and now God in His providence seems to call me off, my voice being enfeebled.' Enfeebled with age the good man's voice might be, but his heart was right. Referring to the service on a certain Sunday, he says: 'The song of the fifth Revelation was sung. I was ready to burst into tears at the words, "bought with Thy blood."' Good music is good indeed, but there may be something even better still.

If the meeting-house and its services played so large a part in New England life, we may easily see how important was the place filled by the minister himself. In laying out a new town settlement some of the best town-lots were set aside for his use, these being sometimes a gift outright to the first settled preacher, and sometimes set aside as glebes or 'ministry land.' At Sippican, in 1680, the first and second house-lots drawn were appropriated with two meadows and two lots in the best of the woodland 'for the minister and the ministry.' At Rochester, in 1697, the proprietors of the lands gave a 'whole share of upland and meadow ground to the minister, upon condition that he continueth in the work of the ministry among them till prevented by death.' It was the custom also on starting a new settlement to build a parsonage for the minister, to the construction of which all the town contributed, some giving work or money or the use of a horse or ox-team, others supplying boards, stone, bricks, logs or nails. It was the custom too to allow free pasturage for the minister's horse; and in 1662 the Town Court at Plymouth judged it 'would be very commendable and beneficial to the towns where God's providence shall cast any whales if they should agree to set apart some part of every such fish or oil for the encouragement of an able and godly minister among them.' At Newbury the first salmon caught each year went to the minister; and in most places the 'minister's wood' was a recognised institution, each church member bringing his portion of wood for the minister's fire to the parsonage door.

At first the minister's stipend was settled by voluntary agreement, but in 1657, when the first generation had passed away, an Act was passed in Plymouth ordering a rate to be levied in each township for the maintenance of a teaching ministry. In Massachusetts, as early as 1637, an order of the court imposed a rate for the maintenance of a minister on all the inhabitants of Newbury, whether church members or not. But, however maintained, voluntarily, or by tithes or rates levied upon willing and unwilling alike, the ministers in the towns of the United Colonies exercised powerful influence, political as well as religious and intellectual, were usually treated with respect and regarded as privileged persons. There were exceptions, of course, but perhaps even these only proved the rule. We read of a man at New Haven who was punished by the town for venturing to say that he 'received no profit from the minister's sermons,' though possibly the punishment might more fitly have fallen upon the preacher rather than the hearer; a man at Plymouth who 'spoke deridingly of the minister's powers,' and another at Andover who 'cast uncharitable reflections' on his pastor, were fined and deprived of the sacrament. Such things as these occurred, but as a rule friendly relations obtained, and the New

England ministers of religion exercised a wide and wholesome influence on the rising communities among whom their lives were spent. In those infant settlements they had often to be many men in one: preaching and praying on Sabbaths and lecture days; preparing young men for college; giving medical and 'chyrurgycal' advice as doctors; sought after for legal counsel and adjudication as lawyers; and often having to work on their own land as farmers; they most of them lived earnest and laborious lives, and were 'pious and painful preachers,' doing their best for their flocks, both for this world and the next.

The tithing man in a New England town was an unique kind of officer, the connecting link between the secular and the spiritual. For it was his function, as his name implied, to have ten families under his charge, and 'diligently inspect them,' especially on the Sabbath, to see that they regularly came to meeting, and with foxtail wand keep them awake when they were there. He had also to enforce the learning of the catechism by the children of these ten families, and sometimes to hear them say it. He had, too, to watch licensed houses of entertainment, and make complaint of all disorders and misdemeanours committed therein; to report to the justices all idle persons, profane swearers, Sabbath-breakers, and the like offenders; and to warn tavern-keepers not to sell more liquor to men who in his judgment had had sufficient already. In addition to these varied duties, the tithing man warned out of the town undesirable people who might come to be dependent; administered the oath of fidelity to new inhabitants; watched to see that no young people walked abroad on the eve of the Sabbath; and marked and reported all those 'who profanely behaved, lingered without doors at meeting-time on the Lord's Day, sons of Belial strutting about or sitting on fences, and otherwise desecrating the day.' In case of any of these malpractices, the culprit, on conviction, was first admonished, and then, if incorrigible, set in the parish stocks or confined in the cage on the meeting-house green. The somewhat close surveillance of the life of the community thus set up by what has been called the Puritan theocracy in New England, has no doubt done much to associate the ideas of narrowness and intolerance with the name of Puritanism. While endeavouring to enforce religious observances and the moralities of life by means of external restraint, it probably meant well, it has been said, but as a religious system it became repellent and unlovely, and looked out frowningly upon the innocent pleasures and winsome graces of life. Matthew Arnold gave voice to a wide-spread feeling when he said that the voyagers in the Mayflower would have proved intolerable company for Shakespeare and Virgil. It may be so, or it may not. Perhaps in the case of Shakespeare we may be forgiven if we hesitate to accept this opinion, for the many-sided dramatist was in sympathy with all sorts and conditions of men, found something to interest and much to speculate upon in the most ordinary forms of life around him ; moreover there is not a little which seems to indicate that he had sincere respect for much of the earnest-minded Puritanism of his time. As for Virgil, we may admit the probability that if he had lived some eighty years later than he did, and had happened to be sailing for Italy in a certain ship of Alexandria, he might have found even the Apostle Paul 'intolerable company;' and when he heard him say, one morning, in the midst of the storm—'There stood by me this night an angel of the God whose I am, whom also I serve,' like his countryman, Festus, Virgil would probably have said, 'Paul, thou art beside thyself, thy much learning doth turn thee to madness!' Still, all the same, Paul's passionate love to Christ was a grander, truer thing than Virgil's offering worship to the genius of the emperor; his consecration to the service of humanity more ennobling than Virgil's half-sceptical devotion to the gods of the Pantheon. When it is assumed that the men of the Mayflower were narrow-minded, uninteresting and commonplace, it is forgotten that one of them, William Brewster, was in his younger days the trusted and well-beloved friend of one of Queen Elizabeth's Secretaries of State; that in the Netherlands he consorted for months with some of the great ambassadors of the time; and that as a Cambridge scholar he was found capable of instructing the students of the Leyden University where he dwelt. It is forgotten too that another of the voyagers in the Mayflower, William Bradford, proved his capacity and largeness of mind by giving us a *History of Plymouth Plantation* which, by its racy English, its far-reaching insight and quiet strokes of pathos and humour, might have beguiled even Shakespeare himself for an hour or more. Finally, it is forgotten also that even among the rest in that historic ship there were, Samuel Fuller, a trained physician and a gentleman, John Carver, deemed meet to be the first governor of the Colony, Miles Standish, a member of an old Lancashire family, who had seen military service in the Netherlands, and Edward Winslow, a Worcestershire gentleman of name and repute. With such companions and many others of the rank and file marked by strength of character and mother-wit, an Atlantic voyage may have been stormy, but it need not have been dull.

Then again if we come to the Puritan successors of the Pilgrim Fathers, the men who went over to New England between 1628 and 1643, many of them, it is no exaggeration to say, were of the flower of the English nation. John Winthrop was a country gentleman living on his own estate, and representing in his profession of the law the culture and refinement of the time; Isaac Johnson and John Humphrey

were the brothers-in-law of the Earl of Lincoln ; Theophilus
Eaton was a prosperous city merchant ; and many others
of the men of Massachusetts and Connecticut may for
social position and culture as well as strength of character
be taken as favourable specimens of the best portions of
the English society of their time. So too with the
ministers of religion who went out to the Colonies. They
must be very distinguished men indeed who would be
entitled to look down patronisingly upon men like John
Cotton of Boston, John Davenport of New Haven, Peter
Bulkely of Concord, Francis Higginson of Salem, Thomas
Hooker of Hartford, Henry Dunster of Cambridge, John
Harvard of Charlestown, John Eliot of Roxbury, and many
more of the nearly ninety Cambridge and Oxford graduates
who helped to build up the intellectual and spiritual life of
the New England Colonies. Whatever difference there
may be between these men and the best in our own time
arises simply from the difference between the seventeenth
century and the nineteenth. If they seem to us narrow
and intolerant in some of the actions of their lives, they
were yet striking examples of large-mindedness and
tolerance when placed in contrast with men like Whitgift,
Bancroft, or Laud.

Judged by the light of to-day, they may be said to have
made some grave and serious mistakes. They suppressed
the expression of hostile opinion, and they persecuted in
some individual cases men and women, who, however wild
and impracticable at the time, might have proved harmless
enough if left to find their own level in their own way.
The most strenuous advocate of the Puritans, too, will
scarcely deny that there was in the New England mind
as formed by them, especially after the first and second
generations had passed away, a certain intellectual hardness, a lack of interest in the productions of artistic genius,
a foolish contempt for the minor elegancies of life, letters,

and manners. Some of this may doubtless be owing to the hard conditions of toil under which many of their lives were lived, and something also to the distance the colonies were removed from the ancient centres of civilisation. But this is not the whole explanation. In the eloquent words of a native of New England of our own time, the Puritan 'has not remembered that to some minds a relish for what is lovely in fancy and in art is as native as colour to the violet, fragrance to the rose, or song to the bird ; that God's own mind must eternally teem with beauty, since He lines with it the tiny sea-shell, and tints the fish, and tones the hidden fibres of trees, and flashes it on breast and crest of flying birds, and breaks the falling avalanche into myriads of feathery crystals, and builds the skies in a splendour, to a rhythm, which no thought can match. It has been a narrowness, though a narrowness that has had depth in it, and that has not been merely superficial and noisy. And it has been a narrowness for which the Puritan has suffered in the diminution of his influence in the world, and in the darkening of his fame, more than others for conspicuous crimes.'[1]

Still, when all this has been said, and allowance has been made for all possible drawbacks, there remains about these men a certain moral grandeur. They had great and high qualities, the solid virtues on which stable commonwealths are founded, and they created such colonies as no other men in those days did : colonies that grew into a great nation, which has not even yet reached the summit of its greatness. There was in these makers of New England a grand masterful sincerity, a noble courage of conviction, an overwhelming sense of the authority of righteousness in human life, and an ever-present consciousness of God's personal rule over the world, in spite of all its confusions. These men felt, as few

---

[1] R. S. Storrs. *The Puritan Spirit.* Boston. 1889.

men have ever felt, the greatness of that human soul for
the redemption of which Christ has died; which has to
work out its earthly history before the background of
eternity, while passing thither to its mysterious destiny;
and there was ever before their thought the glorious ideal
of a kingdom of the heavens yet to be realised on the
earth.

> 'O prophets, martyrs, saviours, ye were great,
>   All truth being great to you: ye deemed man more
>   Than a dull jest, God's *ennui* to amuse:
>   The world for you, held purport: Life ye wore
> Proudly, as kings their solemn robes of state;
>   And humbly, as the mightiest monarchs use.'

LIST OF WORKS

QUOTED OR OTHERWISE REFERRED TO.

	PAGE
Account of the Hospital of St. Mary Magdalen, near Scrooby	44
Ainsworth (H.), *Counterpoyson*	23
Ames (W.), *Manuduction for Mr. Robinson*	149
Antwerp Church Records	56
Assize of Clarendon	18
BARRY (J. S.), *History of Massachusetts*	6
Bay Psalm Book, the	348
Bentivoglio, *Relazione di Fiandra*	125
Bernard (R.), *Christian Advertisements and Counsels of Peace*	130, 143
—— *Faithfull Shepeard*	82
—— *Isle of Man, the, or, the Legall Proceeding in Man-shire against Sin*	78
—— *Plea for Infants ... concerning Baptism*	78
Birch MSS.	374
Borgeaud, *Rise of Modern Democracy*	16
Bradford (W.), *Dialogues*	22, 119
—— *History of Plymouth Plantation*	5, 6, 57, 76, 129, 132, 246, 354
Brodhead, *History of New York*	185
Browne (R.), *Treatise of Reformation without tarrying*	36
—— *True and Short Declaration*	31
Bunyan (J.), *Holy War*	78
CAMDEN SOCIETY	18
Carleton (D.), *Letters*	160, 161, 163
Colonial Papers	175, 185, 227, 339
Confutation of the Rhemish translation	161
De Regimine Ecclesiæ Scoticanæ	161, 163
Dexter (F. B.), *Influence of English Universities in Development of New England*	266, 307
Discourse of some troubles in the ... Church at Amsterdam	115
Domesday Book	45
Doyle (J. A.), *English in America*	219, 266, 338
ELLIS, *Original Letters*	51
FISKE (J.), *The Beginnings of New England*	267, 321
Foxe (J.), *Acts and Monuments*	23
Freeman (E. A.), *Introd. to American Institutional History*	240
GARDINER (S. R.), *History of England*	288
Gray's (Archbishop) *Register*	50
Grindal's Life	27
Ground of the First Planting of New England, the	253
HALL (J.), *Apology of the Church of England*	152
Hanbury (B.), *Historical Memorials*	181
Harleian MSS.	38, 85
Harmony of the Confessions	250
Harrison (R.), *Little Treatise*	32
Hatfield MSS.	65, 291
Henry VIII., Letters and Papers	53
Howard (J.), *Survey of the State of Prisons*	82
Hunter's *Collections concerning the Early History of the Founders of New Plymouth*	43, 64, 65, 70

	PAGE
Hutchinson (T.), *History of Massachusetts*	5
Joyce (H.), *History of the Post Office to 1836*	62, 63
Lamentable Complaint of the Commonaltie	29
Lansdowne MSS.	36, 95
Lathbury (T.), *History of Episcopacy*	85
Leland's *Itinerary*	53
Manchester, MSS. of the Duke of	179, 180, 185
Mather (C.), *Magnalia Christi Americana*	314
Morton (N.), *New England's Memorial*	5, 200, 203, 262
Motley (J. L.), *United Netherlands*	113
Mozley (T.), *Reminiscences*	86
Nederlandsche Archief voor Kerkelijke Geschiedenis	120
Newburgh's *Chronicle*	17
New York Historical Collections	262
Parallels, Censures, Observations	83, 91
Perth Assembly	161, 163
Planter's Plea, the	271
Prince's *Annals*	5
Privy Council Register	54, 64
Proceedings of the Koninklijke Akademie	118
Raine (J.), *History and Antiquities of the Parish of Blyth*	45
Robinson (J.), *Appendix to Mr. Perkins' Six Principles*	95
—— *Just and Necessary Apology of Brownists*	154
—— *Justification of Separation*	143
—— *Manumission to a Manuduction*	136, 149
—— *New Essays: or, Observations Divine and Moral*	137
—— *People's Plea for the exercise of Prophecy*	152

	PAGE
Robinson (J.), *Religious Communion, Private and Public*	148
—— *Works*	83, 84, 96, 100, 128, 131, 136
Rogers (R.), *Seven Treatises*	313
Seebohm (F.), *English Village Community*	258, 259
Smith (J.), *New England Trials*	227
Smyth (John), *The Bright Morning Starre*	91
—— *The Retraction of his errors*	91
Stark (A.), *History of Gainsborough*	88
State Papers, Domestic	26, 28, 30, 37, 57, 60, 63, 75, 162, 167, 170, 270, 324
Storrs (R. S.), *The Puritan Spirit*	356
Strype, *Annals*	44
—— *Life of Grindal*	27
Surtees' Society	65
Thompson (P.), *History of Boston*	104
Trewe Markes of Christ's Church, the	26
Vision of Piers Plowman	18
Wall (T.), *More Work for the Dean*	32
Washburn (E. A.), *Epochs in Church History*	291
Wilberforce (S.), *History of the Protestant Episcopal Church in America*	6
Winslow (E.), *Brief Narration*	191
—— *Hypocrisy Unmasked*	180
Winsor (J.), *The Mayflower Town*	329
Winthrop (J.), *History of New England*	286, 301, 332
—— *Life and Letters*	299, 330, 331
Wolsey (Cardinal), *Twelve English Statesmen*	50
Wordsworth (W.), *Ecclesiastical Sonnets*	4, 18
Yates (J.), *Persons Prophesying out of Office*	152
Young's *Chronicles*	105, 129, 131, 279
Zurich Letters	25

INDEX.

ABIGAIL, sailing of the, 273
Act against heretics, 20
—— of Supremacy, the, 21
Adventurers, the, 242, *seq.*
Ainsworth, Henry, 117
Alden, John, 203
Allerton, Isaac, assistant governor, 219
America. *See also* Connecticut, Massachusetts, New England, and Plymouth.
  Crown Colony established in, 340
American Democracy, the father of, 321
—— Federal Union, the first, 335
—— self-government, origin of, 16
Amersham, Separatists at, 21
Ames, William, on Communion, 149, *seq.*
Amsterdam an asylum of liberty, 113
  first Protestant Church in, 117
  picture of Church life in, 118
Anne, arrival of the, 238
Argall, Captain, 173
Arminian and Calvinist controversy, 133
Arminius, followers of, 133
Arnold, Matthew, *quoted*, 353
Articles of the Church at Leyden, 175
Assize of Clarendon, 17
Austerfield, 65, *seq.*

BABWORTH, its Rector, 77
Balowe, William, 20
Barneveld, John of, 134

Barrowe, Henry, 37
Barrowists or Brownists, 97
Bawtry, 43, *seq.*
Bay Psalm Book, the, 348.]
Bellingham, Richard, 104, 268
Bermudas, Presbyterianism in the, 179
Bernard, a prison reformer, 81
  his influence on Bunyan, 78
  his transient sympathy with congregationalism, 83
  his writings, 78, 82, 130, 143
Blackwell, Francis, 184
Blossom, Thomas, on John Robinson, 252
Bolton, John, 23
Boston, Lincolnshire, 103
  John Cotton's Ministry in, 307-312
  Puritanism in, 104
Bowland, Thomas, martyr, 26
Bradford, William, 65, *seq.*
  in Leyden, 126
  chosen Governor, 219
  third time elected Governor, 241
  his writings, 5, 6, 22, 43, 57, 76, 119, 129, 132, 246, 354
  death of his wife, 208
  his death, 337
  quoted, 22
  on John Robinson and Richard Clifton, 97
Bradfords, social position of the, 69
Bradfurth's (Robert) will, 69
Bradstreet, Simon, 268
Brethren of the Second Separation, the, 85

Brewer, Thomas, 131
  prints prohibited books, 160, *seq.*
  arrested, 162
  surrender to English authorities, 165
  imprisoned, 167
  his release, 168
Brewster, William, 54
  appointed Post of Scrooby, 61
  his religious zeal, 93
  persecution of, 98, *seq.*
  in Leyden, 126
  prints prohibited books, 160, *seq.*
  his kindness, 211
  death of his wife, 254
  his death, 336
Bright, Francis, 277, 284
  withdraws from Salem Church, 287
Britain, rural economy of, 258
Bromhead, Hugh, 85
Brooks of Queenhithe, 23
Browne, John and Samuel, 287
  sent back to England, 288
———, Robert, 30–33
  his writings, 31, 36
Brownists, the, 97
  Confession of Faith, 175
  decision to avoid the name, 190
  Robinson, J., in defence of the, 154, *seq.*
Builli, John de, 43
Bulkely, Peter, 314
Bunyan influenced by Richard Bernand, 78
Burgess, Dr. John, 269
Burial Hill fort, 263
Burleigh, Lord, 32
Bury St. Edmunds, Congregationalism at, 32
  its Abbey, 33
  revolt against ecclesiastical domination in, 35
  stronghold of the ancient faith, 33–35

CALVINIST and Arminian controversy, 133
Cape Cod, Pilgrims land at, 201
Carleton, Mr., suggests a settlement of the Puritan question, 169

Carleton, Sir Dudley, informs against Brewer and Brewster, 160, *seq.*
Carver, John, 131
  his death, 218
Catchpole, the office of, 103
Charity, arrival of the, 241
Chaucer hostile to priestly system, 19
Chauncey, Charles, 318
Child born in New England, the first, 206
Church discipline in Virginia, 173
Church Fellowship, covenant of, 286
  qualifications for, 292
Church Government, divergent views on, 119
  Robinson and others on, 128, 145, *seq.*
Church life in Amsterdam, 118
Church in Leyden, 129
Church of England, Robinson on the, 156
Church Service, *see* Ritual.
Clough, A. H., quoted, 158
Clyfton, Richard, his character, 77, 97
  at Scrooby, 94
  remains at Amsterdam, 127
Colchester, Separatists at, 22
Colonists, ill-disciplined, 230
Communion, religious, Robinson and Ames on, 148, *seq.*
Communistic System at Plymouth, 234
Compact of the Pilgrim Fathers, 201
Company of Massachusetts Bay, the, 276
Concord, the founder of, 314
Confederation of New England Colonies, 331, *seq.*
Confession of Faith, Brownist, 175
Congregationalism, by whom founded, 30
Congregationalists, early, 30
Connecticut, constitution of, 320
——— Settlement, trouble with Indians, 321
Constitution of the Puritan Colony, basis of the, 201
Contra-Remonstrants, 133
Copping, John, 33, 35

INDEX. 363

Cotton, John, 105, 268
  his ministry at Boston, 307-312
  his death 337
Courtenay, Archbishop, 19
Covenant of Church fellowship, 286
"Covenant of the Lord," the, 74
Cradock, Matthew, 275
Crown Colony established in America, 340
Cushman, Robert, 131
  his death, 251

DAVENPORT, John, 323
Davison, William, 55, *seq.*
  his fall, 58
Delfshaven, the start from, 193
Democracy, rise of, arrested, 16
—— transplanted, 16
De Rassières, Isaac, 260, *seq.*
Dorchester, emigrants from, 272
Dort, origin of the Synod of, 135
Downes, William, of Scrooby, 69
Dudley, Thomas, 268
Dutch opinion of the Protestants, 132
—— Sabbath breakers, 159
—— settlement in New England, 260
Duxbury Settlement, 328

EAST ANGLIA, Congregationalism in, 30
East England's share in the Reformation, 266
Eaton, Theophilus, 323
Education in New England, 338
Eliot, John, 317
Elizabethan Free Church described, 25
Endicott, John, 273
Episcopal Government *versus* Presbyterian, 290, *seq.*
Episcopalianism in New England, 243
Episcopalians ejected from Plymouth Colony, 247
Epworth, 78
Exiled Protestants, fellowship of, 24

FEDERAL UNION, the first in America, 335
First Comers, number of the, 240
"First Encounter," 207

Fitz, Richard, 22, 31
  his Church described, 25
  persecuted to death, 26
Forefathers, number of the, 240
Fort on Burial Hill, 263
Fortune, arrival of the ship, 224
  capture of, 226
Fouler, Gyles, 26
Four Sisters, the ship, 280, 283
Foxe, quoted, 21
Free Church, Elizabethan, described, 25
Free Church Martyrs, the first, 33
Freedom of worship, early asserted, 15-21
Freeman, E. A., quoted, 240
Freewill, strife concerning, 133
Fuller, Samuel, physician, 274

GAINSBOROUGH, Separatist Community in, 85, *seq.*
Gascoyne, Adam, 54
Gayton, Mr., 35
George, the ship, 279, 283
Gifford, Robert, 84
Goffe, Thomas, 275
Gomarus, followers of, 133
Gorges, Sir Ferdinando, 172
——, Robert, 243
Government in New England Colonies, 240, 304, *seq.*
"Governor and Company of the Massachusetts Bay," the, 276
Graves, Thomas, 281
Greenwood, John, 36-39
Grindal, Archbishop, 53
——, quoted, 27

HALL, Bishop Joseph, on Separation, 142
Handscomb, Mr., 35
Hanson, John, 69
Harrison, Robert, 32
Harvard College founded, 338
Harvard, John, 318
  his munificence, 338
Heath, Richard, quoted, 123
Helwisse, Thomas, 100
Heretics, early persecution of, 20
Hickmans, the, 87

Higginson, Francis, 271, 278
  his death, 303
Hobart, Peter, 318
Holland, development of industry in, 113
  Protestant exiles in, 110, *seq.*
  Sabbath profanation in, 159
Holy War, Bunyan's, inspired by Bernard's *Isle of Man*, 78
Homiletics, a study in, 82
Hooker, Thomas, 319
Hough, Atherton, 268, 269
Howard, John, anticipated, 81
Humphrey, John, 275

INDIAN attack on Settlers, 206, 227, 233, 321, 339
—— chiefs avow loyalty to James I., 222.
—— welcome to the Settlers, 213, *seq.*
—— treaty with Settlers, 216
—— hospitality, 220
—— massacre of Virginian Settlers, 227
—— plot revealed, 230
Indians, conflict with, 206, 227, 233, 321, 339
  Eliot's influence on, 317, 318
  war with, 339
Insurrection against Protestantism, 74
Ireland suggested as Puritan Colony, 169
Isle of Man, Bernard's inspires Bunyan's *Holy War*, 78
  synopsis of, 81
Islington, Congregationalism at, 31

JACKSON, Richard, 98
James I. and Nonconformity, 180
Johnson, Francis, 38, 91, 114, *seq.*
——, Isaac, 275
  his death, 303

KILHAM's (Alexander) birthplace, 78

LAUD and Colonial Administration, 319
  and Episcopacy, 291
  his treatment of Puritans, 270
Lay-preaching, controversy on, 152, *seq.*
Legislature in New England Colonies, 304, *seq.*

Leland, quoted, 46, 52
Lever, Thomas, 24
Leverett, Thomas, 268
Leyden, 121, *seq.*
——, exiles' Meeting-house in, 124
  its University, 122
  fierce theological controversy in, 133
  lay ministry in, 154
  reason for leaving, 158, *seq.*
Leyden Brethren decide for Virginia, 182
Leyden Church, Articles of Religion, 175
  life in, 129
  flourishing condition of, 253
  letter to Plymouth Church, 252
Lincoln, Lord, 267
Lincolnshire and Nonconformity, 268
Lion's Whelp, the ship, 279, 283
Little James, arrival of the ship, 228
Lollard movement, the, 20
London, Separatists at, 22
Lyford, John, 244, *seq.*

MANHATTAN, Dutch settlement at, 260
Man, Thomas, 21
Marian Church, the, 22
Martyrs for Free Church principles, the first, 33, 35
Massachusetts Bay visited by Settlers, 222
Massachusetts Bay Company, 295
  charter granted, 276
  its equipment, 280, *seq.*
  prosperity of, 306
  its charter annulled, 340
Massachusetts Settlement, the, 265, *seq.*
  its relations with Plymouth Colony, 329, *seq.*
Massasoit, Indian chief, 215
  his illness and cure, 229
  Pilgrim embassy to, 219
  Pilgrims arm in defence of, 222
Masterman, J. H. B., quoted, 4
Mather, Cotton, 314
  quoted, 267
Mather, Increase, 314
——, Richard, 314

INDEX. 365

Maurice, Prince, 134
  his death, 251
Mayflower, the, 280, 283
  sailing of the, 184-208
  size of, 188
  arrives at Cape Cod, 201
  return to England, 217
Merchant Adventurers, 242, seq.
Middleburg in Zealand, Congregational Church at, 32
Minister, the, in New England life, 350
Ministers, Bernard's advice to, 82
Minister's calling, views on the, 284
Ministry, a lay, controversy on, 152, seq.
——, Ordination to the, 285
Monastic orders, influence of, 75
Morrell, William, 243
Morton, George, arrives at Plymouth, 238
——, Nicholas, 44
——, Robert, 43
Motley's *United Netherlands*, quoted, 113
Mozley, Rev. T., on Gainsborough town, 86
Music in Puritan service, 348

NAUNTON, Secretary, and Brownist printing, 160, seq.
Netherlands Republic, foundation of, 113
Nevile, Gervase, 97
Newbury, Separatists at, 21
New England. See also America, Connecticut, Massachusetts, and Plymouth.
  attempt to establish an Episcopal Church in, 243, seq.
  first child born in, 206
  first Puritan exodus to, 184, seq.
  importance of the minister in, 350, legislature in, 304, seq.
  Lincolnshire and Dorchester, emigration to, 272, seq.
  picture of worship in, 344-50
  second Puritan exodus to, 265, seq.
  third Puritan exodus to, 295, seq.
New England Colonies, Confederation of, 331, seq.

New Haven founded, 325
New Plymouth, 262
Norwich, Congregationalism at, 32
  pastors of the church at, 95

OLDHAM'S revolt, 245
  expulsion, 247
  Ordination service, 285

PARTRYCHE, martyr, 26
Patent of land granted to colonists, 224
Penry, John, Welsh martyr, 114
Pequot Indians, overthrow of, 322
Perkins, William, 95
Persecution of heretics or Separatists, 20, 22, 24
—— of Scrooby Brethren, 97-103
Piers Plowman, 18
Pilgrim Fathers. See also Leyden Brethren, Pilgrim Settlers, Plymouth Colony, Puritans, and Scrooby Brethren.
  character of leaders, 307, 354
  four pioneers, 116
  departure from Holland, 191, seq.
  their voyage, 199
  sight Cape Cod, 200
  their compact, names of signers, 202
  number of, 240
Pilgrim Settlers. See also Pilgrim Fathers, Plymouth Colony, Puritans.
  first expedition in New England, 205
  conflict with Indians, 206, 227, 233, 321, 339
  land on Plymouth Rock, 207
  welcomed by Indians, 213, seq.
  troubles and hardships, 211, 217, 223, 235, 302
  treaty with Indians, 216
  defend Massasoit, 222
  visit Massachusetts Bay, 222
"Pilgrimage of Grace," the, 74
Plymouth Colony. See also Pilgrim Settlers and Puritans
  agreement with Adventurers, 257
  attempt to introduce Episcopalianism, 243, seq.

Plymouth Colony—*continued*.
  breach with Board of Merchant Adventurers, 249
  communistic system in, 234
  ejection of Episcopalians, 247
  form of government, 240
  growing prosperity, 255
  its progress, 327, *seq.*
  mortality, 260
  relations with Massachusetts, 329, *seq.*
Plymouth Company revived, 186
—— Plantation, 209-237
—— Rock reached, 207
Popish ceremonies in 1507 . . . 27
Post system, early English, 61, *seq.*
Post, the office of, 64
Prayer, remarkable answer to, 237
Preachers, Bernard's advice to, 82
Preaching, lack of, 28
——, controversy on lay, 152, *seq.*
Predestination, strife concerning, 133
Presbyterian government *versus* Episcopal, 290, *seq.*
Presbyterianism in the Bermudas, 179
Priestly system, early revolt against the, 17-21, 35
Printing, Brownist, in Holland, 160, *seq.*
Prison reformer, an early, 81
Protestant exiles, fellowship of, 24
Protestantism, insurrection against, 74
Psalms in Puritan worship, 348
Puritan Colony (*see also* Plymouth Colony), basis of its constitution, 201
  Patent of land granted, 224
Puritan clergy, their zeal and influence, 76
—— community in New England; its characteristics, 341, *seq.*
—— discipline in New England, 351
—— exodus to New England, the second, 265, *seq.*
—— exodus ceases, 325
—— leaders; their greatness, 354
—— " narrowness," 353-6
—— worship in New England, 344-50
Puritans, *see also* Scrooby Brethren.
  and the Virginia Company, 174, *seq.*
  first idea of founding a colony, 169

Puritans—*continued*.
  decide upon Virginia, 182
  Laud's treatment of, 270
  not Separatists, 270

QUINNIPIACK Settlement, 325

RALEIGH, Walter, quoted, 58
Randolph, Thomas, Postmaster-General, 61
Rassières, Isaac de, 260, *seq.*
Reformation, hostility against the, 74
  pioneers of the, 17
  principles, 16
  seeds of the, 19
  slow spread of the, 26
  share of East England in the, 266
Reform Church of Holland, 254
Religious teaching, lack of, 28
Rembrandt's testimony to the Gospel, 123
Remonstrants, 133
Rich, Lord, 36
Richardson, Mr., of Bawtry, 69
Ritual, questions of, in New England churches, 287, *seq.*
Robinson, Archdeacon, 95
Robinson, John, 94, *seq.*
  at Norwich, 95
  in Leyden, 124-128
  his charge to pilgrim band, 196
  his intellectual eminence, 132, 137
  his saintly character, 94
  his writings, 83, 95, 100, 128, 131, 136, *seq.*
  in defence of the Brownists, 154
  on Church Government, 128, 145, *seq.*
  on the Church of England, 156
  on the Church at Leyden, 130
  on lay-preaching, 152
  on the military spirit, 242
  on Separation, 142
Robinson, Isaac, 253
Romish practices prevalent in 1507 ... 27
Rough, John, 22, 31
Rural economy, early British, 258

SABBATH observance, compulsory, 173
—— profanation among the Dutch, 159

INDEX.

Salem, 272, 275
    arrival of Puritans at, 284
Salem Church; its first pastor, 285
    troubles in, 287
Salem covenant, the, 286
Saltonstall, Sir Richard, 275
Samoset the Indian, 213
Sandys, Sir Edwin, 172
Scrooby, 40, *seq.*
    antiquity of, 45
    Church, 46
    Palace, 49, 52
    centre of anti-protestant rebellion, 75
    formation of the church at, 92
    Wolsey at, 50
Scrooby Brethren; arrival in Holland, 110
    persecution of, 97, 100
    resolve to emigrate, 99, 106
    captured in the attempt, 103, 108
    resolve to move to Leyden, 120
    their Meeting House, Leyden, 124
Separatism, early organisation of, 20
Separatists, *see also* Scrooby Brethren.
    in New England Churches, 288, *seq.*
    first voyage across the Atlantic, 116
    increase of, 22
    in London, 22
Shepard, Thomas, 315–317
Sherman, William, 280
Silvester, Mr., of Alkley, 69
Skelton, Samuel, 277
    chosen pastor of Salem Church, 285
Smyth, John, of Gainsborough, 83, 88–92
    his last book, 91
Speedwell, the ship; departure of, 194
    springs a leak, 198
    size of, 188
Standish, Miles, 131, 205, 211
    appointed military commander, 212
    Robinson's fears of, 242
    visits England, 251
    his death, 337
Stanhope, Sir John, Postmaster-General, 59

Staresmore, Sabin, 178
Statute against heretics, 20
Still, Dr., 36
Stoke, Separatists at, 22
Suffolk's contribution to Puritanism, 267
Summer Islands, Presbyterianism in the, 179
Superstitions at Bury St. Edmunds, 34
Symmes, Zachary, 314
Symson, Cuthbert, 22, 31
    Martyrdom of, 24
Synod of Dort, origin of, 135

TALBOT, the ship, 279, 283
Tattershall Castle, 268
Thacker, Elias, 33, 35
Tisquantum, Indian, 214, 219
    death of, 229
Tithing man, his office, 352
Toller, Thomas, 84

'UNDERTAKERS,' the, 257
Upcharde of Bocking, 21

VIRGIL and religion, 353
Virginia, Church discipline in, 173
Virginia Company, the, 171, *seq.*
    crisis in, 184, *seq.*
Virginian settlers massacred, 227
Voyage of the first Pilgrims, 199

WEAVERS, pioneers of the Reformation, 17
Wesley's birthplace, 78
Wessagusset. *See also* Weymouth, 243
    Colony started at, 229
    troubles at, 230
Weymouth. *See* Wessagusset.
White, Roger, on John Robinson, 252
Whiting, Samuel, 315
Whittier quoted, 345
Wickliff, originator of Free Church influence, 19
    date of his death, 20
William of Occam, 18
Will of Robert Bradfurth, 69
Wilson, John, his conversion to Puritanism, 313
——, Lambert, 282

Winslow, Edward, 131, 229
    receives Indian Chief, 215
    his death, 337
Winthrop, John, 104, 275
    elected governor of Massachusetts Bay Co., 296
    sketch of his life, 296-299
    voyage to New England, 299–301
    death of, 337
Wolsey, Cardinal, 50, *seq.*
Wolstenholme, Sir John, 178
Worcester, rise of independent thought in, 17
Wordsworth quoted, 4. 18
Worksop, its Vicar, 77

Worship, form of at Salem, 287
    freedom of, early asserted, 15–21
    in New England, picture of, 344–50
Wray, Sir Christopher, 35
Wright, Robert, 37

YALE UNIVERSITY, foundation of, 338
Yates, John, on lay-preaching, 152, *seq.*
Yeomen, social position of Elizabethan, 69

ZEALAND, congregational church at, 32
Zouch, Sir William, 165

THE END.

www.ingramcontent.com/pod-product-compliance
Lightning Source LLC
Chambersburg PA
CBHW020307240426
43673CB00039B/736